Llama for Lunch

Lydia Laube, who believes that to travel hopefully is better than to arrive – and she sometimes almost doesn't – is one of Australia's favourite travel writers. Lydia can never resist a challenge, and her previous best-sellers, *Behind the Veil: An Australian Nurse in Saudi Arabia*, *The Long Way Home*, *Slow Boat to Mongolia*, and *Bound for Vietnam* tell of her sometimes alarming adventures in far-flung places of the globe.

When she is not travelling the world, Lydia Laube chases the sun between Adelaide and Darwin.

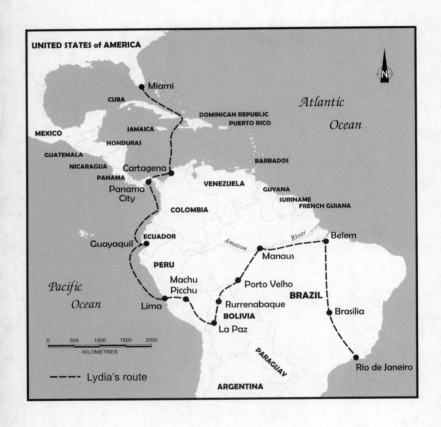

Llama for Lunch

LYDIA LAUBE

**Wakefield
Press**

Wakefield Press
1 Parade West
Kent Town
South Australia 5067

First published 2002
Reprinted 2004

Cover designed by Lahn Stafford Design
Llama silhouette by Jonathon Inverarity
Typeset by Clinton Ellicott, Wakefield Press, Adelaide
Printed and bound by Hyde Park Press, Adelaide

National Library of Australia
Cataloguing-in-publication entry

Laube, Lydia, 1948– .
Llama for lunch.

ISBN 1 86254 576 6.

1. Laube, Lydia, 1948– –Journeys–South America.
2. South America–Description and travel. I. Title.

918

Government
of South Australia

A R T S A

Wakefield Press thanks Fox Creek Wines
and Arts South Australia for their support.

Contents

To the memory of my mother,

Mildred Mary

1 Fright wigs in Chicago

On the last day of autumn, after a ghastly, bitterly cold week I shivered out of bed at three in the morning. It was dark and raining when I clumped into the freezing Adelaide airport. Thank goodness I was on my way to summer in another hemisphere.

I progressed onto the plane for Sydney committing only the minor misdemeanour of setting off the alarm buzzers with my excess of gold buttons. Unusually for me I fell asleep after breakfast was served: I am normally too busy listening for faulty engine noises or looking out of the window for flames. The elderly woman next to me said that she was originally from the United States and returned often for a visit. She was taking the same route as I was to Chicago, via a night's stop over in Tokyo. When she heard that my ultimate destination was South America, she told me that she had known someone who had been horribly murdered there.

Murphy was at it again. It seemed that everyone I met lately had a tale of woe to tell about South America and the dire fates that had befallen friends – kidnappings, muggings and all manner of foul play. One of the least appealing was the story of a Dutch girl who had been attacked in broad daylight on her first day in Lima. She had been stripped, robbed and left naked in the street. I decided that hiding cash in my undies was no longer a good idea.

In Sydney I very nearly missed the Tokyo plane. I couldn't find the ticketing counter and, instead of going straight on as

I was directed, I went around the corner and came back again to where I had started, as though I had been trapped in a revolving door. By the time I was headed in the right direction my name was being called for the final time.

The plane was a huge two-storey affair that was packed solid. I had requested an aisle seat – necessary for emergency evacuations, not to mention quick trips to the loo. But in front of me was lumped a bulky Australian youth decorated with an apparently permanently attached baseball cap that loomed above the back of the seat and obscured my view of the video screen. The food was okay, but served in midget-sized portions. On the other hand, a bottle of wine was supplied with the meal and the girl next to me drank only a little of hers and kindly donated the rest to a worthy cause. I drank it, purely for medicinal reasons of course: it helps to calm white knuckles.

Then we were coming down through a lot of murk and turbulence into Tokyo's Narita airport. I had booked my luggage through to Chicago and had just a carry-on bag. O bliss! Now I realise how great it is to travel light. But it didn't make a convert of me.

A courtesy bus trundled me to my hotel, where I had a very small but nicely appointed room. I discovered that the hotel also ran a free service to the local village every hour, a vast improvement on the taxi fare of eighty dollars Australian. While waiting for the next bus I went up to the hotel's ninth floor beautiful bar where you could sit in front of a long plate-glass window and admire the view in comfort. Unfortunately the prices were enough to make you want to jump out of the window and a very haughty waiter looked absolutely horrified when I asked for a glass of water. Twenty dollars Australian for a beer is a bit rich. A New Zealander I met downstairs later said that a steak sandwich cost one hundred and fifty. I've bought a whole ruddy cow for less than that.

In the town a light drizzle fell as I sloshed up and down

cobbled lanes and narrow brick-paved streets that wound around and around and were home to many diminutive eating places. I entered one that was built of bamboo, had rice paper windows and was crammed with men, long wooden tables and a minute bar. After much deliberation, food of some description, I have no idea what, was ordered and I waited while the men drank saki from large brown bottles. After a very long time the food arrived, but I left still hungry as it had only been microscopic amounts of raw fish, rice and soup – nothing guaranteed to stick to your ribs.

In the morning I made up for these dietary deprivations by attacking the hotel's buffet breakfast, anticipating future meagre repasts. Back at the airport I waltzed through 'exegration' (the opposite of immigration) and found myself on another massive chock-full double-decker plane. This time, however, I didn't need to see over the person in front because, wonder of wonders, every seat had its own little TV screen. On take-off it showed you, via a camera in the plane's nose, what the pilot could see (we hoped!) from the cockpit. As the aircraft trundled out to the runway, there was the tarmac speeding away underneath. I found this disconcerting – it was something I would rather not have witnessed – but my eyes stayed compulsively glued to it.

Having seen the plane safely in the air I concentrated on the video program. You could switch between six films or play games. The flight lasted twelve hours, crossing the Pacific Ocean then flying over northern USA. We left at half past eleven in the morning and, spookily, arrived before we left, at nine the same day. The sun was rising on one side of the plane as it was setting on the other.

The descent to Chicago's O'Hare airport, the busiest in the world, through a murky sky, was extremely bumpy. The next day I heard that a plane had sat on the tarmac for eight hours unable to take off due to the bad weather.

My first impression of America was that I could have been

anywhere – all these huge modern airports look the same. The one difference was that all the staff I saw were Afro-American. I asked the airport shuttle-bus driver if he would take me to the Three Arts Club in Dearborn Street, where I had a booking, and was safely landed on the doorstep. It was still only half past ten and check-in time was not until one, so I had to sit in the drawing room almost stupefied from lack of sleep, with my internal clock insisting that it was long past bedtime. You'd think they could have let me at a bed. The room was ready. Rules are cast in stone to some people.

But I had been impressed when deposited here. The Three Arts Club is housed in an elegant building in a lovely tree-lined street that contains three-storey apartment blocks, a coffee shop and a classy boutique hotel called the Claridge. The street verges have gardens surrounded by little fences and more of the same front the buildings. Dearborn Street runs all the way down to the centre of Chicago, a few kilometres away.

Looking back I realised that until I reached the club I had not understood one word of the English that had been spoken to me since I left Australia. I was beginning to think I'd gone deaf. Most of the announcements on the Japanese planes had been, naturally enough, in Japanese and the subtitled English ones might as well have been. And in Chicago everyone I had spoken to so far had been African-American and I found their distinctive patois hard to decipher.

The Three Arts Club is a great place. Built in 1912 as a residence and club for women, it was executed in the grand manner of the age. On the front of the building one brass plaque confirms its age and another states that it has been declared a National Trust building. It has an imposing entrance flanked by columns and the facade sports bas-reliefs of three women in flowing Greek robes who represent the Three Arts – music, painting and literature. Constructed of dark reddish brown brick, it has four storeys and a flat roof-top area. A flight of steps up from the street gets you in the front door, then another brings you to a set of double doors where you press a hefty brass bell for admission to a massive lobby. On one side of the lobby is an immense room that contains a stage and an entire wall of French doors that open onto a large and lovely courtyard where a fountain tinkles into a pool that has a statue of a small naked boy in its centre. Around the courtyard sit wrought-iron chairs and tables, and huge flower pots from which cascade red, pink, and white petunias and impatiens.

The drawing room, a long, high-ceilinged chamber with a polished wooden floor on which lie a few worn but good old oriental rugs, is on the other side of the lobby. In here are some lovely pieces of well-polished antique furniture, several elegant couches and, in one of the cabinets, some fine antique china. Next to the drawing room is a gallery called the tea room; attached to it is a small library. All the ground-floor rooms have many glass doors onto the courtyard, which creates a feeling of light and space and makes them ideal for art exhibitions and functions. Behind the reception rooms lie the spacious dining room and kitchen and a couple of guest bathrooms and toilets that have been preserved in their original condition. The elaborately decorated ceramic pissoir on the wall of the Gents is a work of art. The basement is used by the residents as a TV room and the washing machines are also housed there in a Dickensian dungeon that has a welter of enormous pipes overhead like the engine room of a ship.

By one o'clock, when I was finally allowed into my room, I was a total zombie. I had tried taking a walk, but it had been pointless – I felt as though I was walking around underwater. I fell on the bed and slept for three hours until, it being dinner time (and only imminent death can keep me from a meal), I got up and took myself down to the dining room.

Before each meal you had to go to the office and collect a ticket to give to the cheerful kitchen staff, who all looked like they came from south of the border. The food was very good but it leaned heavily, especially at breakfast, on sweet stuff like waffles, pancakes, Coco pops and sticky buns. I counteracted this with cheese and lots of lovely fruit. You could order eggs any way you wanted them by writing your request on a piece of paper and giving it to the attendant, who would disappear into the nether regions of the kitchen to appear shortly after with the goods. You could never complain, as I have been wont to do in other places, that there wasn't enough to eat. But best of all was the wonderful, freshly brewed coffee.

The next morning I woke very early and did not feel really rested. My time clock was out of kilter. When I was respectable I headed off to the book fair, the putative reason for my visit to the States, by taxi and found out the hard way that it is obligatory to tip the driver at least ten per cent of the fare. Book Expo America, an annual Mecca for those in the trade, was being held this year in Chicago's McCormack Centre. Irreverently referred to as 'the mistake on the lake' by the locals, it is a monstrous 2.2 million square feet of convention space. I'd never seen anything like it. It started with a ginormous entrance hall that a couple of air strips would be lost in while upstairs, in an unbelievably huge area, were four thousand or more stands for exhibitors. All kinds of books were on display: children's, educational, novels, travel, foreign language, even some erotica. Every time I tried to walk around the exhibition space I failed and after an hour or so had to return for a rest. But boy, you could collect some loot here. I could have amassed hundreds of free books on my rounds. It broke my heart to leave them but I did get a couple to read on my travels. There were also give-away pens, mugs, phone cards and bags. But before you hop on a plane en masse I should point out that the fair is only for book sellers, publishers and buyers with special dispensation for the odd writer. And some were very odd, I noticed.

At four o'clock I returned to the club by the free shuttle

bus that dropped people from the fair at various hotels. I crashed on my bed and again only got up to feed. Then I woke in the middle of the night. It took me four days to wake at the right time in the morning.

Next day at the fair I had lunch at McDonald's. Their food outlets were everywhere and everyone seemed to eat their food, *and* freely admit it. Not like at home where most people I know do it on the sly and would never confess to it on the rack. A Coke from a machine cost five Australian dollars. I was horrified. I found the States high-priced due to the awful rate of exchange for our dollar at the time – parking downtown was advertised at eight dollars an hour as though it was a bargain!

On the last day of the fair I managed to get through the wine tasting and book signing that had been arranged. A line of people waited for me to appear. This would have been more flattering if my publishers hadn't been giving my books away.

On the way back the bus driver said that she would take the scenic route. It certainly was; along the edge of Lake Michigan and past the sensational-looking museum and art gallery and other grand public buildings. Passing a pretty park she explained that the lone grave that stood in it surrounded by an iron fence was there because, when all the other remains had been moved, this person's relatives couldn't be found to give permission to relocate him. The driver also told us that the great fire of Chicago in 1871, from the ashes of which the modern city grew, was alleged to have been started by Mrs O'Leary's cow kicking over a lantern. I think the cow may have been much maligned.

My room at the club was large and pleasantly old-fashioned and had an adjoining bathroom that I shared with the person next door. After three days and nights of creeping around in the bathroom so as not to disturb my neighbour, I discovered that she was a permanent resident who was away

7

on holiday. I could have been having jazz parties in there. My room had a Spartan look because the cement floor was painted red and had only a smidgin of carpet in its middle. The furniture was old, functional stuff that included a comfortable bed and two big central-heating hot-water radiators, monstrous iron affairs that were fixed under the windows. Massive pipes lumbered through the room from top to bottom, I had no idea to what purpose. Part of one wall had been built in sections to provide two walk-in wardrobes with a rail for a curtain in front of them. The bathroom was extremely ancient-looking but everything was painted shiny white and it was squeaky clean.

From my position on the third floor there was a pleasant view from the two original, old sash windows that were located in each outside wall. They looked into the roof tops of other apartment buildings one floor below me. I could see a wooden-paling-edged balcony that had an Asian look and the backdrop to that was a spreading tree that gave me pleasure to contemplate.

The club was rather like a boarding school, or worse, a reformatory. Everyone was pleasant but the list of rules was endless. You even had to make an application in writing to use the lift. One morning I found three police officers bristling with guns in the dining room. During the night the club's female guard had seen a man lurking in the back alley. I got the feeling that they might be a little edgy about men here. It wasn't as though he could have got in.

One night a wedding was in progress when I arrived for dinner. Two large white bows on the pillars that flanked the front door warned me of this, and once I was inside I saw that the reception rooms had been divinely decorated. Large bowls and urns of white flowers had been placed around the courtyard; drifts and drapes of white gauze tied with bows and frills wafted around the French doors. We lesser beings who merely lived there couldn't go through these rooms now, but had to circumnavigate to the dining room via the back stairs and the basement. The next day there was another wedding with more beautiful flowers and decorations. During the ten days of my stay several functions were held in the courtyard while we were eating dinner and we could watch them through the glass doors – it made me feel like an orphan putting her nose to the window. I couldn't help but notice that the guests were eating better stuff than we were (and wasting a lot of it) and the devil whispered to me that fifty per cent of them were too fat to need feeding anyway. But we residents did well out of these bun fights. The orphans in the storm inherited the flowers, great bowls of vibrant colours on our dining tables. And we also scored some very fine left-over food.

The evening that the fair finished it started to drizzle with rain and by the next day it was raining good and hard and was really cold, just fifty degrees Fahrenheit. I wasn't prepared for this weather clothing-wise but I put on all the woollies I had and went out prepared for a great adventure with Chicago public transport. Two ladies at the tourist bureau in the McCormack Centre had emphatically denied that there was such an animal as a subway. When I asked about those steps I had seen going down under the street they gave me blank looks, consulted each other and decided that, no, there was definitely so such thing. Unconvinced, I started walking in the direction that I thought I had previously seen the subway entrance but found myself in the wrong street and ended up strolling all the way downtown along Dearborn Street. I took my life in my hands every time I crossed the road because, naturally, I looked the wrong way, and the traffic was coming at me from the other direction.

On the edge of the city I discovered that I was underneath the overhead train which goes around the loop of the city centre. Not very imaginatively, it is named the Loop. This seemed foolproof, so I mounted the steps to a platform to try it. The only flaw was that you have to know which part of the loop to get on at and which direction the train is going. I had no idea how to even get started with a ticket – you needed to play all sorts of games with machines that required money. But kind people helped me. I didn't have enough change so the woman attendant and a woman passenger between them managed to rake up enough money to subsidise me. Nice, I thought, here I am pan-handling in America. This happened again at the next station, where the guard gave me the ten cents I was short. I rode six of these trains and in between spent a couple of hours sitting on windy stations above the city waiting for them.

First I waited for the purple line because I thought it was a pretty colour then I discovered that it didn't run at that time of the day so I got on another train. This one went out to Midway airport after completing its loop, but eventually after an interesting ride I was back in town and heading in the right direction. Getting off I boarded another train but, discovering that its destination was the outer suburbs, I decided against another foray out of town and got off again. Five trains later I arrived at the station where I could change to the subway that would return me home. I had a marvellous time, with many people pointing the way and many wrong turns, but you can ride for two hours on the one ticket for three Australian dollars and I certainly got my money's worth.

I saw many acts of kindness on the subway. A well-dressed black woman gave her seat to a blind man, an elderly white man was given a seat by a young man. Another time one young man stood for an older person and a young bloke grabbed the seat so the fellow next to him promptly gave up his seat.

In the subway there were intriguing signs; one huge one advertised 'DIVORCE for ninety dollars'. But subways are grotty, unpainted cement-coloured dungeons – the sort of place I'd never go at night.

On one of my rides around the Loop I spotted the marvellous Chicago Library and leapt off to inspect it. With nine extensive floors, it is impressively big and as you ascend slowly by escalator past its walls of white marble you feel as though you are being lifted up through a bright, light, gorgeous space. On the seventh floor, just for curiosity, I searched among the literature and found Australian writer Miles Franklin's *On Dearborn Street*.

Another floor had computers where you could collect your e-mails or surf the internet for free. I said to the young man standing in line behind me, 'If you want to get on the net fast, show me how to get my e-mail.' He did and, much to my surprise, I retrieved a message. Wonderful – I have made it into the twenty-first century! The message had been put on after I retrieved it, if you can work that out. I don't like it. It's not natural. I feel as if I am in a time warp. How can you read something before it is writ? I could be drummed out of the Luddite society for this. Later, when I phoned home to ask how Madame Josephine, my cat, was behaving I discovered that it was fourteen hours beforehand. Still, I felt very pleased with myself. I'd found the Library, used the Loop, travelled the subway and discovered the internet. Wow!

Jaunting around on the Loop felt strange because, although you are elevated, the buildings around you are so high that you really don't see anything of them except their middle bits. You can see the tops of a couple if you look way, way up but there are so many of them crowded around you it becomes claustrophobic. I wondered why the city fathers had decided to make buildings so high and who used them all. Everything here seemed excessively big. Sears Tower, built in 1974, has one hundred and ten floors and, until recently, was the tallest building in the world. The tower is so high that to stand underneath and try to see the top you need to tip your head back until you hurt and then you can only just glimpse its summit. From a distance on the train the tower is long, thin and angular and its black facade makes it look sinister, like Darth Vader. And as for parting with sixteen dollars to ride to the top floor, forget it. This acrophobic would have to be paid to do that. I panicked on top of the Eiffel Tower, refused to get back in the open-fronted lift to go down again and ended up walking down thousands of stairs on the fire escape.

Most of the houses of the suburbs were wood or clapboard, two or three skinny storeys high and appeared European in style to me. But now and then I saw groups of two-storeyed brick houses, dreary affairs of boring identical boxes. On trains to the suburbs many people went to sleep. Every so often there would be an announcement admonishing passengers not to litter or indulge in other antisocial behaviour. And I was astounded to hear a promise to prosecute me if I solicited on the train. Solicited for what? I hate to think. Heaven forbid that it might be that which is not spoken of in polite circles.

Out among the masses it was impossible not to notice how many fatties there were. I don't mean pleasantly plump, but colossally gross. And sadly, many of these unfortunates were amazingly young. Some of the weight-disadvantaged wore most unsuitable clothes, such as tight lurex outfits in screaming orange, or skin-hugging terry-towelling short shorts that looked revolting. Now that I had seen the glut of sweet goodies that you get offered from breakfast onwards and the fast-food outlets, cafes and restaurants that abounded, I began to understand.

I mastered the international phone card I'd bought before leaving home. You punch in a stream of numbers, give your pin number and away you go. It's pre-paid and costs far less than locally made calls, especially in places like South America, where the rates are breathtaking.

My visit to the United States and the book fair had been an afterthought. South America was my aim and anything but an aircraft my choice of travel. I had not been able to find a ship crossing the Pacific at the time I wanted to travel but before I left home I had managed to book a passage from Miami to

Lima in Peru, via the Panama Canal on a German freighter. I had no idea what I would do when I reached Lima but I wanted to cross the South American continent overland and travel as far as I could on the River Amazon. This incredible river had stirred my imagination for as long as I could remember but I had delayed visiting South America because I was afraid – its reputation as a dangerous place is well-documented. At last, however, I had summoned the courage to take it on.

My ship didn't leave Miami for another three weeks. I wasn't sure where I wanted to go in that time but I wanted to travel by train and even though Chicago is the centre of the country's railways, I found that I couldn't get a train to the west coast and San Francisco except by taking a devious and horrendously priced route. So I bought a first-class sleeper ticket south to San Antonio in Texas and a connecting bus ticket to the Mexican border town of Laredo. I had decided that Mexico would be warm and cheap – and I could learn some Spanish in preparation for South America.

At one of Chicago's drug stores – they don't just sell drugs but are more like a supermarket – I asked the disinterested black girl who was supposed to sell stamps if I could buy some. She told me that they would have none until tomorrow, and admitted, when pressed, that when they had them they cost six dollars for a book of twenty.

'How much are they each?' I asked.

She looked vacant. 'Six dollars for twenty.'

'No, how much for one?'

She had no idea. She didn't know and she didn't intend to put herself out to find out. She just played with her hair.

I found it extremely hard to find a place that changed money. I went to where the current tourist-bureau publication said this feat was performed and after patrolling up and down the street several times finally found the shop. It was upstairs and at the rear of the given address. It also sported a sign saying that it had moved months ago. Someone directed me elsewhere. Strangely most banks won't change money. Several more directions later, some in opposite ways for the same place, I finally came to rest at a magnificent bank with malachite coloured marble all over the place in a riot of pomp and splendour.

Another day I set off to explore the streets surrounding the Three Arts Club on foot. This area is a pleasant leafy suburb that formerly housed the affluent in grand mansions, some of which remain. They are different from Australian stately homes in that they mostly have little or no front yard and are, like the lesser houses, right on the street. Small areas of lawns and flowers are dotted between the footpaths and the road among shady trees, and the sound of birds is everywhere.

Downtown looking for the post office, I asked several people the way but I never did find it. I was directed to a place with a clock tower that one woman said must be it. Passing a beauty shop where a big fat African-American with a big fat gold earring sat in the front window having a manicure, I came to this building. It was the old railway station that had been converted to an art gallery, but a computer shop next door sold stamps – logical.

On a frightful day that had suddenly become hot and windy I decided to go to Chinatown. I nearly got my head blown off waiting on the station platform, then got on a train going the wrong way and ended up back in the Loop. I then took the line promoted as the scenic route, but the view was just the same once you were out in the suburbs and, even though I went a long way to the end of the line, it didn't change. One line dives underground after leaving the city and continues for four stops then emerges into the sunlight like a monster rushing out of its hole. Standing in the gloom of the dingy subway cave waiting for the monster is a creepy feeling. Suddenly, with a tremendous racket it comes roaring up out of the bowels of the earth accompanied by great gusts of wind.

Entering Chinatown you walk through a gate ornately carved with dragons and are transported into streets lined by authentic Chinese shops. The people you pass are speaking Chinese. I came upon the Chinese branch of the public library and, having certain needs that were demanding to be met, entered the premises. Libraries are always a good source of a loo.

I set off to return to the city taking one of my famous short-cuts. I thought that the street I walked down must take me to the train station. It didn't. It led into a semi-enclosed alleyway. Halfway down it, with no one else in sight, I thought, Good grief, what a perfect place to get mugged. It was not a pleasant stroll and, emerging at the other end, I discovered that I was now really on the wrong side of the tracks. Not a soul was around except a group of black people who appeared to be living under the trees off to one side. I tootled past them as fast as I could then started on a path that I calculated must lead to the train line. But I was now in some kind of railway works. Round and round this I trudged until it ended at a high reinforced barbed wire fence. The place was deserted. I could have done what I liked in there. The gate had been open when I walked in so I wondered why they had all that barbed wire to keep people out. Backtracking to where I had started, I followed the road again for a long way and finally found the station. This time I resisted the urge to board a train going in the wrong direction and miraculously ended up where I belonged.

My last day came. I returned my towels, had my room checked to get my deposit back and, having booked the lift in writing in advance, waited for the escort without whom no one could use this precious piece of machinery. What did they think I was going to do with it – go for a joy ride?

Built in 1925, Chicago railway station has a stupendous, spacious, brightly lit entry hall containing long polished wooden seats. From there you progress to waiting rooms, cafes and shops. I was allowed into the wonderful Metropolitan Lounge, a place reserved for 'sleeping-car passengers'. Not 'first-class', I noted, for this egalitarian society. But what a contrast the Metropolitan Lounge was from the station's other waiting rooms, where hordes of folk were crammed in front of television sets blaring out soap operas. The Metropolitan Lounge had comfortable leather couches and club chairs, and free coffee, juice, Coke, buns, bikkies, baggage storage, telephones, TVs and marble bathrooms.

I jettisoned my bags, drank some coffee and walked over the bridge on the Chicago River to the downtown area. Now Chicago showed me some of its famous wind. It was incredibly strong. You had to walk perpendicularly to avoid being flattened. I nearly got blown off the bridge into the water and everyone I passed looked really weird with their hair standing straight up on end like a fright wig.

2 South of the border

Back at the Chicago railway station I sat beside the world's most boring woman, who told me she was reading a Christian romance novel. Apparently there exists a publishing firm that produces only this type of book. More power to them. I availed myself of another free drink. Fortunately this was a most comfortable place to read or knit while waiting, as I had been thrown out of the Three Arts Club at eleven and my train didn't leave until five. As soon as it was decently possible I moved away from the Christian woman and sat next to a smartly dressed black woman who turned out to be a publisher of travel books.

By listening to the announcements and speaking to other waiting people I discovered that, much as the railway's publicity department would like you to be impressed by its efficiency, every train runs at least two or three hours late. One man said his last train had been fourteen hours in arrears. My train departed ninety minutes behind time.

Walking out of the waiting room onto the train platform I had been surprised to find that it was already dark. Then I realised that the platforms were underground. I dragged the small bag that I was taking on board with me for kilometres along a long train and was shown into a compartment by a conductor. I was partly unpacked when he told me that I was in the wrong carriage. Then I had to walk more kilometres back again.

The railway personnel mostly gave me the impression of

being slightly off the planet. They didn't know what was going on and they didn't much care. A *National Geographic* survey found that one in seven Americans could not identify the United States on a map of the world. I rest my case.

My first-class compartment was a pokey little hole containing two seats that metamorphosed, with great difficulty, into a bed. Supposedly designed for two people, it was hard enough for just one to get in or out of – it would been a circus for two. My young black conductor, Lazy Boy, didn't help. He left the operation on the bed so late that I performed it myself in desperation. I really needed sleep. And what a struggle it was! Lazy Boy was really strange. Everything I asked him, he didn't know. His attitude was so laid back, he was almost flat out.

Not long after leaving Chicago the train stopped for a further half an hour's delay. Looking out of the window I saw several men moving along the line and the conductor said, 'Ah, they've gotta walk the train. That could take some time'. Apparently there was a fault in the air brakes. It was comforting to know it had been fixed. Or had it? No one said. Later several more unscheduled stops occurred.

At dinner everyone complained that you didn't get anything unless you asked for it on this train. 'Where's the sweet on the pillow the brochure advertised, or the early morning coffee?' But up a small flight of steps from my compartment on this double-decker train was a permanent supply of good coffee, bottled water, juice and Coke to which you could help yourself. On the top level there were bigger compartments with showers and toilets. As they were higher, they afforded a better view of the countryside – down at my level you mostly saw only the trees that were planted thickly along the railway line, although later these did thin out and I could see that everything was beautifully, verdantly green.

By the time I was allocated a dinner sitting at half past seven I was famished. I dined with three pleasant people who had massive, good-looking Texas rib-bone steaks that didn't, contrary to the description, contain a single bone. I had catfish with a black pepper coating. It was delicious, and I followed it up with a sinfully sweet desert.

After I had fought my way into my bed I tried to sleep, but whoever was driving this train had a mania for the horn – and leaned on it heavy, long and often. I was told that engine drivers had to sound the horn three times at every crossing. Well, the crossings must have been legion.

I woke up in Arkansas to discover that my breakfast sitting was now on. So much for the promised wake-up call. Dashing to my ablutions, I tried to use the shower down the corridor but I couldn't work out how to get the water to stay on, so I had a sketchy wash. The first time I had used the toilet the night before I had almost brained myself senseless. I had pressed what I took to be the flush button above the loo and, lo and behold, a clunky great baby-change table came crashing down on top of me. I've always suspected that babies are a danger to your health.

Presenting myself for breakfast, I sat outside the dining room for half an hour waiting my turn then, finally up at the trough, waited another hour for my bacon and eggs because one of the children at my table had ordered pancakes and they had run out of mix. Pesky child. The whole table had to wait. Eventually the pancake mix was obtained – maybe they got it at the next station. I had a communication problem with the ordering of the eggs. The waiter didn't understand fried eggs. You had to ask for easy or hard over or whatever, but when at last it arrived around lunch time, the breakfast was decent.

The trees along the line were a type of pine unfamiliar to me. The flourishing green crops were soya beans, a dwarf kind of maize that is used as cattle food, and a corn with a kernel-like wheat that is also used as animal feed.

In Little Rock someone hurled a huge pile of Sunday papers under my door. They contained a staggering amount of advertising pamphlets, confirming that this is a society inclining to the materialistic.

This train had one superior feature – electronic press buttons that opened doors between carriages, no struggling with a heavy door on a rocking train. But otherwise it was not a patch on Australian long-distance trains that run dead on time, are superbly well organised and have marvellous, willing service. Lazy Boy treated me like a nuisance.

It was Sunday in America. All the little towns of two-storeyed houses that we passed through had masses of cars outside their churches. We travelled further south until we were deep in Texas, where the country became less green and a lot like Australia in places. By dinner time that evening we were running three hours late, but it didn't matter to me as I had a long wait scheduled between the train's arrival and the departure of my bus. I ate an enormous tender steak then, returning to my compartment, saw that someone had interfered with my case, which I had left on the spare seat. A small purse had been left outside it. There was no way that I had done that. Nothing had been taken – the purse had been empty – but it made me feel peculiar. Earlier I had seen Lazy Boy acting suspiciously in another compartment and, as all the passengers from down this end of the carriage had been at dinner together, he seemed the prime suspect.

I slept a little as it got dark and at half past one in the morning we arrived in San Antonio. The air-conditioning on the train had been too cold and it was lovely to step down into the balmy fresh air. I was told that the four o'clock connecting bus to Laredo would come to the railway station door to collect me. In the waiting room I tried to sleep but it was a small crowded room and the carved polished wooden benches, although mighty attractive, were hard on the rear end and not conducive to a snooze. I read my book and talked to a hugely fat but agreeable woman.

I finished my book. I asked the station master about the bus a couple of times and was told that, yes, it was on time. Far be it from me to nag, but at five I finally said, 'Has the bus forgotten me?' And it was decided that it must have. The station master, a handsome, friendly, Mexican-looking man – almost all the locals here looked Mexican and were pleasant – tried to phone the bus depot but got no answer. He then gave me a voucher and sent me off in a taxi. The ease with which he made this arrangement left me thinking he'd probably had plenty of practice at it.

By the time I arrived at the bus station a faint pink glow of dawn was in the sky. The next bus to Laredo left in ten minutes. It was a Greyhound and supposedly a good bus but the seats were uncomfortable and the air-conditioning freezing. Halfway into the two-hour trip we stopped for a feed at McDonald's. I slept a little and then we were in Laredo where, to my surprise, everyone spoke Spanish. The taxi driver greeted me with 'Buenos Dias'. No one understood me when I spoke English.

I wanted to leave my big bag in storage at the bus station but the change machine didn't work. An affable chap who was washing the windows helped me get the bag in the box and minded it while I went to get change from the desk. A taxi took me a long way out of town to Motel Six, where I had booked a room. This district, just off the busy freeway, was a desolate place surrounded by a concrete jungle. By now the temperature was over one hundred degrees but I had a comfortable room so I took to my bed.

A good five-hour sleep later I went in search of dinner. I had used the phone in my room to ring a few travel agents and ask about the train to Mexico. No luck, it doesn't run any more. If I had known this beforehand I would have taken a bus direct to Mexico from the Laredo bus station.

In the diner next to the motel I ordered a dish of chicken breasts and vegetables that sounded delicious. But everything came fried and oozing fat. The huge chicken pieces were coated with thick slabs of breadcrumbs and the veggies were hidden in deep balls of batter. A large potato was piled high with cream and margarine and the whole mess was accompanied by a mountainous pile of heavily buttered French toast. At least it was filling.

At eight in the evening it was still a hundred degrees of very dry heat, no inducement for a walk. I went back to my room to watch television. There were about seventy channels. I was amazed by the advertisements permitted – cigarettes, medicines, divorce and anti-cancer drugs. Eating, getting un-married and taking medicine seemed to be generally very popular. I went to sleep watching the television and slept soundly for another eight hours.

I had heard that it could be a two-hour hassle to cross the border to Mexico but it was actually a breeze. In the morning at the Laredo bus station everyone treated me kindly again. This certainly seemed to be a friendly kind of town. I needed seven dollars in quarters to liberate my suitcase. Buses from Laredo run frequently to Nuevo Laredo just across the border and I only had an hour to wait for the next one. In the functional – well, uncomfortable – waiting room an old man peddling tacos for a dollar came up to my perch. That was breakfast.

In the fullness of time the bus arrived but the driver warned me not to get on it. He said it smelled very bad. I put my head in the door to perform the sniff test. It sure didn't smell like violets but I'm not as fussy as some folk; years of bedpans have seen to that. I think an inconsiderate person had left a baby's nappy in a rubbish bag. The driver said he'd take anyone who was game. One Mexican woman and I decided to brave it rather than wait. Once again everyone spoke Spanish and expected me to do so too.

We headed off. It is just a five-minute ride across the Rio Grande, which isn't all that grande but forms part of the 3326-kilometre Mexico–USA border. On the bridge long double lines of cars waited to cross from Mexico but there was no one waiting on our side. Once over the bridge I had to go through customs, but there seemed to be no immigration officials. I stepped off the bus, said that I was carrying nothing prohibited, walked through a shed, pressed a button that said 'passe', identified my bags and got back on the bus. No one looked at my passport.

Now I was in Mexico, a large country of almost two million square kilometres that borders Guatemala and Belize in the south and the USA in the north. It has coasts on both the Pacific and the Gulf of Mexico and two north–south mountain ranges that frame a broad group of plateaux varying in altitude from 1000 to 2300 metres. In the original land grab from the Indians, the area that is now Texas was part of Mexico, but in 1836 the territory seceded from Mexico to become an independent republic. From 1839 to 1841 an area of the Rio Grande valley of Mexico also declared itself separate and independent, proclaiming the Republic of Rio Grande with Laredo as its capital. The US annexation of Texas in 1845 precipitated a war with Mexico which the US won in 1847. After this the Rio Grande was established as part of the border and the Mexicans built the town of Nuevo Laredo, on their side of the river.

Mexico's civilization began long before that. The first people came down through America from Siberia across the land bridge that existed 60,000 to 80,000 years ago. By the time of Christ the great city of Teotihuacan was being built. It incorporated the Pyramid of the Sun, still the third-biggest pyramid in the world, and the Pyramid of the Moon, which is only slightly smaller. The Mayan culture flourished from 250 AD to 900 AD. The Mayans had a system of writing and calendars that accurately recorded earthly and heavenly events. Religion played a major role in early Mexican cultures but their gods were cruel, demanding frequent human sacrifices, usually by beheading or being thrown into a well, and blood-letting from ears, tongues and penises.

The Toltecs, who became a power around the thirteenth century AD in central Mexico, worshipped a feathered serpent called Quetzalcoatl until he was displaced by Tezcatlipoca – 'Smoking Mirror' – the god of warriors who demanded a regular diet of warm and often still-beating hearts. Wars were fought to obtain a steady supply of these organs from captured enemy soldiers.

By 1426 the Aztecs had become the most powerful people in the valley. They were also warlike and sacrificed prisoners, believing that this was necessary to keep the sun rising every day. In four days in 1487, twenty thousand prisoners were slain to dedicate a temple.

I found an intriguing description of a ball game that all early pre-hispanic Mexican cultures seemed to play. After the game one or more players would be sacrificed. No one knows whether winners or losers were chosen for this grisly end but I can't see it catching on in Australian Rules.

Nearly three thousand years worth of Mexican culture was destroyed in two years by the Spanish after their invasion in 1519. They annihilated the civilisation and reduced the native peoples to slaves or second-class citizens. In Mexico the Spanish leader Cortes is considered the villain of the piece. By 1821, when the fight for independence from Spain was successful, the population of Mexico consisted of native Indians and Mestizoes – a mixture of Indians, Spanish immigrants and African slaves. Now Mexico is a federal republic and, although it had been an almost entirely agricultural economy before 1910, it is one of Latin America's most industrialised countries. Ninety per cent of the eighty-one million population is Catholic. The missionaries of the sixteenth and seventeenth centuries won the local people over by grafting Catholicism onto the Indian religions, and witchcraft and magic still survive.

In Nuevo Laredo my financial expenditure took a turn for the better. Taxis had no meters but travelling quite a distance to find a hotel cost only five dollars. My first choice of hotel was full but the taxi driver took me elsewhere. At the Fiesta Hotel the receptionist said, 'Ah, Australian! Crocodile Dundee!' It seemed everyone who had heard of Australia associated us with crocodiles. The night before the TV in Laredo kept advertising that 'Croc week is coming'. The show they were referring to was that Australian fellow who over-acts with a lot of snakes and crocodiles.

The receptionist also told me that the train I had hoped to take from here into Mexico was no more. 'There was a train but not now,' he said. It had stopped running the previous week. The story of my life!

But all was not lost – the receptionist said that there were many buses going south during the day. All I would need to do was go to the station and wait for one.

My room was a few steps off the main street, up and down which I walked several times looking for it before I realised that this narrow path lined both sides with small grotty-ish shops was indeed it. Although unimpressive it stretches for two kilometres in one direction – south. In front of the shops lots of makeshift stalls sold tourist trash, as well as some decent handi-crafts, while posters on the walls advertised bull fights. I had expected downtown to be big and elaborate like Laredo across the river, but this was a totally different world. Still, it was pleasant enough, and no one hassled me to buy his wares.

My hotel room was Spanish in style and had a huge bed, much black iron-work placed against white-washed brick walls, a white tiled floor and heavy, black, wooden doors. I knew I was back in the Third World when the first room I was taken to had no light bulbs. We moved on to another. This room had only a couple of missing bulbs but the shower-head sat on the floor. The mattress on the bed was almost as old as I am and sagged nearly as much.

Next morning, when I tried to wash my hair, I found that the hotel's accoutrements did not run to hot water. I had to brave a cold shower. But my room did have good air conditioning and that was important in the heat.

I ate dinner at a cafe on the main drag. It must have catered to tourist tastes as I had the blandest enchaladas fobbed off on me as Mexican tucker. The meal's one redeeming feature was that it was cheap. The next day I found a local cafe and ordered one dish. It came complete with bean soup, salad and many side dishes but the food was still uninspiring.

At the station I found that a bus left for Monterrey, three hours south, almost immediately, but the bus to San Miguel de Allende, on the central plateau of Mexico, which I had chosen as my destination, did not leave until six in the evening. I took the Monterrey bus thinking that I would find another from there to San Miguel. I was most impressed by the Mexican bus. It had decent leg room and comfortable seats but it came complete with the obligatory screaming video. I inserted my ever-ready ear plugs and could still hear comfortably. The film was a dreadful James Bond but the subtitles helped me learn some Spanish. Everyone working for the bus line was polite. They found the bus for you, gave you a seat number and stowed your bags. There was even a toilet on the bus, albeit a cantankerous one. From the outside the door wouldn't open without a strenuous wrestle, and once inside it wouldn't shut.

We hadn't gone far into Mexico before we were stopped at a check-point. A soldierly type climbed onto the bus and videotaped us all, while others searched the baggage compartment under the bus. We were stopped and checked several more times along the way. Later, in San Miguel, I learned that highwaymen and bandits rob buses in the remote areas of the north. I was glad that I found this out after I had survived the trip through the most isolated part of Mexico unscathed.

On leaving Nuevo Laredo I had thought that I was now going to see the Mexico of legend, but the country didn't look particularly exotic. It was early summer and the sparse bushy scrub of the northern desert was still quite green although there were no trees. There was little sign of habitation, though a few cows appeared now and then as we drove further south, indicating that a ranch was out there somewhere. Later we progressed to clumps of trees, not pines and fir as in the USA but scrubby bush trees.

We came upon infrequent buildings that were square and flat-roofed with lean-to verandahs tacked on to their fronts. Some of these houses were crazily warped and their tin roofs rusted and sagging. In this 'great wasteland of the north' villages were few and far between along the road, although I saw one tiny place that consisted of a small congregation of primitive dwellings and a dog so skinny that its legs splayed out as though they didn't have the strength to hold it up.

Apart from the cows and the dog I saw only an occasional lone eagle, hawk or buzzard. Grazing animals had pushed the native mountain lions, deer and coyotes into isolated areas. Still common are armadillos, snakes and rabbits but I saw none. I read that the tropical forests of the south and east continue to harbour howler monkeys, jaguars, tapirs, anteaters, toucans, and reptiles such as boa constrictors, while iguanas and other lizards are found in warm parts.

Then we were driving through desert where prickly pear and cacti shaped like strange, long toilet brushes poked up into the sky. Most of the world's fifteen hundred species of cactus are found in Mexico. The sides of the road were dotted with shrines made of wood, cast iron, concrete and metal that commemorated road accident victims. Each time relatives or friends visit the site they leave a pebble or stone and cairns are created. A grim warning for the traveller.

Monterrey bus station is enormous. I encountered six waiting rooms in front of the various bus starting gates and several garishly decorated religious shrines where nervous passengers could seek fortitude. The entrance to the toilets was lit up like a nightclub by a big neon sign under which a woman guard was stationed. You put a coin in a box and she moved a turnstile to admit you. When I first saw this alluring-looking place on the far wall of the station I thought it must be something interesting, like a casino.

Sitting in the adjacent waiting room listening to the sound of constantly dropping coins, I decided that the toilets were doing a roaring trade. But it was worth the point two of a peseta you paid to get admitted. The walls were tiled all the way up to the ceiling but the doors didn't lock and reached only to your shoulders – just high enough to cover your personals and the business end of you. Toilet paper was not provided in the stalls. This ensured that you didn't play with it or, worse, put it in your pocket. A big communal roll of paper hung on the wall by the entrance door and as you came in you were permitted, under the eagle eye of the attendant, to take some. Later I found some places that didn't even allow you this liberty but doled you out a ration. Unfortunately I didn't realise this until it was too late to go back for some.

I had thought I would find a bus to San Miguel de Allende leaving fairly soon but there wasn't one until nine that night so I had a long wait. Depositing my bags in the cloak room I went into the VIP lounge. I had a first-class ticket so I figured I was entitled to use these facilities, but I was soon disabused of that notion. A guard woman very nicely asked to see my ticket and then directed me back out with the common herd. I was curious to find out who these VIPs were who rode on buses – the lounge was huge but it was empty.

I spent the day hanging about the waiting rooms, trying them all in turn, alternately reading or knitting and watching the people. Many Mexican men are extraordinarily hand-some in their ten-gallon hats, cowboy boots and silver-buckled belts. Some are very dark-skinned. I had noticed the change in people's looks as soon as I had arrived in San Antonio and from there on it seemed every man wore a ten-gallon hat. I did not see one sombrero in Mexico, just ten-gallon white-straw or black-felt cowboy hats. Had they seen too many Western movies? At one stage a forty-year-old man sat next to me engrossed in a comic book.

I had expected a bit of spitting but it was the nose-blowing with the fingers onto the shiny terrazzo floor that I found off-putting. I filled in an hour having lunch in the expensive restaurant, which was baking hot. Conversely, it had been freezing in the VIP lounge so I'm glad I didn't stay there – sour grapes!

In the evening I saw a bus pulling in that I thought was the one I wanted. I confirmed this with a gorgeous Mexican man who appeared to have something to do with the staff, and he helped me take my bags to the departure point. I went off to buy a bottle of water and when I returned another man was standing guard over my bags. He proceeded to give me, I think, a lecture along the lines of: 'You shouldn't have left them.' I thought it was kind of him to care. I had been warned that Mexico was the land of machismo and a violent country where you must take all precautions against theft. And that pocket-picking and purse-snatching was common – not to mention highway robbery on buses and trains, especially at night in the north. And Mexico City was reputed to be so bad I had decided not to go there.

The extremely comfortable, but extremely cold bus was almost empty. One other woman, six men and I made up the complement of passengers. After an hour and a half's travel we stopped for thirty minutes and continued to do so regularly for the rest of the way, probably because we had only one driver, who was closeted like a jet pilot in a curtained cabin at the front of the bus. Noise emanating from in there sounded very much like a television. Was he absorbed in his favourite soap opera? Asleep? Dead? You'd never know. Our driver had to contend with tremendous winds, rain and wet roads coming up into the mountains. We were catching the edge of a hurricane that was causing havoc further south and was spreading across the country.

The first stop we made was at a shop that was really just a cement-floored shed with a few metal racks scattered with a meagre supply of goods. I tried to buy some provisions but the stock leaned heavily to biscuits and drinks and all I got were some ghastly sweet wafers. Back on the bus I slept off and on and it didn't seem very long before it was a quarter to five in the morning. I snoozed again and then it was seven o'clock and getting light. There were, thank goodness, no videos on this bus.

Approaching San Miguel de Allende the bus stopped in out-back country at a run-down farm house where an old man in a ten-gallon hat and cowboy boots got off. The beginnings of the town were very ordinary looking; shabby ramshackle little square boxes of houses with flat roofs. The bus station was small but pleasing with its religious shrine and a lavatory entrance once again lit up something gorgeous – green on one side for males, pink on the other for females and in between colourful pastoral scenes painted on the walls and flowers, albeit plastic, everywhere.

I taxied to the youth hostel where the taxi driver asked me for fifty pesos. I said, 'No. Twenty five.'

'Si,' he said and smiled.

The hostel was a quaint place that fronted right onto the old cobblestone street. At first glance these streets look as though they contain nothing except decrepit walls, then you notice that there are gates in the wall. The hostel's gate had an open grille above it and a plaque in the wall that declared its identity. A big piece of wood hung down on a rope and you pulled this to ring a bell and summon help. I pulled the rope and inside the gate discovered a lovely courtyard filled with plants and flowers.

But I soon learned that this was not the place for me. According to the guide book the hostel had single as well as double rooms. The proprietress denied this. She had one double, which she refused to let to a single. That book has a lot to answer for. But the woman was very helpful and directed me elsewhere. The San Bernado Hotel where I eventually came to roost, was the first hotel so far since I'd left home that hadn't insisted on the money up front. I didn't have enough Mexican pesos to pay but I was assured that this was okay. I wrapped myself in a thick Mexican blanket, fell on the bed and slept for four hours.

3 Illegal!

When I woke I got smartened up and went to look at the town. San Miguel de Allende is a colonial town of old buildings and cobbled streets in a beautiful hillside setting that affords splendid vistas of plains and mountains in Guanajuanto state. The entire town has been declared a national monument to protect it.

There had been irrigation-based agriculture here since 200 BC. After the Spanish invasion, a barefoot Franciscan friar called Fray Juan de San Miguel started a mission here in 1542. Later a Spanish garrison was established to protect the road from the south to the mines of Guanajuanto, which for two centuries produced up to forty per cent of the world's silver as well as gold, iron, lead, zinc and tin and are still important sources of silver and gold. Ranchers and crop-growers followed the road and San Miguel grew into a thriving commercial centre where the silver barons built sumptuous homes and lived opulently on slave labour.

San Miguel was also the home of the Mexican revolution. Ignacio Allende, who was born here in 1779, organised the uprising for independence. He was executed in 1811 before independence was gained, but in 1826 the town was re-named San Miguel de Allende in his honour.

In 1938 the Escuola De Bellas Artes was built and in the forties painting classes at the school attracted artists from all over Mexico, the United States and other countries. This high, unpolluted place has a superb light. Writers and other arty types gravitated in the painters' wake and from the 1950s the Instituto Allende's Spanish courses have attracted foreign students. But I didn't see many foreigners – they don't come south until it is winter up north.

The San Bernado Hotel (everything possible here was San something) was a joy. An unprepossessing walled exterior presented to the street, but once inside the immense, carved, creaking wooden doors I found a tiled foyer that opened onto a delightful courtyard filled with pots, plants, creepers and a life-sized whimsical statue of a musician complete with guitar. A red-flowered tachoma vine with a trunk like a tree wound up three storeys to cover the flat roof top and pergola. On one side of the courtyard was an extremely high wall covered with creeping vines. A fountain with a pool at its feet was set in the wall. On the other side were guest rooms that opened onto the courtyard on the ground floor or the verandah on the floor above. The courtyard and balconies were surrounded by brick arches in which stood pedestals and embossed earthernware pots that overflowed with bright red and pink geraniums, impatiens and bougainvilleas.

The floor of my second-storey room was tiled, as were half the walls, and inset in the floor tiles, as well as in the roof of the bathroom, were thick, old embossed glass bricks, twelve inches square. You walked on them as well as using them as skylights. On my balcony I had a comfortable chair covered with leather, and an iron garden seat. From the balcony two tiled steps led up to my wooden door with its glass insets, either side of which were wooden framed windows with iron grilles. Inside, my room had fine old carved furniture, a big comfortable bed, reasonable lights and, in the bathroom, the weirdest window – it had an open hole in its centre. At night I stuck a carrier bag over it to keep out the cold.

I should have realised when I first entered Mexico and saw containers for used toilet paper alongside the loos what the significance of this was. But the penny didn't drop until, arriving at this hotel and throwing a wad of paper down the loo, I spent the rest of the day trying to unblock it. The antiquity of the Mexican sewerage system does not tolerate paper in its drains. Just because it was called toilet paper didn't excuse that use of it.

At the hotel reception desk, Dino, the resident spaniel, wandered in to have a sniff of me. I saw no stray dogs in Mexico, just a few well-cared-for pets.

I had been practising Spanish since before I left home and had a set of cassette tapes and a book along with me. I was getting better at it and managed to say, 'Where is the bank please?' to the hotel receptionist. The response was a stream of instructions I failed to understand, but after walking around for two-and-a-half hours I discovered that I was billeted close to the central square, the Plaza Principal, also known as The Jardin, which is the focal point of the town. On one side of it was the seventeenth-century parroquia, a pink, sugar-coated Gothic church with strange, pointed, soaring pinnacle spires that could be seen all over town and which were a nineteenth-century addition designed by an untutored local Indian said to have scratched the plans in sand with a stick. I believe it – it looks like it was designed by a blind man and built in the dark. The clock on the church struck regularly at a quarter past the hour but never got the time right.

I looked in the parroquia, discovering that was the word for church and not the parrots I had been asking the girl at the hotel about. Never mind. Inside the church was stupendous – just how I think churches should be – but I wondered whom the Spanish made do the building work. It was constructed of rough stone and had a huge cupola of brickwork high up in the roof, but at ground level everything was very ornate. There were several altars, the main one superlative, some magnificent glass chandeliers, pretty coloured-glass windows and a battalion of gilded statues. In the front courtyard the inevitable fountain burbled away, surrounded by ancient trees that, by the width of their trunks, looked as though they were planted when the church was built.

The centre of the piazza sported an elegant rotunda where on this day a band played martial music to lorry-loads of children who were massed around it. The uniforms they wore differed for each school, but the girls all wore long, white socks and looked neat and smart.

I walked many kilometres, saw a great deal of this lovely town and found all kinds of delights. But you had to watch how you stepped on the uneven old cobble stones of the street and the narrow footpaths made of rough-hewn stone blocks. Passing windows grilled with fancy metal bars and glazed with patterned glass, it seemed that everything had the touch of time on it. I encountered wooden doors with tiled facings, carved panels and peep windows barred with simple slats and spools or delicate iron scrollwork, personalised knockers, huge hammered metal key holes and handles, overhanging ancient lights, textured walls and swinging wooden signs. It was like a living museum.

I finally worked out that all the funny little hole-in-the-wall places that I had been walking past in my search for the shops were in fact what passed for them in this town and, once I poked about inside, I realised that they actually had all I needed. From the outside each shop looked to be merely a wooden door in a wall and the small signs above the doors hadn't registered with me. Some of the shops around the piazza were tiny jewels packed full of gorgeous trinkets, ornaments and jewellery meant for the rich or tourists. And some were teeny cafes that contained two minuscule tables and seats for only four people.

The central area of the Jardin was constantly being swept by women with old-fashioned straw brooms. Most things were done the old way here and, as most floors were tiled, everywhere I went someone always seemed to be sweeping or mopping – even in the big bank, which possessed a bit of carpet, a woman scraped away with a straw broom. Despite all this cleaning activity, I saw much rubbish strewn about on roadsides and empty blocks as I rode around the outskirts of town in local buses.

I bought the local English-language newspaper and read it on a bench under the Jardin's trees. The major news of the week was contained in a long article concerning the only person who seemed to have died lately in San Miguel. It described in gory detail how he fell down on the steps of the church, hit his head and 'pools of blood came out'. The departed had been unidentified for a while so all his clothing was described minutely by the reporter. Then came a harrowing tale of how his relatives came and looked at him through the glass window of the morgue. There was a blow by blow account of the proceedings, concluding with the comments of onlookers outside the church who had said 'what a good thing it was that he had just been to confession', and 'how fortunate for him to have died in a state of grace'. No one mentioned that going to church seemed to be a health hazard. I wandered into several churches but managed to avoid starring in the local paper, perhaps because I wasn't in a good enough state of grace. All the churches were much the same in degrees of grandiosity and over-the-top decor.

As I walked along I decided that the folk here must be honest. I saw vendors' carts left unattended in the gutters protected only by a piece of cloth that had been thrown over the contents and tucked in at the corners. You wouldn't be able to do that down in Mexico City from what I'd read.

I was completely floored by the beauty of the town's bank and wondered why all banks couldn't be like this. Entering from the street through big wooden gates and a little portico, you came to the teller's desks, which were on one side of yet another open courtyard full of natural light where flowers bloomed around a fountain. Mexicans seemed to be able to make all kinds of mundane places attractive. Unfortunately this didn't always go hand in hand with efficiency. For some unfathomable reason the bank only changed dollars between half-past-nine and eleven in the morning. And later, between one and four, came siesta when everything shut.

The market was just a short way down the street from my hotel. It had a big veggie section packed with many stalls of fresh produce where I bought some delicious guavas. There were also stalls that sold huge glasses of fresh juices that I tried and found scrumptious. Women sat on the ground with cactus and prickly pear fruit laid out neatly in green rows on mats. The rest of the goods were pretty ordinary – clothes, shoes and tourist junk. No one harassed me. I could stop and fiddle with the goods to my heart's content. I sat on a stool at the counter of a makeshift stall and had hamburgerzitas – better than McDonald's and you got chips too. The chips were fried in corn oil, not cooked all the way through and came covered with sweet tomato sauce. The hamburgerzita had a slice of ham to keep the meat patty company as well as cheese and salad.

Street food stalls, where people sat on tiny stools alongside the gutter or walls, offered food that looked yummy. There were tacos and corn cobs grilled on braziers. After drinking my fijoa juice I watched the proprietress washing glasses with water from a tap on the wall and realised that it probably came from the canal. I'd passed the canal on my walk. It was a stinking horror of filth.

In a small shop I bought a bag of local coffee, bananas, bottled water and laundry powder that was sold from an open drum for a peso a kilo. It smelt like Omo, looked like Omo and was blue, so I can only hope it was. Seeing some bottles of hair colour I decided that if I rinsed my hair a bit darker it might make me look more like a local. Most Mexicans look half Indian. There are 1.7 million descendants of ancient Aztecans in the country.

And now I looked like one of them. I hadn't meant to come out jet black like an Indian but, as usual, what I had hoped would be a light golden brown had turned out a definite light golden black. Maybe it worked. People now seemed surprised whenever I said 'No, hablo espanol'.

That evening I ate at a small cafe close to my hotel. When I sat down at the table I thought that the red cloth had a pattern of black dots on it but the dots, resenting my intrusion, arose en masse and flew away. The waiter casually flicked their retreat along with a tea towel. Then I saw that the whole place was swarming with flies. They left me alone, however, while I ate a solid meal of enchaladas stuffed with cheese and drank delicious fresh orange juice. After dinner I was chewing gum to clean my teeth and, good grief, there was tooth filling in the gum. Lots of it. Oh, no, not again! This had happened to me in China. Why was it that the minute I got to a third-world country I lost a filling?

At seven in the morning, before it was even properly light, I was awoken by the sound of clanging church bells – and what I hoped were firecrackers and not a revolution going on outside. At first I thought that this day must be Sunday, but it wasn't. The bells started again at twelve and I decided that if this happened on a week day, I couldn't wait to see what Sunday brought. On Sunday the usual morning bells tolled and then at half past eleven and twelve more bells joined in and the lot went berserk. You couldn't miss going to mass here – the bells wouldn't let you.

During the day I found the library. According to my map it was straight down the street, turn right and you can't miss it, but real life doesn't work that way. After a fruitless search I asked for help from a woman who was carrying some books. I had walked past the library twice. I had been expecting something set back off the road in a large building with a huge sign, but this library was entered through the usual heavy wooden doors in a high wall. Only a small plaque set in the wall gave away its identity. A portico led into a cobbled courtyard dotted with chairs and tables shaded by umbrellas, where a fountain trickled dreamily in the centre. Tall pencil pines fronted by flowering plants stood sentinel around the four sides of the courtyard, while bougainvillea massed with purple flowers climbed the surrounding arched walls. Under the arches and colonnades at the far end were long wooden tables and chairs. In this enchanting, peaceful spot I spent a couple of happy hours and decided it was so wonderful I could live there. I gave it my vote for the best library in the world. The Chicago Library gets the vote for the most magnificent but San Miguel's is the most delectable.

Cool, quiet rooms full of books radiated out from the courtyard and up a set of stone steps was a restful cafeteria in an upper courtyard filled with flowers and bird song. Up more rough-cut stone steps that took you out on the roof I found the stone office that housed the computer room. It faced the massive old stone walls and arches of the church next door, which looked like a fortress from the street. With a little help from a bystander, I used the internet to send an e-mail.

Returning from the library, I unwittingly walked past the corner of my street and went all the way around the town and through the square to come back the way I had gone. I did this twice more before I recognised where I was. What's new!

Every now and then in the streets I would pass a water spout in a wall, beneath which was a sickle-moon-shaped tiled receptacle for the water to fall into. In the past people would have come there to get water. When it rained heavily, as it did some days, you would only have to stand outside with a basin.

I found a shop that sold small, round local cheeses and bought one. I think it was made from goat's milk. It tasted rather home-made and could have been anything, but it was okay with the toast I had been able to buy in packets like bread. My hotel didn't run to meals, so in the morning, after boiling water with my immersion heater, I made coffee in the little metal filter I bought in Vietnam. With cheese, toast and a banana, what more could you want for breakfast? Bacon, eggs, sausages and a steak for a start.

Mexicans were unfailingly friendly to me. As soon as I spoke to them they would smile. They didn't know what I wanted, I could have been about to complain, but they smiled and seemed happy to help me. Even with my fractured Spanish I got by reasonably well.

The weather was divine in the mornings and warm in the afternoons, but on my first night in the town I nearly froze. The evening had been reasonably cool so I had a hot shower and got into bed. Half an hour later I was almost asleep when the cold fell on me as though someone had chucked a bucket of water over the bed. My whole body went into spasms of shivering. I got up and put on all the warm clothes I had, including long-johns and a cardigan, but still I shivered. In the morning I asked for another blanket and during the day a very heavy one materialised on the bed. I doubled it over and, of course, sweated all through the next night. Now I understood why there was a large, obviously well-used, open fireplace in my room. Even with this as encouragement I don't think I'd survive the winter here.

This was the wet season, which lasts from May to October, and the nights were stormy. Active volcanos dwell in this mountain area and after I returned to Australia I heard that an earthquake had killed many people in San Miguel.

I loved my delightful room, especially the minute street-front balcony where I put out food for my friends the sparrows, who came every morning for breakfast. On my first morning a couple of sparrows had flown down to sit on the electricity wires strung across the street close to the balcony. They had perched there for so long looking hopeful that I wondered if they were accustomed to receiving hand outs. I put some of my crumbled toast on top of the balcony rail and within minutes they were eating it. Other little birds hopped around in the courtyard below the other side of my room, filching the fallout from the budgies that spent their days in cages hung on the wall.

Standing at the hotel reception desk in the early morning when I first arrived, I had heard the loud cheeping of birds. The sound seemed to be emanating from the reception room itself but, although I looked around, I couldn't see any cages. I asked the receptionist about this and she pointed to the floor. On a low bench I saw a stack of cages piled three high and covered with a cloth. Underneath the cover a dozen budgerigars were chirping to let it be known that they wanted to go outside to their places on the wall. The sparrows hop in and out of the creepers and crevices of the walls all around the cages and I wondered how the poor little budgies watching them felt about this. As I observed the sparrows flying around in the mornings, zipping in and out among the roof tops and landing on my wires, I thought of the bumper sticker that my hang-gliding nephew displays: 'Hang gliders know why the birds sing.' I bet the caged budgies know why the birds sing. I wondered if they still longed for the feel of the wind beneath their wings.

One night as I came out of the cafe up the road from the hotel, I noticed a huge black cloud hanging over the nearby hills. Back at the hotel I climbed up to sit on the roof patio and watch this marvellous, inky cloud stream down off the mountain dragging the rain behind it and bringing the storm. At first a few big splatters fell and then a deluge followed, accompanied by deafening claps of thunder and brilliant stabs of lightning. As soon as the rain began two of the hotel girls rushed outside to bring the budgies in.

Another evening we had the grandmother of all storms. I had got used to it raining a little most evenings but this was excessive. At four o'clock the sky was dark and lowering and it was raining a little, but by five, when I had gone out for a walk, it was throwing it down by the bucketful. I walked around for a while looking into some attractive, drowned courtyards but, much as I love a storm, after half an hour I gave up. This town was not built for hoofing about in such an assault. Even with my brolly aloft I got soaked and the turmoil was no longer fun. The houses had no gutters – water simply ran off their flat roofs by means of a whacking great pipe, which sent it splashing down into streets that were soon awash in torrents. Too bad if your car happened to be underneath a pipe.

At the hotel I sat on my balcony above the courtyard, thrilled by the stupendous thunder and lightning right over-head, while rain poured from the roof pipes and splashed to flood the courtyard, thoroughly washing the flagstones and making everything sparkle. In my room, water started rushing through the unglazed bathroom window and very old wooden French doors that opened onto the balcony on the street side. I thought I'd soon need a boat. Fortunately the floor was tiled, so no damage was done.

During the night more heavy rain fell and at one time I woke to find that my feet were wet. I couldn't work out how this had happened until I looked up and saw that the roof was leaking from a hole where a light had once been suspended. I had already noticed the remains of old kerosene light fittings in the verandah alcoves and other places in the hotel. I was surprised that the electric power held out through this onslaught – there were a few big flickers. I didn't look forward to telling the housemaid that I'd wet my bed.

When morning dawned the sun shone brilliantly and it was bliss to sit on a low wall waiting for a bus. This is one way to see life, I mused – sit in the gutter with a few of the local people. The bus driver must have had child-care duty that day, as he had his two-year-old baby girl with him. In these tin buses there was a flat area like an extended dashboard alongside the driver on which there was usually a box for the fare money, or else the money was simply spread on a piece of cloth. There didn't seem to be any fear of theft. Neither was there a feeling of danger in the streets. People carried handbags and wore bumbags without fearing robbers. I noticed that people also paid as they got off the bus rather than when coming aboard. This driver had squeezed a rug into an indentation next to his money and his baby slept on it unconcerned. Later the wee one sat up on the front of the dash and watched the oncoming traffic. What a good little girl. There was not a peep out of her.

At times I saw other people working with a child in tow. A school teacher who was taking a group of older children out held a tot that was sucking on a bottle by the hand. I don't think it was in school.

Turning my attention, reluctantly, to my damaged tooth, I decided to ask directions to a dentist from the man who ran the book shop at the library. A waspish little fellow, he was the only English speaker I'd found, but so far his track record wasn't good. It was he who had directed me to a mythical book shop when I asked him where I could buy a Spanish dictionary. He was the sort of person who goes to live in foreign climes, considers the place his own and gets jealous of anybody else elbowing in. When you ask these people something they tell you the answer very fast and in the local accent so that you won't understand. The book shop, I discovered much later by accident after several fruitless searches, was in a street called Jesus, but it was not pronounced the way it was written in English and he sure as all hell wasn't going to write it down. But he did tell me the address of a dentist down the road, probably hoping I was going there to endure much pain.

Once at the dentist's I discovered, by pantomime, that 'El Dottore' was away. I got another dentist's address but was told not to go there until Monday. I supposed I'd live till then. I ate lunch in a tiny local cafe, unfortunately called the Colon. A set meal called *comida* – lunch – began with scrumptious tomato-based soup with melted corn chips, chunks of white goat's cheese and avocado in it. I am such a messy eater that I normally never eat soup in public, but now I splashed it all down my front with gay abandon and didn't give a hoot. I'd watched the locals at table and decided that anything goes. They slurped soup and shovelled food into their mouths with rolled-up flat bread. I was in my right element here. Following the soup came a thin beefsteak that was small, tough, but tasty and covered with a delectable meat sauce. It was like a lucky dip trying to find the meat but there was plenty to mix with the sauce – the cheese on top of it, rice and the ubiquitous bean paste that you are given with every meal as a side dish.

But no chilli. I asked for some and was given a big bowl from which I ladled liberally. I had expected Mexican food to have lots of chilli.

Lastly came a teeny sweet so small you could have put it in your eye. I think it was meant to be a creme caramel. The entire meal cost about five dollars including great coffee. Mexicans eat three meals; *desayanyo* (breakfast), *comida* (lunch) and *cena* (dinner), but lunch is the main meal of the day. Most meals contained the staples: tortillas – patties of pressed corn – and beans.

While eating I stared across the road at the San Francisco church, the dark old stone wall of which goes straight up like the rampart of one of those grim medieval castles that were built expressly to keep out marauders. The wall was a huge stone blob roughly made from rocks with no hand or toe holds on its face, but there were small octagonal windows set into it way up high. These windows and little holes in the stone work close by were inhabited by pigeons. It must have been nesting time because every now and then one deter-mined pigeon, who between times rested in nearby window ledges, kept trying to invade one of the nesting sites. The occupier, equally determined, would repulse his incursion and back he'd go to his ledge to prepare for a fresh assault. Again and again he did this. Talk about a slow learner.

I'd stopped worrying about looking the wrong way when crossing the road. Motorists here were too polite to run you over. The policeman even stopped the sparse traffic for me. Buses seemed improbable in the tiny streets but they managed – it helped that they were quite small. Volkswagen beetles seemed to be the car of choice. Even official cars were old-style VWs.

One morning dawned a day of fiesta – Dias Los Locos, the day of the crazies. The church bells had started at seven the night before. They were followed by cannon shots, then more bells joined in until all three nearby churches were clanging away: San Francisco down on the corner with its lovely big peals, the parroquia in the piazza and the little tinny local church's bell that could hardly be heard as they all tried to outdo each other. On and on they rang, stopping now and then for a cannon shot or two. It was deafening. And it started again early the next morning.

The day before I had seen a couple of elderly nuns wearing old-fashioned habits preparing for the festival by filling the local church with great bowls massed with beautiful flowers. The hotel staff also deposited roses in bottles covered with silver foil at strategic spots. There were wonderful flowers galore here. Everywhere I went I saw people walking about with armfuls of gladioli, roses or carnations.

In the morning everybody in the town was out. Rows of children had been sitting on the edges of the blocked-off streets for an hour or more. I went for a walk and had to make a wide detour to get back to the hotel; the town centre was so packed you couldn't move in it. Then, quite unexpectedly during my detour, I finally came upon the no-longer mythical bookshop. But wouldn't you know, the sign read 'closed for the holiday'.

The parade, luckily for me, passed under my window, and

I stood on my balcony to watch. Men walked in front of the high vehicles holding up the overhead cables with forked sticks so that they could pass underneath without fear of electrocution. Good thinking. Everyone wore a mask. The very popular Bill Clinton mask was most realistic. It had big red kisses all over it, a silly fatuous grin and the head was slightly on one side. It really looked like him. One float demonstrated local anti-American feeling. It portrayed US border guards returning Mexican would-be immigrants across the Rio Grande, illustrating a recent case where two men drowned while trying to swim back. Clowns and costumed dancers threw confetti and sweets to the crowd from the floats. Among all this racket one dear donkey placidly plodded wearing a funny hat and garlands of flowers and pulling a small float.

There seemed to be a contest in Loud. Every truck bore the biggest set of speakers its owners could find. The revellers, dressed up and dancing on the rough cobblestones, looked set to party on all night. The procession took eighty minutes to pass. The next day I wasn't surprised to see bandaged ankles adorning the walking wounded.

Never mind dancing, just walking around was hard on the feet. The town slopes uphill from east to west from the square and those cobblestones are murder after a while. It must have been tough on the poor horses in the old days. I heard a horse clip-clopping past my room late one night but apart from a couple that were pulling drays, I didn't see any in the town though there were plenty of donkeys on the outskirts.

It was a high step up from the street to the narrow sidewalks and I was told that this was the height at which it was convenient to alight from a carriage. Sidewalks were also only wide enough for one person, so if you met someone coming the other way one of you had to step down into the gutter and give way. Some of the wide doorsteps came right over the footpath and left only six inches to walk on, and old ladies were given to sitting on their steps as though this was now their role in life. The ones who were begging sat on the steps of churches or municipal buildings.

San Miguel seemed to have more than its share of old women, but there were not many beggars. All of these were old people, a few men but mostly old ladies who, enveloped in their shawls, looked like bundles of rags. All old ladies wore shawls over their heads and shoulders in the traditional manner. Now and then I saw a tiny antiquated one wrapped like an untidy parcel. She hobbled along, bent almost double, so slowly that I couldn't see how she kept moving.

Early on Monday morning I set off by taxi in search of the dentist. Her surgery was a long way out of town, up on a hilltop in a posh private hospital that was painted brilliant blue and could be seen for miles. Of course I was in the wrong building at first. It was the emergency department. Mind you, after I got the bill I needed the emergency department. Directed to the correct building, I saw a door on one side of it and, walking in, found myself in the drug cupboard. Very handy. I could have had anything I desired, no need to hold up this lot at gunpoint for a fix. Hastily correcting my error before I was arrested, I entered the right door and was sent upstairs, where a charming girl told me that she was the secretary, as well as the nurse, but that the dentist wasn't there. Two out of three ain't bad, I guess. But I should have known that no one started work here until at least ten. I waited. La Dentista arrived and said that she would see me at one o'clock. This was kind of her as I realised that this was her siesta time. I hoped she wouldn't nod off over my tooth.

I decided to go back to my hotel and return later. Standing outside the hospital I saw a bus come by with 'Centro' on it. Why not? I thought, and jumped on. I paid two-and-a-half pesos – fifty cents – and to my total confoundment arrived back almost at my door. I was glad that I had braved the rigours of the crammed, jolting little bus. Made entirely of tin – even the seats were tin – it was a peasant-class bus but squeaky clean. When the next one I took – once I got the hang of it you couldn't get me off them – stopped at its terminus, two boys – this bus was more upmarket than most, it had a conductor as well as a driver – got out kerosene tin buckets and scrubbed that bus from one end to the other. Inside and out they sloshed away, having a wonderful time. And every time I went past the buses standing on the main streets of the town, they were being washed. So much for Mexico being dirty, as I had been frequently told in the States when I said I intended travelling there.

Returning to the dentist for my one o'clock appointment, I thought that, with the superior knowledge of buses I had now acquired, I could do the trip again but in reverse. I got on a bus labelled 'Central', which you'd think would be the same as 'Centro'. Not on your nelly. At least I was now understood when I asked directions of the drivers – well, I guess it's not too hard to say, 'Ospedale de la Fay'. But it turned out that the bus I had boarded went past the turn-off, so I was put off at the corner at the wrong end of that horribly steep hill. It was a terrific climb and I only just made it in time.

The charming dentist spoke good English and chatted pleasantly while she X-rayed the offending tooth. Then she told me what needed to be done and proceeded to stuff a great big piece of rubber in my mouth and clamp it in place. A lot of people have wanted to do that before now, I can tell you. Was this precaution to protect the dentist or me? Her, I think. After this device had been inserted, the nurse and dentist took turns squirting water and liquid goo into my mouth. The sucker, which was meant to save me from drowning, didn't quite reach the fluids as the bloody rubber thing was in the way. There I lay, being put through the water torture. I was not able to swallow, as I couldn't lift my tongue. To have a lot of water shoved in the back of your throat while you are lying down is decidedly not nice – but at least there was no pain.

To take my mind of my imminent asphyxiation I stared at the purple – yes, purple – gloves of the perpetrators of this crime. I could see Edna Everidge wearing those gloves – they matched the mauve walls nicely. The rest of the gear my tormentors wore looked like they were ready for a trip to the moon – they were totally encapsulated in space suits. I, on the other hand, was utterly unprotected from them.

The nastiest cruelty was saved for last. The bill for the repair of one filling was two hundred and twenty dollars.

From the hospital I took one bus down the hill and another to the 'estacion tren' – gee I was proud of myself. Still hoping to find the train I had read about for my return to the States I had asked a young man at the tourist bureau in the piazza about it. He had said that there was a train but that it was unreliable. I found a very fine train station, but except for a small freight office at one end, it was an empty echoing shell. The attendant managed to convey to me that there was no passenger train, only cargo ones. I waited for the bus to have its wash and bought a Coke in a lean-to of a cantina for three pesos as opposed to the ten they cost in town. Cantinas are bars/cafes that are for men only in Mexico so I didn't linger. Then I moseyed on to the long distance bus station where I discovered that there was a bus that goes all the way across the border and on to San Antonio in Texas. The ticket seller told me that the trip takes thirty hours.

I bought a ticket for this bus – which left in two days time – using only Spanish. Every day I had been doing my lessons on the tape recorder and now they were paying off. But Spanish was a puzzlement at times. They don't pronounce 'h', so why do they have it at all? Get rid of it altogether, I say. Then they pronounce 'h' for 'j'. I give up. As my vocabulary improved I realised that I had been calling churches *ciesa* – cheese. And one day, after she had been missing for a while, I tried to ask the girl at reception if she'd had the day off. She looked at me as if I was a bit odd. No wonder. I later found

49

that, in my lovely Spanish, I had asked her if she'd had a wash yesterday.

In the bus back to the hotel an old, dark-skinned Indian woman sat down next to me. She crossed herself at every church and there were a lot of churches in this town. If I hadn't known what she was doing I might have thought she had St Vitus Dance. I wondered why such a poor country spent so much money on churches. Mexican Christianity is a religion of earthy reality incorporating many old pagan beliefs, such as placing eagle feathers on statues of Christ in holy week. This is a means of communicating with the sun god: the eagle ascends closest to heaven.

When I had been at my hotel for nearly a week, I had risen so far in the management's estimation that I received a bath mat. Having qualified as fit to be entrusted with this precious article I wondered what I'd get the next week if I passed inspection again. Unfortunately I didn't find out, as I left after ten days.

At the tourist bureau in the town square I confessed my worries about my lack of the necessary permit to be in Mexico. I had read in the guide book that I needed a tourist card to get out again and that I should have obtained one of these when I crossed the border.

The girl in the office said, 'I'll take you to see someone.'

I thought, Oh Lord, here we go, down to the police station, but instead she took me upstairs where I spoke with the most beautiful woman. She could have been any age, but was probably between thirty and forty, and had sleek black hair that was combed straight back into a large bun from a lovely oval face with honeyed skin and regular features. She wore a pant suit of fine beige wool – they make very fine wool in this district – with a top like a loose buttonless jumper over slacks, and her shoulders were draped with a pretty red and blue paisley shawl. This exquisite woman was so kind to me. In her faultless English she said, 'Of course you realise that you are an illegal immigrant!' Having heard how border officials feel about us illegals – very recently two of these unfortunates had died due to their brutality – I was thrilled to find that I was now in the same category. I would not only be trying to enter the USA illicitly, but also exit Mexico unlawfully. I asked her what they would do to me. She replied, 'You can get another card from the police but they will fine you.'

'What if I get to the border?'

'You may get across without problems or you may be fined.'

She rang someone. Terrific. Now they will probably have a dragnet out for me. At first she was going to send me to the police, but then she rang someone else and after a long conversation she said, 'You can try going back the way you came and maybe no one will notice. But if they do then you will be fined.' Giving me her card she said, 'If you have any problems ring me.'

It wasn't the fine I was worried about, but the stories I had heard of people being put in gaol and having to sell their houses to get out. I decided that the less said the better – I wasn't confessing to any Mexican policeman that I was an illegal. I'm a gambler. If it ain't broke don't fix it, is my motto. I had enough to worry about. Highwaymen, bandits and all those crosses on the side of the road were quite sufficient.

While at the tourist bureau I thought I'd check out the stories I'd heard about robbers and buses. I asked the young man in the office if it was true that banditos sometimes held up the bus I was taking to the north. 'Oh, yes.' He couldn't agree with me more, but he didn't know how often. He phoned a friend, but neither of them could give me an answer, so I decided just to take my chances. He did offer to come to the bus station with me to ask there. This was most obliging of him, but I declined. He then wanted to ask at the police station but I declined this even more emphatically. I was an illegal immigrant.

As the dentist had taken every cracker I had, it was now

necessary to repair again to the bank. The cash distribution system was quite cute. A small room with a glass surround covered by grilles protruded from the side of the building and you entered it and locked yourself in. To my dismay the machine refused to give me any money on my Visa card. Already paranoid about being an illegal immigrant, now I had to contend with being a penniless one. That would make me a vagrant as well. I was much relieved when the next morning the machine condescended to give me some money. It even asked me if I preferred pesos or dollars.

On my last day, as I passed the police station I thought I might ask them about the chances of my bus being held up by bandits. But smack in the middle of the entrance, where you almost had to touch him to go past on the tiny footpath, was a fellow with a huge submachine gun. That put me right off and I kept on walking.

While I was preparing for the overnight bus ride out of Mexico, a marathon for a non-bus-lover, I started to feel squirmy in the tummy. This progressed to squirty. I was in trouble – just when I had to spend thirty hours on a bus. Nice. I cemented my internal workings with Lomotil – I hoped – and bought a bottle of tequila for sedation. It cost seven pesos, just one dollar forty cents. The nice shopkeeper put my Coke and other snacks in a plastic bag, but the tequila he wrapped in brown paper.

4 Tequila sunrise

On a lovely morning I ate my farewell Mexican breakfast of omelette, coffee, juice and toast under the vine-clad pergola of a nearby restaurant. Then I checked out of my room and took what I meant to be a short cut to a craft shop I had heard about – but you guessed it, it turned out to be another of my long cuts. I ended up on the edge of town, where I found a street market and an old bloke selling gem stones. They were most probably almost all cut glass but the opal was genuine. After some solid bargaining, I bought a pretty opal egg for fifteen dollars in order to rid myself of my remaining pesos.

Never having managed even a whiff of the craft shop, I returned to the hotel and stationed myself in the portico on a long polished wooden seat to read and watch the comings and goings until it was time to take a taxi to the bus station. As I disengaged from the taxi, three diminutive and exceedingly grimy urchins rushed up wanting to carry my bags. They were in no way big enough for this task but, as I still had some Mexican coins to unburden myself of, I let them 'help' me inside.

After a while I asked someone to watch my luggage while I patronised the wonderful green and pink loo, inside which I was accosted by a maiden in distress: a large-ish Mexican girl wearing a trendy outfit of black skin-tight pants topped by a vest. It didn't take long to work out her problem. The zipper of her pants had seized up at the top and she had an urgent need to get it down. After struggling with the recalcitrant zipper for some time I told her, in pantomime, that it was hopeless. 'Shall I cut it?' I asked. 'Yes yes yes!' I cut as neatly as I could, then went back to my bag and returned with a large safety pin. The girl at the turnstile, a witness to the drama unfolding, refrained from charging me more coins to re-enter and, after some tugging and pulling, I secured my new friend back in her pants. She covered the damage with her jacket and went on her way relieved. Giving away a precious safety pin was my good deed for the day. They say a good nurse always has a safety pin and a pair of scissors and I never go anywhere without mine.

The next entertainment in the bus station was the entry of a pair of Americans. One was a very large, blind man sporting a big black leather hat and a black cape that made him look like an overweight Zorro. Attached to a female helper, he tapped along with a white cane. The helper was also very large, as well as far advanced in age. The blind man was about fifty; she could have been a hundred. If she was the helper then Lord help him.

I wondered what they might be doing on a bus in the middle of Mexico. The helper seemed to have no idea what was going on. She tried to get into the disabled persons' toilet but it was locked. This threw her completely. So she went back to the desk and they showed her where to go. The regular toilet was next to the disabled one but she had failed to see it – and *he* was the blind one. She then made an attempt to get into the regular toilet but couldn't work out what to do with the coin machine or the turnstile. The desk staff rescued her again. This pair of innocents abroad were obviously leaving Mexico, so I pondered what she had been doing all the time she had been there. Later she fronted the desk again and they tried to explain something else to her. She called the blind man to her aid and the poor fellow got up and tried to walk towards her voice, but went in the wrong direction, tripping over bags. She didn't have the nous to go and get him.

Finally they sat down behind me and I was forced to listen to one of the most inane conversations I have ever heard.

'You can have fruit if you can peel it.'

'You are supposed to peel it?'

'Yes you can have fruit if you peel it.'

'Well we did peel the fruit.'

'Yes you are supposed to peel the fruit.'

When they got on the bus she bumbled around and couldn't find their seat numbers until I helped them. It was pathetic. I don't know how they got home. Strangely I later came across two other blind people travelling on buses, a young black girl who was totally with it and an American man, with his dog.

The bus left San Miguel with only five people aboard. Great, I thought. But a couple of stops later it filled up. This bus was not the White Star line on which I had come to Mexico and that travelled pretty much direct. This bus stopped at every excuse – and each time the driver would say, 'Five minutes,' but it would be twenty or more. A woman who spoke a little English sat next to me and we stumbled through a conversation.

When night came I managed to sleep, thanks to my tequila. It was so awful I mixed it with a carton of chocolate milk to disguise the taste. My neighbour told me I had slept well and, having woken up with my mouth wide open and snoring, I had to agree.

Countless stops and starts later we arrived at Monterrey bus station in the early morning. I knew this place well from my time spent there before. Breakfast was a burrito, a hot edible full of ham and other goodies and very tasty. I was having a little gastro trouble but it wasn't serious. Then we were heading for the border crossing which, due to my illegal status, I was dreading.

Crossing the border took three hours. We were stopped and inspected at several check points coming up to the border and once there we had to get off the bus outdoors under a tin roof and go through immigration procedures. This was where I needed my missing tourist card. Passengers with those highly delectable objects went quickly through a mobile baggage X-ray apparatus that was mounted on the back of a truck, and then got back in the bus. But I had to get in line with the Mexicans who needed entry permits for the USA. One at a time, passengers were allowed into the tiny air-conditioned hut that served as the office. There was only one official to process the long line and it was very hot waiting outside. Several times I tried to sneak one of the white entry cards that they all seemed to have and a pile of which sat in a box near the door, but each time I was defeated. It turned out that I had to have a green card anyway. We were there for ages and somehow I ended up last in the line.

When the officer finally looked in my passport he said, 'You don't have an original entry stamp for the United States.' This was an unexpected blow. Then I remembered that at Chicago airport I'd had trouble because the airline had given me the wrong form for immigration. I said that I thought that my passport had been stamped anyway. Terrific.

The officer said, 'No. There is no stamp to say you have been legally admitted to the USA.'

Really terrific. He made a couple of phone calls, went through my passport again and made more calls. By this time I was in a state. Now I was an illegal alien of both countries. Fortunately no one had mentioned the Mexican permit I was deficient in. After a long time another man came in – he seemed American, whereas the other was a hybrid Spanish type. This latest person took my passport and after several efforts found the elusive stamp. It was small and very faint but it was there! What a relief. The officer filled out a green card for me, I signed it, they took six dollars from me – the price the Mexicans paid – and away I went rejoicing. I actually saved nineteen dollars, the price I should have paid for the tourist card on the way in. Not to mention the thousands of dollars fine I had been sure would be my fate. But there are better ways to save a few dollars.

The last one back on the bus, I sank relieved into my seat. My neighbour then told me that 'the chauffeur' had wanted to take the bus and leave me. I said, 'He couldn't do that, my luggage is on the bus.' She replied that he had said I could come on the next bus. I was stunned to think he really was going to leave me out there in no-man's land. She told me that he said, 'The bus will go without the foreign woman.' But the entire bus load of passengers had stood up and said, 'No no no!' So he waited. I was immensely grateful.

In Texas we stopped at a roadhouse. This place had really dreadful food – fried, heavily crumbed and greasy, or dried up as though it had been waiting for an owner for hours. The staff spoke only Spanish and had trouble understanding me when I asked for chicken. I received two lumps of foul – fowl – oleaginous chicken coated with something even I couldn't eat. I pulled it off, chucked a lot of chilli on what was inside to kill the bugs and ate it. The chicken was accompanied by a lump of some sort of fried suet that was supremely awful.

I had intended to take the train from San Antonio to Miami but when I rang the train booking number from the bus station I discovered that this was not to be. There was no train for three days and it did not go direct. You need to change trains in Orlando, Florida, which means staying overnight. At that rate I wouldn't get to Miami in time to catch the *Atlanta*, the ship on which I had booked a passage to Peru.

There was nothing for it but a Greyhound bus. The Mexican bus lines only came as far as here. At the Greyhound station a pleasant black American lady told me that there was a bus leaving in an hour that was going all the way to Miami. It would take sixty hours. Two more nights on a bus! I'll never make it, I thought. But there was no other option.

57

Although I could have done the trip in stages, I decided to get it over with in one fell swoop.

I didn't have long to wait in the dreary bus station, thank goodness. It was vastly inferior to the Mexican ones. The bus was too. No arm rests between the daggy seats, very cramped leg room and no seat numbers allocated. You just got on and fought for a position. Being a good fighter I got a decent seat but before long I had someone sitting next to me: a small Hispanic fellow who didn't say two words to me – mainly because he couldn't, I guess – even though we spent the night together! By this time I was not the best in the abdominal department and decided to eat nothing and drink only lemonade. I didn't really feel like eating. It's usually time to call the ambulance when I lose my appetite and by the next morning, though I didn't feel in the least ill, even the thought of food turned me off. I no longer needed tequila to sleep a lot. All that day I couldn't wake up. After the Hispanic gent got off in the morning I was alone on the seat so I lay down. I don't think I missed much. I had imagined that Texas ranches would look like Australian back country but they were different – very green, with lots of trees.

On and on we went, stopping many times. In the evening the bus became crowded again and now I shared my seat with a very, very large American man. He wasn't fat, just big with hair everywhere possible, and he wore a big bushy coat. We struck up a conversation during which he told me how he had worked in the Caribbean as a construction manager.

Another night passed. The bus ride wasn't the nightmare I had expected but I hadn't been prepared for it. I had no toothbrush, nothing to wash with and no change of clothes. I became grottier and grottier.

Every time the bus stopped, which was often, the passengers poured off, only to return with armfuls of chips and boxes of take-away contained in masses of disposable packaging. Food was served in a box and a plastic bag and there were styrofoam cups in horrendous numbers. I saw one woman buy armfuls of chips, dips in plastic tubs and soft drinks to the value of twenty-seven dollars. That's fifty-four Australian! No wonder the kids here are fat. It's really sad to see a six-year-old with an enormous stomach sticking out in front like a dreadful old man with a beer gut so big he can hardly walk.

All the next day we travelled down through Florida, finally arriving in Miami West at a quarter past four in the morning. No one had told me that this bus terminus was a long way from Miami Beach where I planned to stay. By now it was forty-eight hours since I had eaten. I was okay but felt washed out. I waited in the dismal bus station until half past five and then rang the youth hostel. They said I could have a room right then although check-in time wasn't normally until two. The taxi across town and over the causeway to the beach cost fifty dollars, but I was glad just to find a place to lie down that wasn't moving.

At the hostel I found that there were no private rooms available, and settled for a four-bed dormitory. Creeping up the stairs I snuck in, collapsed on a bed and was immediately out like a light.

I spent most of the day sleeping or lying about lethargically. Around mid-morning I felt hungry and forced myself to get up. I was still in a grubby state, having slept in my clothes, but, more in need of food than cleaning, I went to the cafe downstairs and had eggs and hash fries. This was a mistake. Lesson learned! I resumed a fluids-only regime.

I had alighted from the taxi at the hostel in balmy pre-dawn air, but the day quickly became boiling hot. About lunch time it rained very heavily and soon afterwards the day became frightfully humid. It felt just like Darwin in the build up to the wet. In the evening I surfaced long enough to talk to one of my room mates, a likeable English lady.

Next morning I pronounced myself cured and, feeling fit as a flea, went in search of fodder. I found a place called Chop

Chicken across the road that had decent food – not fried, breaded or crumbed rubbish. I ate as though I believed that food was about to be abolished, then worried that I, too, would soon be joining the obese brigade.

The youth hostel was located in the old Clay Hotel which, in its past life, had been the home of Desi Arnaz and a gambling casino owned by Al Capone. The front part of it was a beautiful Art Deco building and the dormitories were in attractive, Spanish-style blocks at the rear. However the dorms were dog boxes inside, with little room to move between the two sets of bunks and no space for your luggage.

My room was filthy, but it did have a fridge and an adequate bathroom. Of the four of us in this room, one got up and left shortly after I arrived. The English girl I had spoken to the first night went off in the afternoon to find somewhere better. I tossed up whether I would join her but in the end couldn't be bothered. The fourth inmate was a gorgeous Argentinian with whom I practised my Spanish during our brief encounters. She rushed in, gave everyone great big kisses on each cheek, said, 'I am Elenora,' got cleaned up and went out on the town at ten at night and didn't return until lunchtime the next day. She did this every day. The phone rang every twenty minutes all day and late into the night and it was always some man looking for her. In the end I took the phone off the hook after she left each night.

There was a supermarket across the street and the prices were not the only shock I received there. The first time I visited it I saw two American girls sitting on the footpath against the shop wall. They were clean and nice looking, but I could not believe what they were doing. Begging. As a small black man went by they asked him for money and he gave them some.

From the foyer at Clays, where you could make phone calls seated in comfortable cushioned cane chairs, I rang the ship's agent, who informed me that the *Atlanta* was sailing on time.

I rang a hotel in Lima and booked a room for when I left the ship, hoping I had got the message across. You never know.

An attractive young German, who said he was working in Miami, sat down and talked to me. I learned that he wanted to go to Australia by ship. When I left he followed me out and we walked together for a while. He said I should come to a nearby bar later that gave free drinks to ladies after ten. I told him that, unfortunately, these days I couldn't stay awake until ten, let alone after. Travelling is tiring stuff. Still, I hope this practice catches on in Australia.

Apart from tourists you don't see many Caucasians in this part of Miami. To my astonishment hardly anyone spoke or understood English in shops and cafes. They all spoke Spanish to me – maybe it was the hair, I still looked like an Indian. The gorgeous mad Argentinian who came flying in like a whirl-wind before racking off until the next day told me that my face is Argentinian. I hope that's good.

Miami Beach had a deco area with many beautiful old pastel-coloured buildings that curved in the typical fashion of the era. The post office was semi-circular and lovely out-side, but not so nice inside. A sign warned, 'No loitering or soliciting,' and there were no seats or comfortable spots if you had the desire to defy the admonition.

I had serious doubts about entrusting my letters to the dilapidated blue objects found in the streets that were alleged to be mail boxes. They looked more like rubbish bins to me and nothing reassuring was written on them about collec-tion times. I was floored by the amount of packaging and waste that occurred here. I bought two stamps and was given them in an envelope too small to do anything with but immediately throw away.

I made another phone call to the ship's agent who said, 'I've been looking for you. There is a problem with the ship.'

Oh, no! The bloody thing has sunk, I thought. It was still afloat, but on the way down the coast from New York one of the crew had been diagnosed with hepatitis B. The ship had pulled into the next port and put him ashore, and now the vessel was quarantined until the medical authorities cleared it. The options for me were to take a refund, sail on the next ship in a month or, if I still wanted to sail on the *Atlanta*, to produce proof of full vaccination against hepatitis B. Fortunately I had this qualification and could prove it via my yellow vaccination book, a copy of which I had to fax to the agent. Just as well I'd had inoculations against everything known to man and recorded them. The ship would now be sailing a day late. Sadly the crew member who caused all the ruckus with the hepatitis died an hour after he was returned to his home country, Burma.

My room mates at the hostel were now an erudite Turkish professor of English called Aisha and a tiny ballerina from Canada as well as the fun-loving Argentinian, with whom I enjoyed fractured conversations.

Trauma struck. I got flea-bitten. I worked out that it must have happened when I sat in the foyer making phone calls and leant my arm on the padded chair. There were cats everywhere in the hotel at night. The cause dawned on me as I leaned on the cushions again the next day and my arm started to burn as though it was being bitten.

On the scheduled sailing day the *Atlanta* was delayed yet again and boarding time was put off until midnight. I hung about in my room for as long as I could before it was turf-out time and, suddenly, I was homeless and on the street. Then it started to rain. I headed for the library and read the local papers until the rain stopped, then set off for the library at the other end of town which I was told had access to the internet. This was the signal for the heavens to dump a deluge on my head. Wow, that storm was something else.

The bus stop outside the library was said to harbour a bus that would take me across town to my destination, but another bus had broken down at the stop, so when the bus I wanted came it zoomed around the broken bus and didn't halt. I walked. It poured more, and despite my trusty brolly I got soaked again. When the thunder claps and lightning flashes intensified I took refuge in the foyer of an apartment building and talked to a couple of people who were also sheltering there. Half an hour later it was still pelting down so I sloshed out into it again and found another bus stop. A helpful man came along and said, 'Go across the road. This bus costs one dollar twenty-five because it goes over the toll bridge, but the local bus is only twenty-five cents.'

Coming out of a second library I found rain still bucketing down. Four metres of water radiated out from the gutter so that the bus couldn't pull in to collect me. While the driver waited patiently, I took off my shoes and, starting to wade to him, promptly fell into a hole up to my knees. I squelched soaking wet onto the freezing, air-conditioned bus, much to the amusement of the other passengers.

Back in the hostel lobby in my dripping wet, floppy pants I selected a wooden seat and avoided the flea-harbouring cushioned chairs. This was the fourth of July holiday weekend and many people had come from New York and other parts of the north to celebrate it in Miami. I talked to several of these holiday-makers in between reading a book during my long wait. Everyone complained about the dirtiness of this hostel. A young Englishman said he planned to sleep at the airport rather than spend another night in the filthy, smelly room he'd had here. And that had been the second room he had been shown. The first was even worse and he had refused it.

Finally it was time to go to the ship. My taxi had a Turkish driver who said that Miami felt like South America. Miami was beautiful by night with all the lights along the wharf and the streets of town. This was Saturday night and, even this late, mobs of people crowded the streets. I asked the driver why some stood in big throngs on the footpaths, and he told me that they were waiting to get into nightclubs. What a scene.

It was a long drive to the wharf. At the gate we asked for the *Atlanta* and received directions, but I was apprehensive that the ship might not be there yet.

The wharf was a huge place. We drove past cruise vessels and cargo ships and along an enormous pier stacked so high with containers that you could see nothing beyond them. Finally there was a break in the wall of containers and I saw a ship that, praise be, had *Atlanta* painted on its prow. She was much bigger than I had expected – two hundred metres long and 36,000 tonnes, I learned later. Her decks were piled high with containers and men scrambled all over her busily working. As it was well after midnight I thought that I might be told to come back tomorrow and not interrupt them, but a smiling Chinese officer came immediately to shake my hand and welcome me aboard. Then he shepherded me up the gang-plank while a sailor came on behind with my bags. The rain had stopped and it was one of those clear, damp nights that are so lovely in the tropics.

The beaming boy who bounded up the corridor to meet me, and who looked about sixteen with his very short hair and happy face, turned out to be the Polish captain, Wojciech. He seemed genuinely pleased to see me, sent the other officer away and showed me to my cabin. I worried that he might be desperate to get back to work and kept saying, 'I won't hold, you up,' but he stayed, chatting and being pleasant.

My cabin was sparkling, immaculate, and as big as a state room on the *QE2*. It was a shock to find myself in such a large space after the claustrophobic dog kennel that I'd inhabited for the past few days. I could have held a dance in the bathroom and there was enough room for three people in the shower alcove if I should feel so inclined.

From the centre of the cabin roof, however, an air conditioner blew out the most ghastly blast of cold air. It was like being in a howling blizzard. Trying to fathom how to turn it down, I cruised all around the room examining every switch, but none did anything to lessen the cold. I saw that the machine had two knobs on it so I stood on a chair to fiddle with them, turning them up and down to no effect. Then I noticed some buttons on the other side. I got up again to play with them, but the chair, a comfortable swivel job, started to swing. I hung onto the round vent of the air conditioner but now this also began to swing to and fro. I felt as though I was riding a hurdy gurdy so, deciding that it wouldn't be nice to break a leg on my first night aboard, I desisted. Instead, I stuffed some clothes in the vents. They immediately flew out. I stuffed in a sheet, which fared a bit better, but I was cold around the ears all night. Next morning one of the crew showed me how to turn the air-conditioner down. Easy when you know how.

All the good wooden furniture in my cabin was either built-in or nailed to the deck. I wondered what the loop and chain in the floor were for until I found that they were to tie down the chair if the sea got rough. One wall had a porthole that opened onto the deck and next to it hung a wooden cabinet under which stood the bar-sized fridge. The upholstery and carpet were greyish-blue wool and a couple of pleasing modern prints hung on the pale grey walls. The bathroom had royal-blue towels and curtains. There was a wardrobe, a single bunk that was built into the side of one wall, a big desk under the porthole, a coffee table, a couch and a ship's clock on the wall. On the desk was a phone and a CD and tape player and radio (on which I managed to get radio stations in port but which didn't work at sea).

As I didn't get to sleep until two in the morning I thought that I wouldn't be expected to front for breakfast, so it was quite late in the morning when I went down to meet the kitchen crew. They turned out to be all ever-smiling Burmese. Even the notices on the wall beside the kitchen door were written in Burmese script. The crew fed me coffee, cold boiled eggs, and toast topped with ham, cheese and pineapple. At lunch I met the other passengers, Laura and Len, a pair of retired Americans. He had a droll New 'Joisey' accent. She was gentle and motherly. They told me that we were keeping good company. Novelist Arthur Hailey and the president of Lufthansa had travelled on cargo ships of this line.

In between meals and while we waited for departure I was glued to a riveting book about a woman, who could not sail, crossing the English channel in a small boat during the second world war while a German U-boat hunted her. Storms at sea and shipwrecks – good comforting stuff for an about-to-be sailor.

Now and then I ventured out on deck and, from a safe distance, watched the containers being loaded. I was told that the trucks at the front of the ship were for the ship's last port of call, Valparaiso in Chile. A great contraption with a crane in its middle ran along a railway line on the wharfside. Then an arm dropped down from it like one those penny arcade gadgets in glass cases that pick up toys, if you are lucky, and four prongs grabbed a container off the back of a truck that had been conveniently driven underneath. Then up and over it went to be neatly and effortlessly placed on the deck.

We sailed at six. A large tugboat delivered the pilot on board. He turned the ship in the narrow channel and then took his leave by hopping back onto the bobbing boat – no mean feat seeing, I had been told, he had recently had a hip replacement. We steamed off and soon the row of tall buildings on the shore were gone. The sailors blasted the decks with a fire hose to clean off the soot and grime of port and an hour later I went out on deck and found that we were alone on a dark blue sea. There was a stiff breeze, the sun was setting and we had left the murk of Miami long behind.

5 Pirates and Panama

Next morning the ship was pitching and rolling on a swell that came at us side on from the west, while a wind from the same direction slowed our progress. I was on my way back from breakfast when an ear-piercing shriek from a siren began and did not stop until all the passengers had assembled on the bridge for boat drill. And a very thorough drill it was too. We had to put on our lifejackets and play with all their attachments, as well as learn to tie a knot on the cords so that we could be pulled up out of the sea by a helicopter. All thrilling stuff, if somewhat daunting. I thought I'd rather stay with the lifeboat than go dangling about lost in space, looking like bait on a hook to the sharks waiting below. By comparison, the lifeboats with their covered tops seemed very modern and comfortable. Of course, the pirates that infested these waters might come along to jolly things up a bit.

During the day we passed along Cuba's eastern shore and the ship made up some time. By afternoon the ship was doing twenty-one knots and skipping along on a calm ocean. I could feel just a faint rocking as I walked around the deck. Out on the dark sapphire blue of the sea there was only an occasional white pencil line to mark a wave, while the centre of the cream-coloured foaming wake that spread out from the ship's side was a pure, clear aquamarine. Later I could feel, by the lift of the ship, that the speed had increased.

After dinner the captain took Laura and me to inspect the bridge. It was a massive, immaculate affair containing lots of electronic stuff that was a complete mystery to me. The duty officer told us that we were now eight kilometres off the southern tip of Cuba and about to turn to start sailing around it through a channel that was narrow, but well buoyed.

As dusk fell I could see the buoys flashing close by. I walked to the bow passing along rows of containers stacked under covers. The extreme end of the ship was open and had a look-out platform that you could climb up on to – like the gadget that daft woman in the movie *Titanic* was about to commit suicide off – and I sat up there for a while. It was glorious, but the wind was fierce. It tore at my clothes and flapped them behind me until I felt quite pummelled. Thunderhead clouds were massed along the horizon. Out of the dusk another ship in front of us took shape as I watched us overtake it. It was also a container carrier but the rows of lights strung along its sides gave it a festive look.

There were white caps all over the face of the sea the next morning. They didn't appear big until you looked at the troughs between them and imagined yourself down there swimming. When my apple rolled off the desk and went sashaying around the floor, I looked up at the porthole – one moment I could see the sea and the next, whoops, it went down, and there was only sky.

That day the weather was overcast and it rained a little. In the afternoon a couple of large birds landed on us for a rest. By the time I went to bed the sea was quite rough. I heard my glass sliding back and forth across the desk and got up to move it so that it wouldn't go bump in the dark. I woke during the night and felt the ship starting to roll and by dawn, although the sea didn't look any bigger, there was definite pitching and heaving.

I woke next in Cartagena, Columbia. The engines stopped sometime around six in the morning and I looked out to see that we were tied up to a wharf, not alongside but rank-parked. The ship next to us was a grim, grey job from which containers busily came and went. The weather was very humid – my sunglasses fogged up as soon as I stepped out on deck.

I found that all the ship's doors had been locked, even the laundry, as a precaution against theft. Why the laundry? I wondered, thinking that it would be hard to get down the gangplank clutching the washing machine unnoticed. Then Martin, the German first mate, told me that the precautions were also supposed to hinder stowaways. So for the first time I locked the door of my cabin. Martin also told me that he feared for his life in Columbia and never went ashore there. On a previous trip on another ship he had seen two men acting suspiciously and on investigation the seals of a container were found to be broken. The loot discovered hidden in it, eighty kilograms of heroin, had an uncut value of two million dollars. The ship's guards were found to be involved and it was known to all that it was Martin who had pointed the finger.

That night we turned our watches back an hour. I was thinking about climbing up to change the ship's clock on my wall when, to my surprise, I saw that it had turned itself back. It must have been centrally controlled – I hoped.

At breakfast we were joined by the Cartagena port captain and his offsider, some sort of ship inspector. When our ship's captain told us that we had to leave port early and therefore couldn't go ashore, the port captain gallantly offered to take Laura and me for a quick tour of the town in his car. Unfortunately he then received a call to go to another ship immediately, so that excursion was cancelled. Wojciech, our ship's captain, said that we could take a taxi but there was no guarantee that, even if we managed to avoid being kidnapped, we would make it back in time for sailing. I did not fancy returning to the wharf to find myself abandoned in Columbia. As compensation Wojciech took us up to the bridge and gave us each a pair of high-powered binoculars so that we could look at Cartagena as we left.

It was quite pretty. Facing us was a pointy mountain on top of which stood an imposing white building. Was it a presidential palace? On the other side I saw the antiquated castle and buildings of the old town. Two small spits of land, one of which had a small lighthouse on its furthest end, poked out either side to encircle the inner harbour protectively. It was very hot and sticky on deck in the lee of the wind and I thought how pleasant it would be to walk under the trees that lined the edges of these narrow pieces of land.

Leaving Cartagena was effortless. A tug pulled the ship around a little way until we were facing in the right direction and then we were on our own. In the middle of the bay we passed small knobs of land with domes on them for ships to tie up to, and on a plinth in the inner bay a statue was stationed that seemed to be doing an imitation of the Statue of Liberty. A way out in the outer harbour a very big, old fort stood on the edge of an island. Opposite this was a smaller island that sported another fortification. These were built to make the harbour safe from the pirates who used to come here often in days past. Len said with a twinkle in his eye that the fort looked like it needed bulldozing. He made gruff comments like this often just to stir up a bite in response. They were a round couple, jolly and nice. Laura wanted to adventure on shore but Len kept saying, 'I just came for the boat ride.'

In the middle of the harbour, alone on an immense expanse of sea, I spied a flimsy canoe that was being paddled along unconcernedly by a bloke without a lifejacket.

While in port I had turned the snazzy radio on the desk to FM and picked up what appeared to be a local TV station. I thought I might learn some Spanish but I understood only 'si', 'no', 'senor', and not much else. Then a soap opera came on and I understood that perfectly. If you've heard one, you've heard them all. There were long meaningful silences, arguments and recriminations, the obligatory romance scene complete with heavy breathing and the hospital scene with someone groaning and sighing. It had the lot. After this came a cartoon, every word of which I also understood. Three minutes of biff, crash, bang, wallop, were followed by 'Ah Buena!'

The day that followed was a busy one for me. It included a nap before and after lunch and a two-hour chat with the captain. Wojciech was such a charmer and he loved to talk. I had a standing joke with him about the letter of complaint that I was writing concerning the ship. This came about after he saw the list of rules for passengers that I had been given by the ship's agents. They intrigued him no end as he'd never seen or heard of them before. He was especially amused by the stern warning that passengers must wear only slippers in their cabins.

I finally mastered the washing machine. I'd had a big argument with it when it wouldn't give me back my clothes after finishing the wash. Eventually one of the sailors came by and told me its secret. The machine needed to be left alone for a little quality time with my clothes before it felt inclined to release them. Maybe it had formed an emotional attachment to them.

And I learned to ride the exercise bike. Hurrah! a bike that was safely anchored to the floor and couldn't throw me. I had mentioned to Wojciech that I needed exercise and, voila, he ordered a crew member to bring forth the bike and harness it in the TV room. It felt weird to be riding a bike while looking out of a porthole at a pitching, rolling sea. Even though I was pedalling madly, the up and down motion of the waves made me feel that I was riding a horse. The bike behaved admirably for several days but then it took to groaning and making complaining noises. I don't know why – I was doing all the ruddy work.

I did my daily Spanish lessons and argued a lot with Carlos, the person on the tapes. Lord, he was thick – and I was heartily sick of him. Then I acquired a deck chair. At lunch I told Wojciech that there was class distinction on his ship. The deck above me had a plastic chair and I didn't. A chair was produced but I failed to use it that day because I was too busy mastering the video machine (I hope this doesn't get around). After an hour of swearing and pressing all the buttons I could find I watched *Shakespeare in Love*. Absolute drivel but nice clothes.

Wojciech told me some terrific stories about the drugs that had been planted on ships in South American ports. Once on this ship, before he was captain, the crew had noticed that a container picked up in Columbia wasn't correctly sealed. The drug authorities were notified and they found a large quantity of heroin. The captain was taken ashore and arrested, despite the fact that it was he who had actually notified the police. Another time someone was seen swimming in the water near the ship. The police were called and a bag of drugs was found to have been attached to the hull with a magnet. Again the captain was arrested and this time the engineer was also arrested for good measure – the authorities said that underneath the ship was his department. They were held for two weeks. You'd hope that they learned to stay clear of the constabulary from then on.

Wojciech said something that expressed a feeling I'd often had, but never put into words. I had told him that I liked to hang over the bow or the prow to watch the water foam away from under me. He said, 'When you do that and you look down and stare for a while, does the water call to you? Does it call to you to join it?' I knew exactly what he meant. The water has always called to me. Not that I want to drown – it is just a consciousness that you want to be one with it. When I said, 'Yes. It calls to me.' Wojciech replied, 'Ah, you are a romantic.' Funny, I never thought I was.

Out on deck that night, in the delicious warm, velvety dark, there was no moon and the sides of the ship were not lit. I watched great sheets of lighting flashing close on one side accompanied by clashes of thunder – this was the hurricane season.

Five days out from Miami we reached Manzana in Panama at two in the morning. Work began immediately and by morning we had finished loading. The pilot came aboard and we chugged off into a channel marked by buoys, passed through a breakwater made from big chunks of rock that encircled almost all the bay, and sat riding at anchor five kilometres off the coast waiting our turn to go through the Panama Canal. The pilot left clutching his obligatory bottle of whisky, while from the flag drawer we selected and ran up the red and white flag of the canal. Wojciech told me that when entering Libya's waters that country's flag must be higher, as well as bigger, than any other flag on the ship. Fortunately this is easy. If you don't have a suitable exhibit, all you have to do is paint an old bed sheet green. That is the Libyan flag, plain green.

Swinging around out there in the middle of the bay the sea looked fairly calm, but every now and then there was a terrific whoomp as we hit against the swell of the tide and pulled up sharp on our anchor. Chief mate Martin threw his fishing lines in from the bow but with no luck. He said it would be better later when it got dark and he could put the light on to attract the fish.

Meanwhile I watched four ships come out of the canal and sail away across the bay heading north and I counted five other container ships parked and waiting, as we were, to go through the next morning.

After dinner I went aft to check on the fishing. Yuri, the huge Russian bear of an electrician, had joined the hopeful and was jagging for squid. As the sky slowly darkened the lights came on aboard the ships around the bay and made a pretty sight. Night slowly fell and it grew darker until finally I could see into the water with the lantern that had been hung over the side. Schools of small fish flitted and flashed through the beam of light and every now and then a big fish dashed from the shadows to eat one. But no fish was stupid enough to get caught for us to eat. 'Most unusual,' the crew said. Not for me. No one ever catches anything when I am around. Jonah they call me. I gave up and went to bed.

The ship tugged on her chain all night like a dog shaking a rat. I was told that the swell was very strong here – if you fell in you'd be whisked away out to sea and gone forever. The thump of the engines coming on woke me at four but I went back to sleep while we crossed the bay. When the ship was ready to enter the canal at five-thirty, Wojciech called me on the phone. I had a quick shower and was on the bridge just as it was getting light. Ahead of us the lights of the Canal illuminated the sky, on one side the lights of the settlement twinkled, while behind the dawn was breaking rosy pink. It was extraordinarily beautiful, with a surreal quality.

Approaching the first lock we could see the ship ahead of us, a Japanese vessel. Then the gates closed and we watched it rise slowly, slowly, until it looked very high.

The Canal pilot came aboard. He stays on the ship for the entire eight to twelve hours that it takes to go through. The pilot, an elderly American with a great letter-box mouth that made him look like the old-time film star George Formby, said he had been in Panama for thirty-nine years, and that there were now only twenty-five Americans left since Panama had been given back to the locals in 1999. His main interest in me was to find out if I played bridge. I was afraid I had to disappoint him but I offered him a game of poker.

We entered the first lock. The water had been allowed to flow into it until it was level with us, then the gate was opened, we moved in and the gate was shut. The two tugs that had guided us in, one on either side in case our engines stopped and we went in sideways, sheared away and went directly to the next ship behind us. If we had gone in wrong way around there would not have been enough room and we would have been in big trouble.

I could see more ships coming slowly along in a stately line after the ship behind us. There were two locks side by side. The one next to us was empty but the Japanese ship was in the lock in front of us. Once the gate was shut people walked across the top of it on a footpath and in front of us was a cantilever bridge over which buses ferried workers. Water started to pour into the lock, and as the level slowly rose we went up with it.

The sides of the Canal were covered with dense, dark-green jungle that on one side was cut by a road running along the edge. Hovering frigate birds with forked tails circled us while a troop of pelicans lumbered in our wake. Closer to the administration area a few houses stood, but there was still plenty of thick jungle with an occasional palm frond sticking out of it. The pilot told me that all the animals that could be found in Amazonia, with the exception of anacondas but including jaguars, could also be found in this jungle. He said that Panama was a very fine place to live and that he made two hundred thousand US dollars a year. Pity he wouldn't play poker.

The water continued to rise. Only one ship at a time can fit into a lock that is one thousand metres long and fifty wide. That's big enough for the *QE2* – but, while the passage would cost that ship one hundred and thirty-five thousand dollars, the *Atlanta* had to pay only thirty-five to fifty thousand.

The Japanese ship that had been in front of us before was now in the lock alongside us. She was the *Neptune*, a car carrier, painted blue on the bottom and white on the top but up close I could now see that she was very rusty. We came out of the lock and, moving on, came level with the administration centre, which was fronted by five dilapidated train carriages standing on a rail line. There was no other housing so I presumed that only canal workers lived here.

Waiting to go through the next lock we encountered the contraptions they call mules, which took the place of horses some years ago. Some swap! These mechanical monsters run on a track alongside the ship and are attached to it by ropes with which they haul the vessel up, up, into the next lock. Then we were going down again. The water falls nine metres.

I descended to the lower deck to see what it was like at that level and stared at the walls of the lock as we crept through. They were either made of old-looking metal or carved out of rock and bolstered every now and then by a great beam of wood. Some of these beams were badly splintered as though something big had hit them – no doubt it had.

Ahead I could see a tug pushing the Japanese ship into a lock and as we approached the last lock we managed to pass this ship. Passing is not allowed outside the locks but can be done in them. The *Neptune* had broken something so we came out of the locks ahead of her. A little further on we passed a ship that was lying half submerged on its side on the canal bank. A sad sight, it looked as though it had gone aground and tipped over.

By this time I was desperate for breakfast. As soon as I had supervised the *Atlanta* safely through the locks and out onto the Gaton Lake, I went below.

We followed a channel marked by buoys through the immense body of water that is the Gaton Lake. In the middle of the lake were a great many tiny islands, remnants of land that had been flooded. Again, they were covered in thick green jungle and they had no shore line – the jungle flowed all the way down to the water. The lake was very calm. The water was the oily green colour of an aventurine gem stone and it was disturbed only by faint ripples from the soft wave made by our slow advance. From between two islands of vegetation behind us a ship loomed up in our wake, looking enormous compared to the tiny islands. Behind that I could see another two ships and in front there was one more.

One-and-a-half hours later we were still on the flat dark water of the lake. There was no sign of habitation until we came close to the lake's shore on one side. There I saw a tiny cove that had small boats tied in it, and above them a couple of red-roofed houses. A motorised skiff painted the same green colour as the trees came out from there going very fast but creating little movement on the water. Passing a long flat barge that was pushed along by a tug and loaded with what looked like building material, we continued to progress between the marker buoys, green one side, red the other. Later we passed another barge that appeared to be permanently anchored to a buoy and had a small plot of maize growing in the middle of it. I sat on deck in my plastic chair. After making such a fuss to acquire it, I thought I'd better use it.

Suddenly, from behind the uninhabited-looking green jungle, the high-rise buildings of Panama City appeared against a misty grey sky. Floating between the jungle and that eerie sky, the city looked quite unreal, like a mirage. Approaching it, we passed under a wide-spanning bridge, not unlike the Sydney Harbour Bridge, over which much traffic flowed. Then we were in the bay that fronts Panama City and sailing alongside a lengthy causeway on which a road and a row of palm trees led to a small, low, unpopulated island. Another causeway followed that also led to another little island and still two more causeways came after that. The last island was quite high and looked like one of those pointy karsts from south China that seem to have just jumped up out of the sea. This one had a building right on its peak and vegetation around the base.

We anchored out in the bay surrounded by a lot of other ships. Rain poured down on us – I was told that it rained every day here.

During the night we moved to the Panama City wharf. The sea was like a millpond when I ventured out on deck at seven. Not a whisper of wind moved its surface and the air was pleasantly cool. However it soon became steamy and later a fine drizzle fell. I was listening to the *Barber of Saville*, which

Wojciech had lent me. A CD no less, the first for me – whoever said that travel broadens your education told no lie! Out on deck, containers went off and came on, as did a huge tank.

Then it was Saturday and I had been aboard the *Atlanta* for a week. We were now out on the empty, grey Pacific ocean. All night there had been a gentle swell and this day was overcast and humid. We saw whales and dolphins close to the ship. I walked around the decks just before dinner and watched two ships pass. One was a white refrigerated ship that carried no containers and the other a long, black vessel away on the horizon. On one side of our ship seven beautiful big frigate birds flew in perfect formation, gliding motionless so close to the sea that at first they looked as though they had been painted on the water. They had white bodies and graceful, black-tipped wings, which every now and then they would flap effortlessly, then continue gliding as they caught the wind drafts off the ship's side. After a while they flapped a bit more, sped up, and disappeared.

Early in the morning, approaching Buenaventura, a large port on an island off the Columbian coast, we took on the pilot – as well as several guards bristling with guns, ammunition and other lethal means of destruction. All doors on the decks were locked. There were many small, crude boats on the dirty brown water, as well as low wooden canoes in which two men sat with fishing nets heaped between them. The captain pointed out a 'pirate' going fast. He said they were all pirates. Sixty per cent of the people of Buenaventura are unemployed and it is said to be the worst place in the world for crime and, we were told, much too dangerous to go ashore. A tug painted bright red, yellow and blue with a dirty old rag of a Columbian flag hung at its mast came alongside and pushed us broadside into the wharf, belching black smoke as its engine strained.

At lunch Martin told me the story of the pilot who had come aboard this morning. Not long ago he had been kidnapped on his way across the harbour and a ransom of fifty thousand dollars had been demanded. It had been paid by the pilots' association. The chief mate also told me about a German ship that had been boarded by pirates at the wharf in Rio de Janeiro. The pirates grabbed hostages and held them to ransom, and when the fracas was finally over the police arrested the German captain, tied him to a chair, put a bright light in his face and insisted that he was part of the conspiracy. Martin said that captains don't want to take their ships in to the wharf there now. They tie up out in the harbour, but even that is dangerous.

At Buenaventura the water at the wharf was shallow but it has a safe bottom, which means that when the tide goes out the ship can sit on the mud. But you have to leave with the tide. The captain said, 'We go whether the cargo is ready or not.' So at half past nine in the evening, when the tide was full, we were pulled out by a tug. Looking over the side of the ship into the dark I saw the little tug, pulling its hardest to get us out from the wharf and turned around so that we could sail down the river.

It was a long way down to the sea. As we retreated from the wharf we passed a line of container ships tied in a row along the quay, and even those dingy old vessels looked fine at night thanks to the lights that were strung along their sides and on their rigging. The town also looked pretty – which it wasn't.

We passed a red buoy that glowed constantly, then a white one that flashed nine times and was still for three seconds. I had learned in my boating past that those signals all mean something and you can tell exactly where you are by navigational lights. After we passed a couple of bobbing fishing boats I went to bed. It began to rain. I could hear it pelting down outside for quite a while and in the morning all the decks were ankle deep in water.

The weather was considerably colder that day and I had to put on a woollie. At midnight we anchored off Guayaquil in Ecuador, having arrived too late for the high water that would have enabled us to tie up at the wharf. From then on I woke every so often with the tugging of the ship on its anchor. By morning I could feel the ship floating freer and then the tugging stopped. The pilot came out, a jolly person who insisted on kissing me soundly on both cheeks and we commenced our long ride in. It took about four hours to pass up the Guayas River, dodging sand bars among very low water. Large shrimp farms were visible on one side, rows of sticks with a sheet of water behind them that didn't look much but were big enough to show on the radar. The pilot told me that he had done nearly five thousand trips up this river. He called the readings from memory to the man on the bridge.

In Guayaquil the pilot, who seemed to fit the name Jolly Roger, and his gorgeously handsome and perpetually smiling son, Tino, took Wojciech, Laura and me for a tour of the town in a red Nissan van. The tour was a total fizz, but after ten days at sea it was nice to put my feet to the ground again. At least I can say that I have been in Ecuador, not that I'd want to return to Guayaquil with its dreary, scruffy streets where crime is a serious threat. It is Ecuador's largest city of two million people and the commercial and financial centre of the country, as well as one of the Pacific's most important ports.

Our first stop, almost our last, was at a supermarket not far from the wharf. Here, Wojciech bought provisions for the ship. Ecuador had just started to use US dollars for its currency, which made conversion easy. I found the prices about the same as at home except booze was very cheap. There was also a huge counter entirely devoted to perfume. Loaded up with unlabelled white washing powder in clear plastic bags – and looking very suspect – Wojciech returned to the ship. The pilot, Tino, Laura and I had progressed a few feet further when the van broke down in the middle of the street. Laura and I sat and sweated. Jolly Roger and son pushed. No success. We did it again. More people were enlisted to push until – another triumph for People Power – we arrived at the main road.

I looked behind and saw a great horde of men approaching and thought, Oh good, more pushers. Then I noticed that they bore a coffin shoulder-high in their midst. It appeared to be inhabited.

The coffin bearers and the big crowd of mourners passed by. Finally the van was given up as a lost cause and JR went to retrieve his car from the wharf. It was ninety minutes before we were eventually rescued.

The new vehicle was hot and pokey and I couldn't see much from where I was scrunched in the back seat but I don't think I missed much. The city looked a lot like some of the less salubrious towns of Indonesia. There were box-like houses made of cement bricks, hole-in-the wall shops and dirty streets heaped with rubbish even in the affluent suburbs, where all the houses were behind grilles and bars. In the downtown area with its smart buildings we parked and walked on the new riverfront corniche, which was clean and grand but over-populated with large bronze statues and guards toting gigantic guns. One statue was of a rabid-looking pig that dripped water from his mouth in a most unpleasant manner and one was of local hero Simon Bolivar. He was carved shaking hands with a friend, but something in the angle of their hips and wrists looked decidedly camp.

Next we visited a park opposite an imposing twin-towered church. The nineteenth-century park was home to a large collection of iguanas. It was encircled by a high, ornate iron fence with an elaborate gate and contained a cast-iron rotunda, manicured lawns edged with flowers and cobbled paths, on one of which two iguanas were fighting. Many people sat on benches to watch the iguanas, which posed draped along tree branches or skittered evilly across the lawns. It was a horrible sight. Iguanas must be the ugliest specimens in creation – they have the most malevolent eyes. But they do have pretty colours. Laura said her son once kept one as a pet. Yuk. It would put you off your food. Maybe that was the idea.

We drove up a perpendicular road to a look-out high above the city. The view wasn't inspiring but you could see how big the town was from there.

By now it was dusk. A car stopped beside the stone bench on which I sat and the young woman driver spoke to me. Tino told me that she had said, 'It's not safe for you to be here at this time. There are many robbers.' That was enough for me. We headed home. On one side of the hill, with million-dollar-real-estate views, were the shacks of shanty dwellers. The other side was a cemetery crowded with many crypts. The view was rather wasted on the inhabitants of those.

Back at the wharf no one stopped the car at the first two gates, although large guns were much in evidence, but at the third a guard read our passes intently even though they were upside down and he obviously had no idea what they said. We paid Tino the agreed sum of thirty dollars. He offered no discount for the time spent on the side of the road – all part of the tour experience, I suppose. Our dinner had been kept for us. Wojciech had bought some delicious fruit in town – custard apples, guavas, fijoas and tamarillos. He asked me how the tour was. I said, 'If you want me to go again you must pay *me* thirty dollars.'

The crew were still busy loading the ship when we returned, and work continued well into the night, with containers whizzing here and there. Afterwards the ship was very grubby with cigarette butts, papers, cans and rubbish. At six in the morning the engines started. The captain hadn't wanted to leave until the tide was higher but the wharf space was needed. We had to proceed very slowly as the ship had just two metres of draught and you can't go faster or you end up creating suction and get stuck on the bottom.

Walking around the ship I looked over the bow and saw that we were churning up pure mud. The sailors washed the decks to get rid of the filth and soon the ship was squeaky clean again. Out on the water the sky was clear azure and the sea dark, dark blue and empty. I watched a couple of big sea birds and wondered why they flapped alongside us when we were going in the same direction and it would have seemed more sensible to hop on and hitch a ride. I certainly would have.

At about eight that evening the sea produced a few white caps and the ship started rolling. Then it began to buck and heave and continued to do so all night with increasing ferocity. Walking on the deck I would climb uphill and then gallop down with a rush as the waves flew away under my feet. It was like riding a demented camel or a carousel pony that tipped forwards and back. I had to dance a sort of sailor's hornpipe just to keep on one spot in the shower or the water kept missing me. The sea still looked reasonably calm for all its tipping. The captain said that it was the current and that it had cut us back a couple of knots in speed. Los Americanos missed two meals – I gobbled up their share.

Approaching Callao, the port of Lima, we doddled along at half speed waiting for the pilot. The sea all around was pitch black as I watched from the darkened bridge where there was no light except for the dim glow of the navigational instruments. It was a spooky feeling being above the dark sea on this dark ship. I wondered how the navigator knew where he was going – nothing showed except a flickering buoy on one side. Then on the horizon I saw the lights of several ships and later a faint, yellow glow appeared. This turned into shining silver pin-pricks that eventually became twinkling lights strung along the shore.

The pilot radioed that he was on his way and soon a red glow detached itself from the shore lights and came ever closer until there he was underneath us in a boat with a green and a red light atop its cabin. The pilot caught the side ladder and eventually was puffing on the bridge. The captain had warned me that he had a voice like a 'drunk man'. It was more like a gorilla with laryngitis. As he neared me a wave of chemist shop passed over me – cough lollies or mouthwash. Maybe he really was a drinking man.

A pair of tugs positioned themselves either side of the ship to guide us through the narrow entrance of the breakwater – the current was very strong here – then we were inching up to a wharf where trucks with containers on them were lined up waiting. There were no cranes on the wharf. Only the two on the ship were used here. There was a lot of cargo to be off-loaded, so work began immediately and went on all night.

I had to wait for the ship's agent to clear me ashore in the morning. As I waited I watched the antics of the pelicans fishing nearby. Wojciech said you have to be very careful in this port. Pirates try to board ships even before they come in – they come out to get you in little boats. He said he would just run them down and not go around them if they tried this. Even when the ship is tied at the wharf, he said, they try to steal ropes and anything else they can get their hands on. This really is a desperate place. And this was where I was to be put ashore.

The agent finally came and demanded one hundred dollars to allow me to land. Wojciech blew a fuse and we went to lunch while it was sorted out with a higher official. Landed at last, I survived the inspection of a sombre customs woman and was taken to the minister for the interior's office for immigration rites. In this grand shore-side building my passport was stamped. We shook hands all round. Wojciech kissed my hand, I kissed his cheek. I was now on my own in South America.

6 Llama for lunch

Callao is a colonial fortress that was built in the mid 1700s to defend Peru's Spanish viceregal capital, Lima, from English and Dutch buccaneers. It replaced previous fortifications that had been destroyed by earthquake and tidal wave.

As soon as I climbed into his taxi the driver reached over and locked the doors. We travelled all of one hundred metres before the taxi broke down. An inauspicious omen. The driver tried over and over to get the engine going again but finally conceded that we were out of gas. A man selling sweets on the corner was commandeered to help push the taxi to the petrol station. It was a long way. At an intersection we passed an impressive policewoman who was dressed in long black boots, black shirt and jacket and had a white gun holster slung on her hip. At the station I had to pay for the little bit of petrol that was infused into our unwilling vehicle. The driver had no money. After much coughing and belching of black smoke the engine was coaxed into starting again and we continued on.

It was a very long way to Miraflores, the suburb where I had a room booked, and reaching it necessitated asking directions frequently of policemen and passers-by. People seemed kind and friendly. They were, to my surprise, very dark-skinned. I had expected them to look more Spanish than Indian. But they are mestizo, of mixed Indian and Spanish blood. One policeman was the spitting image of a picture I had seen of an ancient Incan leader. He had the same copper-coloured skin, strong hooked nose and ferocious features.

I could imagine him performing a human sacrifice by tearing out a still-beating heart. But this image evaporated when his severe countenance smiled at me.

But what a dump Lima was so far! The guide book had been dead right about the perpetual smog and fog. And, worse in my opinion, it was cold. Yet no other city in the Americas enjoyed such power and prestige in the colonial era as Lima. The long road from Callao wended through a barren, treeless landscape congested with daggy old cars and lined by squalid concrete or adobe box-shaped houses.

When at last we reached the foreshore of Miraflores the houses began to improve, until eventually some were quite grand. Miraflores, 'view of flowers', a century ago was a small resort town where people went for summer weekends, but now it is a prosperous suburb of Lima and I had read that it was a much safer place to stay than downtown. We drove up the main street, which had some magnificent buildings and was crowded with modern shops. But as my taxi circled the central roundabout I saw that it was surrounded by soldiers and riot police with clear plastic shields. Black clouds of strong acrid smoke rose from piles of burning tyres. Seeping into the car, they made me cough. This was scary.

Later I learned that this was the dress rehearsal for the protests planned for Independence Day, two weeks away on the twenty-eighth of July. People were angry because they felt that the last election had been rigged.

After a lot of inquiry and a couple of circumnavigations of the block, Domingo Elias Street and the Pension Yolanda were located. There was no sign on the high wooden fence and the gate was locked, but the number was right so I rattled the handle hopefully. A hatch opened in the gate and an old lady with a sweet face examined me and let me in. This was not the entrance to your average hotel, but the owners turned out to be friendly.

Entering the pension I found myself in a terrazzo-paved

courtyard with steps at its rear that went up to the guest rooms. The place was rather like the house that Jack built, all higgledy piggledy with bits and pieces everywhere. The office was downstairs on one side of the courtyard and the family lived at the back underneath the guest rooms. Climbing the outside stairs you entered a sitting room, and two rooms went off that. Then there was a tiny communal kitchen with another two rooms off it, and from a side door in the kitchen outside stairs ascended to yet another two rooms. The kitchen had a supply of coffee, tea and boiled (I hoped) water, and a fridge that had a shelf labelled for the use of each room.

I moved into a second-floor room off the kitchen. My room must have been under the top-floor bathroom as it often sounded as though water was running down my walls. The room had an attached closet of a bathroom that was painted a screaming lolly pink. I had to ask at first where it was. I had thought that the odd-looking door up a step on one wall, was the wardrobe. Oh well, I hadn't expected the Hilton.

It took a while to work out why I kept coming out of the bathroom with plaster in my hair. Then I looked up and saw that the ceiling was disintegrating and hanging down in ribbons like Christmas decorations. The plumbing was exceedingly ancient and no toilet paper was permitted to pollute it. There was only spasmodic hot water and you had to order it in advance. The furniture, except for a magnificent carved chair and bedside cabinet, had a bush-carpentry look.

The room was freezing cold. I pinched all the blankets from the vacant room next door.

With directions from the hotel I walked to Miraflores's main street. McDonald's dominated the central roundabout where the two one-way main streets with their central parks containing seats and trees met. In the shops I again found that booze was very cheap, especially imported vodka. Maybe the Peruvians had a special deal with the Russkies. At five I returned to the pension absolutely frozen. I piled all the blankets onto my bed and crawled under them to read. I was very tired and when I was finally warm and had finished my whodunit, I slept.

Next morning I looked out of the window of my room into the narrow space between the pension and the neighbour's wall. Against the wall one floor below I could see the outdoor wash trough. From a little above the level of my room a wooden trellis that was completely overgrown with creepers sloped down to rest on the top of the wall. This made a safe haven for many birds and I enjoyed watching and listening to them. A teeny brown hummingbird had a home in among the vines, as well as a dove-grey bird smaller than a sparrow. And the ubiquitous pigeons hung around, one in particular looking rather forlorn. I thought he might be looking for a feed, so I put on the window ledge some crumbs from one of the delicious bread rolls that were left in the kitchen for guests' breakfasts. After lunch, when I was having my siesta, I looked up to see him walking up and down on the window ledge only a metre away. I lay very still and after a thorough inspection of the inside of my room, he commenced to eat.

That day the pension's proprietress phoned a travel agent she knew so that I could ask about buses to Cuzco, high in the Andes, which is, figuratively speaking, the jumping-off place for Machu Picchu. I wanted to see the 'lost city of the Incas' on my way through Peru. To my disappointment I was told that no buses went directly there. The recommended bus takes a circuitous route via the south. But the woman insisted that I should fly. 'Everyone does,' she said. Not me. My aim was to cross the continent overland, anyway I could, but preferably by river once I got over the barrier of the Andes.

I studied my map. The Andes are a formidable barricade that run the entire length of South America; there are few roads anywhere and none cross to the other side of the mountains in Peru. From Machu Picchu I would have to go south to La Paz in Bolivia from where there is a road that travels into the interior.

Deciding to travel to Machu Picchu by the unrecommended bus method, I took a taxi to the bus station to buy a ticket. When my driver neared downtown Lima he peeled off his taxi sticker from the inside of the windscreen and hid it under the dash mat. On the return journey another driver did the same thing in reverse. I presumed that they were unlicensed. To make up for this deficiency (or maybe because of it) they festooned their vehicles with religious medals, pictures and rosaries. Once again the taxi didn't have any petrol and I had to buy some before we went far. I noticed that all drivers wore gloves, scarves and hats against the cold, but they kept all their windows down and froze the poor passenger.

Downtown Lima is no longer the social hub of the city, especially in the evening when the focus moves to the suburbs. The Lima area has been inhabited on a permanent basis for at least four thousand years but the city of Lima was founded in 1535 by Francisco Pizarro, who led the Spanish invasion of Peru. Lima's main square is fringed by beautiful buildings, including a magnificent cathedral. Some of the buildings and houses have enclosed and shuttered Moorish fretwork boxes around their windows and small balconies that reminded me of Saudi Arabia. It was also a bit like San Miguel in Mexico but not as nice. I saw no plants and greenery as I did there. And the weather was putrid – foggy, smoggy, grey and depressing as well as cold. It is apparently like this for almost all of the year. The dense overcasting is called 'neblina' and is caused by the fact that, although Peru is near the equator, the chilly Humboldt current flows up from the south and supercharges the air with humidity without rainfall.

The bus station was very posh and upstairs there was a waiting room that beat the pants off scruffy old Greyhound. A trendy cafe, enclosed by glass, sported a big television set and comfy lounge chairs. At the 'inflammation' desk a lovely girl patiently extracted enough fractured Spanish from me to discover where and when I wanted to go. A first-class ticket to

Ayacucho, which was about half-way to Cuzco and from where I could get another bus to continue, cost fifty sol – there were roughly three sol to an Australian dollar – and the bus left at the respectable hour of ten in the morning. The journey took eight hours, I think I was told. Four well-armed policemen guarded the bus station office, who knows why? But it reminded me of the high probability that I could get mugged in downtown Lima so I did not linger.

The return taxi driver couldn't change even a small sol note. He told me to ask the moneychangers on the street corner when we reached Miraflores. They wouldn't, the stinkers, but a nearby riot policeman saw my predicament and changed a note for me. Four Australian dollars got me an 'all-in lunch' of soup, fish, rice, salad and fruit juice at a cafe. Then I bought a four-page English newspaper for the outrageous price of two dollars fifty and went for a long walk up and down the main street in the afternoon sunshine to thaw out.

Next morning I went downtown to Lima's main market. I wouldn't have wanted to wander around this area too much and certainly not after dark. It was exceedingly grotty. Great piles of rubbish lay in the streets, apparently thrown there in the hope that they might be swept up. In the huge undercover market many stalls were still not open at half past ten. It seems the Peruvians don't get going early – too cold I guess. The cold also kept the meat market from smelling too horrible, but the fish market didn't need a tropical climate to get a pong up.

I failed to find the woollen poncho I wanted to buy for my trip into the Andes. I had thought that Peru was the home of the poncho, but despite searching high and low I couldn't find one for sale. I accosted a woman I noticed wearing one and she directed me to a shop but it offered only lairy tourist stuff made of cotton.

This day was a religious festival and, as it was also close to

National Day, balloons and bunting in Peru's red and white colours were draped everywhere possible. Behind the ornate gates and fence that surrounded the grounds of the presidential palace – which looked a bit like Buckingham Palace – a band resplendent in red, blue and much gold braid, straight out of a Gilbert and Sullivan operetta, played lustily while guards, who were also dressed pretty fancy, stood to attention on the palace steps and outside the gates.

I visited the cathedral. I thought I had seen it all in the way of ornate in Mexico, but this bulky edifice was absolutely stupendous. Inside everything was covered with ceramic tiles, even the pillars and arches. Altar after altar proceeded down both side walls and each one was covered with lights and flowers. It looked almost pagan and it was not hard to see the ancient animistic religion seeping through the Catholicism that took over. But I suppose the glut of glitter is preferable to the previous human sacrifices – certainly it would be if you had been on the day's list. There were catacombs under the church that could be visited but, as it was a religious holiday, long queues of local people waited to enter them – I saw no tourists anywhere downtown – so I gave them a miss.

I left Lima on a cheerless morning and in drizzling rain. The bus was a surprise. It had a toilet, video and even heating and, after lunch, which had been served a la aircraft, the charming conductress passed out bingo cards and called several games. I didn't win the prize – which was probably a washing machine anyway – but it was good practice for my Spanish numerals. The bus driver was encapsulated behind a screened door as on buses in Mexico. I was the only tourist on this bus ride (later I found out why) which, despite few stops, took ninety minutes longer than the promised eight hours to reach Ayacucho.

At first we travelled on the road that ran along the coast, a 2300-kilometre narrow band of some of the driest desert in the world. The Andes divide the length of Peru like a spinal cord and from the coast there is a difference in altitude of almost 13,000 metres within a distance of eight hundred kilometres. But due to the lack of roads into the mountains, the local culture, customs, crafts and lifestyles have been kept alive over the centuries.

Looking out from the window of the bus I decided that a more desolate landscape would be hard to imagine. Everywhere was grey-brown dirt that eventually rose up into the bleak, barren hills of the western Andes. There was no vegetation whatsoever. Everything was the same colour as the smoggy sky, even the occasional hovel and the poor villages of decrepit, square, flat-topped boxes with a few lines of washing flapping on their roofs.

We passed through two toll gates and then began hours of climbing ever higher. The mountains became pointed but they were still bare. Three hours from Lima we saw blue skies and left the frightful climate behind. Now and then there would be a house or two right on the edge of the road and there were many, many – far too many for my peace of mind – crosses and shrines that had been erected in memory of travellers who didn't make it any further. But I loved the quaint green dunnies that guarded the rear of each house. Every one was identical, a tiny outhouse built of green corrugated iron sheets and with a chimney vent poking from its top. Later they were all red, possibly due to a change of district.

Higher and narrower the road wound ever upwards, until finally the mountains were covered in green grass that looked as smooth as moss from a distance. There was even an occasional tree. Higher still and the vegetation was gone and there was snow on the black, jagged peaks and in the crevices on the lee sides of the mountains. In the valley way below I saw an occasional farm house and, on the fields around it, llamas and goats. And once I spied a family living in a Beduin-style black tent with their livestock grazing about them. There were few running streams of water but I saw one river frozen to a huge sweep of solid ice that cascaded spectacularly over a wide stone ledge near the road.

Now there were very steep bends on the road, but luckily not much traffic. We passed only a truck or two. As I rocked and rolled to the toilet in the back of the bus in the afternoon, I saw that everyone was asleep, including the stewardess. When I stood up I was struck by a sudden severe headache, the first sign of soroche, the altitude sickness that is caused by lack of oxygen. I had read that it has no respect for age or condition. I took some paracetamol and it went away.

From very high up in the snows at about 5000 metres we descended to Ayacucho at 2700 metres, arriving late and in the dark of night. I asked the man in charge of the small bus station to help me procure a taxi, which he did. The 'taxi' turned out to be his beat-up old car. He took me to the San Francisco Hotel, a peculiar but adequate place that incorporated much local decoration and was close to the plaza. My room had a television, a touch light that I amused myself by playing with seeing that the television was no use to me, a comfortable bed, a basic bathroom and a small balcony that was really an encased window over the narrow cobbled street.

In the dining room, which came complete with a television set and an enraptured audience, I had a tasty local version of a schnitzel and then took a walk. It was cold but I did not feel it as much I had in Lima.

At breakfast the T-shirt-clad waiter of the previous night now wore a spiffy suit and tie. He looked about fourteen and the cook looked twelve. I walked to the plaza which was sunlit and clean. The sky was clear and a brilliant blue – I realised that I hadn't seen the sun for what seemed ages. The town was rimmed by brown mountains that were so close the houses ran up them, and the flat-roofed colonial buildings and small houses topped with big old rounded tiles were as brown as the mountains. The plaza was reminiscent of Spain, but the court-yards had no pleasing gardens or flowers.

The last obstacle to an independent Peru was overcome in Ayacucho when Simon Bolivar and field marshal Antonio Jose de Sucre defeated the Spanish royal army at a great battle here in 1826. A large church dated 1670 dominated the square, which also contained trees, plants, seats, flowers and a bronze statue of Bolivar on a horse. I noticed that everyone crossed themselves as they passed the church.

The colonnades surrounding the plaza were pleasant to stroll under. They housed shops, offices and the tourist bureau, where no English was spoken – but the man in charge drew me a mud map to help me locate the bus station that sold tickets to Cuzco.

I continued along the pleasant, sunlit cobbled streets until I reached the market. From among a multitude of sacks of beans and seeds of all description I bought, very cheaply, Brazil nuts, bananas, mandarins and bread rolls for the onward bus trip. Judging from the primitive bus station I estimated (correctly) that the posh bus ran no further than here. I also finally found a poncho, in wonderfully warm, but light-weight alpaca, for which I paid ten Australian dollars. All the women I passed in the streets wore the local garb, which I thought most unbecoming – dark-green, black or brown bowler hats, short skirts with several layers of petticoats, a blouse, a woollen pullover, a vest-like jacket, a cotton apron, a shawl, and a rectangle of cloth slung around the back and across the shoulders as a carry-all. No wonder they all looked dumpy. And they wore their hair in two long plaits joined by a piece of wool. At least I didn't have to worry about what I looked like – there were no fashion stakes here. Studying a woman of the Andes standing alongside her llama, I concluded that the llama was the better-looking of the two. But I loved the rubbish cart. A man rode on the back step of it tolling a big, brass hand bell. Shades of the plague, bring out your dead!

For a couple of sol I lunched on a huge bowl of delicious soup, made no doubt from all of yesterday's leftovers, and some curry and rice. The meat was almost inedible but the rest was tasty, especially when I added the chopped chilli in vinegar mixture that was served as a condiment.

Ayacucho had one memorable attribute in its favour. I saw no ashtrays and no one seemed to smoke. I guessed that the altitude prohibited it.

I was up, protesting, at five in the morning and reached the bus station when it was still dark. I waited, leaning against a wall with the other passengers, who were all locals, alongside the smallish, oldish bus. By the simple expedient of removing the door handle and putting it in his pocket, the driver kept us out of his bus until he was ready to go. Baggage was heaved up on the roof. Thank goodness I was now in that part of the southern hemisphere where winter is the dry season. The window alongside my small, uncomfortable seat had been broken in some trauma and it had been repaired by sticking a piece of plastic over the hole.

Standing up front by the driver was the look-out man, whose job it was to shout out if he could see anything coming around the blind corners – of which there were many. As we moved through the town and outskirts the look-out man canvassed for passengers. When the seats were all taken, passengers sat on the floor.

Half a kilometre from town the road turned into rough gravel, and from there got worse. No one looked at our tickets until we were well under way. Then it was discovered that one Indian woman had no ticket and no money to buy one. While the conductor argued, she remained mutely defiant with eyes cast down. He gave up. When a paying customer claimed her seat she sat on the floor next to me. Boy, was she on the nose! As the throng at the front thinned she camped on the engine cover alongside the driver. He even gave her a blanket to sit on. She rode the whole way to Andahuailas, twenty-five sols' worth, free.

This journey took twelve hours. The going was rough and

slow but not slow enough for me at times. Villages were hours apart and the road took countless kilometres to cover every short distance as it had to make many loops to climb some mountains and many circles to wind around others. Clouds of dust eddied through the innumerable cracks in the floor of the bus and before long I was coated in a film of grime.

We didn't take the narrow road with its many blind corners slowly or carefully, but it was on the sides of steep mountains, with their sheer drops straight down thousands of metres, that I was truly terrified. Looking down at the crumbly edge of the dirt road directly beneath our wheels, I saw under it nothing but space. In order to achieve the feat of putting our wheels on the extreme edge of the road, our cowboy driver was haring along on the wrong side of the road. Why? Several head-on smashes were narrowly averted by the shouts of the look-out man and the driver backing up. Going downhill he put his foot flat to the boards and roared along, skittering around corners.

At first the countryside consisted of barren, sweeping expanses of mountains, valleys dotted with one or two small cultivated patches and an occasional mud-brick hovel – an infinitesimal mark of human habitation in nature's grand wilderness. What a hard life this must be. Further on, greenery appeared in some of the valleys and there were tiny plots of crop on the hillsides. At intervals I saw a few animals – sheep, horses, cows and small flocks of goats that were always tended by women in local dress. Later, vistas of green valleys flowing to black, jagged, snow-topped mountain peaks extended for ever. Way below in the bottom of one deep valley a wide, pale-jade river flowed fast. Now there were two kinds of mountains – big, fat, rounded green ones and bare, formidable, black ones whose jagged tops had ice and snow on them.

The bus climbed in what seemed endless up-and-down patterns to get over the mountains. Most of the time we were travelling high up near the snowline and at times I experienced a sharp pain in my head and my ears popped like castanets. Our driver, who seemed to have a death wish, casually looked right or left to admire the scenery as he chatted to nearby passengers. And as if he needed further distractions, his dashboard blazed with bobbing ornaments, while a great glittering orb twisted directly in front of his eyes. The only decorations I approved of were the holy pictures and medals. Lord knows we needed them.

We stopped for lunch at a small village cafe that I remember as having the world's smallest hole-in-the-floor toilet. Ten centimetres wide – you had to be a crack shot to hit that, especially from a height. This rough cafe was surrounded by total squalor and all that was on offer in the nourishment line was some pretty ordinary soup – but I ate it anyway. Who knew where the next food was?

Once we reached the side of the mountains that was not in rain-shadow terrain, the land became more fertile and there were more crops, villages and farm houses. We zoomed through the villages in clouds of dust, scattering dogs, goats and pigs – cute white ones and ugly, sway-backed black ones – that narrowly escaped annihilation under our wheels. Later there were towns situated in valley floors where bananas and paw paws grew in profusion and herds of alpacas grazed. Out here also roams, but is seldom seen, the endangered vicuna, which is now protected. Although similar to the alpaca it is not tameable and cannot be domesticated.

People got on the bus to travel between villages. One woman stood in the aisle near me. She wore several shawls, one of which was slung over her back and had some large bumps in it that I presumed to be a baby. Then I saw the southernmost bulge in the shawl emit a stream of yellowish fluid that ended up in mother's skirts. Looking closer I saw three darling little heads sticking out of the top of the bundle, two white baby alpacas and one black one. They were close enough for me to pat before they all got off again at the next village.

At six in the evening we made it to Andahuailas, where I had to change buses for the all-night ride to Cuzco. At the bus office I bought another seat so that I had two seats to lie across for the night. It made all the difference.

This next bus was better than the last. It was comfortingly large and had bigger seats. I had a thirty-cent toilet break in a squalid dump and layered on all my spare clothes in preparation for the ordeal to come. High in the Andes, in an unheated bus, in the middle of winter, is not the best place to spend a night. I survived. I even slept, huddled under my poncho. But the bus windows rattled themselves open every now and then and condensation ran like rain down the windows and wet the floor and the side of the seats. Gee it was cold out there! But at dusk I watched the unforgettable sight of the full moon rising between the black, snow clad peaks of the Andes, the moon a glowing, yellow gold disk in the not-quite-dark, misty grey sky.

After leaving Andahuailas the road deteriorated even more and the bus lumbered along very slowly at times, for which I was eternally grateful. But it still rattled, shook, bumped and rolled. Some time in the middle of the night we stopped for bladder relief, men on one side, women on the other, in the unwritten law of bus travel.

Outside on the road I could see quite clearly by the full moon. We were on a mountainside and way down below in the valley the lights of a town twinkled most beautifully in the clear air.

At about three in the morning there was a terrific bang and thump. The bus braked suddenly then started to back up. At this several women behind me in the back seat began screaming and shouting, 'Basta, basta!' Enough! The driver stopped and tried to move forward again. He couldn't possibly have seen what was behind him. The women and some men screamed again. I couldn't see anything from my seat but what they saw obviously terrified them. It seemed that we hadn't made a bend, had backed up and had a wheel almost over the edge of the precipice. I heard that this happens a lot – that's why there are all those little crosses. I prayed fervently that I wasn't about to get one of my very own.

At half past six in the morning I was in Cuzco, freezing cold at 3700 metres, but still alive. The town is cradled in a high Andean valley. It seems to surge up from the earth in orange-hued adobe brick houses with pottery shingles that match the deep red clay tones of the soil. The old core of the city consists of stones of volcanic granite and limestone that the Incas quarried for their palaces and temples. The Incas inhabited the Cuzco region from the twelfth century. They rose to power when one Incan leader, convincing the people that he and his wife were the children of the sun god, established a benevolent dictatorship.

Cuzco is laid out in the shape of the condor, which the Incas revered and was the fountainhead of the Incan empire, an advanced civilization that had been isolated from the rest of mankind. When the Spanish arrived in 1531 the Incas thought that they were the manifestation of a legend that said the gods would come as bearded white men. The Inca empire was called 'Quechua' which means the four quarters of the world, and the network of roads, trails and steps that radiated out from Cuzco's square, deemed the navel of the world by the Incans, was as far reaching as the Roman Empire. The Incas had three-dimensional clay maps and it is thought that they explored as far as Manaus on the Amazon, 2500 kilometres away.

From Cuzco the Inca expanded their political boundaries, building great stone cities. Like the Romans, the Incas were law-givers, warriors, administrators and statesmen par excellence. They constructed an elaborate system of royal highways along the dorsal spine of the Andes, as well as awe-inspiring suspension bridges. By communal land ownership they made provision for bad harvests, natural disasters and aid for the poor. They had a splendid grasp of architecture and masonry, bevelling stones to fit tightly together. Their buildings have survived better than those of the Spanish. In the 1950 earthquake that felled much of the monastery of Santo Domingo, which had been built over the Temple of the Sun, the inner Incan walls withstood the quake, and were revealed in all their glory.

The social foundation of the Incan and Andean world was the village, a tightly knit community of kinsmen who worshipped the local spirits. This religion continues today in the villages around Cuzco. The Spaniards imposed their culture only superficially.

Cuzco, I discovered, is a real tourist town. A woman tout with a kind face accosted me in the bus station and in my weakened state it seemed like a good idea to let someone else take care of me. Maria was a doll and I'm glad she grabbed me. The Hotel Felice, where Maria deposited me, was adequate, the staff helpful and the price good. I ate breakfast in the dining room and huddled under my shawl in the freezing lobby until a room was ready for me. The hotel had been built around a large central courtyard that had a flagstone floor and was covered by an atrium of perspex. The courtyard doubled as the sitting room. It had a TV that had prudently been built into the wall in a glass case in order to keep the guests' sticky fingers off it. At one side a wooden staircase went up to the balcony of the floor above, which was surrounded by sky-blue, wooden, Moorish-style fretwork arches.

When a bed was produced for me, I fell on it and slept soundly for several hours. My room was tiny, the bedside cupboard was painted tin and the bathroom had a lethal hot water system that required a great deal of cursing to get satisfaction from it. But it was sufficient, as they say, unto my needs. Rested and cleaned I went out to walk the narrow cobblestone streets that wind up and down the hillsides of the town—a dangerous occupation if you are as clumsy as I am.

The ancient stones had been worn slippery smooth by many feet, and I nearly broke a leg. But I got warm walking around in the sun and had a delicious llama roll for lunch, washing it down with divine-tasting fresh juice made from local fat, yellow passionfruit.

I had a wonderful time in the huge market. Row after row of stalls lined the streets surrounding the main building and inside I browsed among piles of buttons, hair ornaments, frilly children's dresses, flowers, fruit and open bags of seeds, dried herbs and medicinal goodies. There were frogs, live, skinned or dried, desiccated corpses of alpaca foetuses, olives in great casks and sugarcane sellers who whirled their great wheels to extract the juice for you to drink on the spot. I bought an alpaca jumper and woollen long-johns for more insulation against the cold.

The next day I joined a tour of the town and surrounding ruins. The bilingual explainer spoke in Spanish then English. The Spanish bits were pretty boring but the English ones were interesting enough.

We visited the three churches in the plaza. Cuzco is crammed with fine baroque churches that have centuries-old, hand-carved pulpits, valuable paintings and dazzling, jewel-inlaid ornaments. The Incas were skilful gold and silver-smiths but unfortunately the Spanish melted down most of the finest examples of these artifacts to decorate their churches. I was staggered at the unbelievable wealth that had been squandered in the churches I saw. The guide told us that Phillip of Spain took so much gold from Peru to Europe in the 1600s that the price crashed, so he told his minions to bung the gold in the churches. They certainly did. Some altars had entire walls encrusted with gold. One altar was solid silver. Another, also solid silver, was mounted on tractor wheels so that it could be paraded around the town and displayed to the populace. Bigger than life-sized dolls, overdressed in crappy taste and covered in gems and glitter, represented the various saints.

Some whacking big paintings hung on the walls, one of them a copy of Leonardo da Vinci's *Last Supper*. This had been painted by an Indian who jazzed it up by depicting a guinea pig and local bread as the food on the table. The inquisition rewarded these pious efforts by executing him for sacrilege.

The guide also said, with more than a hint of asperity, that the Spanish had pillaged the wonderful stone of the Inca buildings to erect their houses and churches.

We drove out from Cuzco to the Inca ruins of Sacsay-huaman, a fortress constructed from huge boulders, some of which were three hundred tonnes in weight. Then we travelled further on to the sacred valley of the Urubamba river to visit the remains of Incan country estates. Everywhere the tour went, sales vultures, waving their tourist wares, were lying in wait ready to ambush us, but they were not really tenacious. Not surprisingly we were taken to a large souvenir shop, where we were expected to leave large sums of cash. I failed to oblige but gave the proprietors a gold star for their toilets, which were almost normal except for their lack of paper and water. I did rather blot my copybook, though, by using the men's. The male and female toilets were divided by a wall, on top of which a doll dressed as a woman, which I failed to see until later, identified the one for the use of ladies.

Near my hotel I found a shifa, a Chinese restaurant, where I had a reasonable dinner. Early the next morning I caught the train to Aqua Caliente, the village nearest to Machu Picchu. Maria, the tourist tout who had now fully adopted me, had arranged a room at a hotel there for me. The elderly local train had leather seats but no heating and was very cold. It chugged out of the station a short way then backed up, doing this several times before I realised that we were on a switch-back and ascending ever higher with each shunt. This was the only way a train could have climbed out of the valley and over the high mountains. Higher and higher we went, passing hovels, broom bushes, eucalyptus trees and an unbelievable amount of rubbish that cascaded down from the hillside houses and was strewn into all the ravines. Dogs galore of every mixture imaginable chased the train or dug among the piles of garbage. On the roofs of houses we passed at eye level I saw small clay figurines of pigs.

Finally the town was far below and we reached the top of the ring of mountains that encircle Cuzco. Way down, about sixteen hundred metres below, I saw the town, a cluster of brown buildings with curved tiled roofs, nestled in the valley. I could see the train track up which we had come snaking out.

Then hawkers began climbing onto the train, mostly women of local dress and odour who bore all sorts of edible goodies. I bought bananas, boiled eggs and bread rolls. Their boarding methods were alarming. They jumped on the moving train's steps and banged on the locked carriage doors until someone opened them. Then they proceeded from carriage to carriage via this outside route. Watching the carriage in front of me rocking wildly, and considering the large baskets and bundles that the vendors carried, this game looked extremely dicey. I was told that this railway had only recently been restored and re-opened after it had fallen down the mountains last year. I was exceedingly glad to hear this.

The railway track had been cut along the edges of the mountains and as we spiralled up and down to pass through them the views down the valleys were superb. And when the train reached the broad fertile Andean plateau, the scenery was breathtaking – gorges and foliaged mountains on all sides. Broad meadows swept over the plateau, interspersed with small patches of wheat and onion crops. I saw different animals grazing – donkeys, goats, cows and pigs. All untended animals were tethered. At one stop a woman milked her cow into a wooden pail beside the railway line.

A small, clear stream bubbled far below in a rocky bed. This stream came closer and closer and grew larger and larger as we descended onto the plateau until it was running alongside the train track. Then it became a river that, by the time we reached Aqua Caliente, was a broad, seething, mass of white water that went falling and tearing along.

Now the train was running on almost flat ground and really rocking on. Slowly the vegetation increased until it became forest, and the mountains that rose steeply around us were fully clothed in tangles of green dotted with splashes of red, pink and yellow flowers. The train stopped at the eight-kilometre peg to let off groups of hikers who intended to walk the Inca Trail to Machu Picchu from there.

At Aqua Caliente – meaning hot water – named for the springs that were almost in the main street, it was bedlam at the station. I was caught in a crush of tourists and touts who tried to shove me into nearby restaurants and hotels. Then I had to run a gauntlet of souvenir stalls that lined either side of the narrow pathway. The hotel owner – the one who had been organised by Maria to meet the train – rescued me, shepherded me to his establishment, threw my bag into a room and shoved me off to catch the bus up to Machu Picchu.

For eight kilometres the road looped around an incredibly steep mountain to reach a dizzying height. Looking down I saw a breathtaking view of the valley – the densely covered green slopes of the lofty mountains that rose from it, the tiny train that stood in the village like a toy on a model railway and, alongside it, the mighty green and white river now reduced to a mere thread.

The bus ejected its load of tourists and, giving the expensive restaurant near the entrance to the ruins a miss, I started the long climb to the top. At first there was a guard rail and a path, then there were only steep steps cut in rough rock, some of them worn smooth and slippery. At the summit, when I had stopped panting for long enough to admire the view, I found that I could look down on the whole of Machu Picchu. Thought to have been the last hideaway of the Incas, this site was never discovered by the Spaniards. Hiram Bingham, an

American explorer, is said to have found it in 1911, but it was never really 'lost' – most local Indians knew about it.

Set among a complex of still-used Andean terraces, some of which are 2500 years old and are estimated to have taken ten thousand workers forty years to build, Machu Picchu is a flourishing ceremonial and agricultural site and the gateway to the jungle marches of the empire. It is not of monumental proportions but is rather a beautiful jewel in a perfect setting, completely in harmony with the contours of the mountain on top of which it sits. The buildings are no more than three storeys high and some builders took advantage of the slope of the land to construct them in tiers. One huge rock at the base of a temple has thirty-two angles cut on it in order to fit the stones. Many buildings have bases of natural rock into which other rocks have been perfectly fitted. The architectural work is wonderful.

Most of the structures are tiny houses. There didn't seem to be any bathrooms and I wondered where the lavatories had been. Looking across to the adjacent mountain I saw workmen the size of ants at the very top of the steep point. They were excavating more Inca terraces. Some of the mountains that surrounded me had large patches of exposed rock and others had razor-sharp edges on their tops and slopes that looked as though they had been cut with a knife. Way below me were plots, houses and temples. Only a couple of the buildings had restored thatched roofs, the rest were open to the sky.

The stones for the buildings had been cut on the spot. The Incas did not have the wheel, so possibly they rolled the stones on logs. They also had few tools. The stones were polished by hand with shards of haematite, an iron-oxide ore.

I came down more steps to the level of the buildings and visited a round temple where the sun strikes a golden ray through the windows to illuminate a certain stone at particular times of the year. And at the temple dedicated to the condor, native to the Andes, the heaviest bird of prey in the world with a wing span of over three metres, I discovered a slab on which sacrifices were performed and from which ran a gutter to convey the blood of the slain down to the carved condor's beak. There were also a stone Southern Cross constellation sign and several sundials.

When I arrived at Machu Picchu the tops of the mountains had been tipped with clouds. Now the clouds slowly descended to wreath everything in fine rain, so I took the bus, which left every half hour, down to the village again. A small boy clad in an Incan tunic and sandals raced the bus to the bottom of the mountain by leaping down the Inca trail from loop to loop of the road. He would wait by the roadside and shout, 'Hola,' at the bus as it passed each loop. This had become a feature and tourists were told to look for him. However, I now know the trick that got him to the bottom first. He was plural. When I walked the trail the next day I encountered five of him.

Back at the hotel I sat by the pizza oven to get warm. The oven was situated on a balcony that served as the dining room and which had a roof, but was open on all sides except one. Very ordinary food was provided here, for large sums of money, on long, communal wooden tables. I shared a table with Klaus and Claire, an interesting middle-aged German couple. I tried a Pisco Sour, a local specialty rather like a marguerita, that was made from Seven Up and singani, a spirit distilled from grapes and lemon juice.

My hotel room didn't cost much but, although it had a surfeit of beds, it had no refinements whatsoever. There were no cupboards or shelves, not even a hook to hang your clothes on. In the bathroom you had to be a contortionist to get at the toilet paper, which was secured to the wall behind the toilet. The hot water was provided by another of those inventions of the devil, a plug-in instant electric element. The element is like those in electric kettles and is inserted in the shower head to heat the water as it flows past. It is connected to the electricity supply by a plug in the shower wall over which water flows. It gave me electric shocks in between cutting in and out with alternate blasts of cold, then boiling water.

The Aqua Caliente train returned to Cuzco at six in the evening and pandemonium ruled at that time. After this the hotel was utterly quiet and I slept well. It was still raining when I went to sleep but I woke to a decent morning. The sun was shining and the sky was as blue as it gets. It was very cold at first but I soon warmed up after a good breakfast of great coffee, fresh papaya juice and bread rolls sliced and toasted on the end of a fork on the oven fire.

After breakfast I took the bus up to Machu Picchu again. The ruins looked even better in the bright early sunshine and there were few tourists before the train arrived to disgorge its hordes. Wandering around virtually alone, when it was peaceful and quiet, I was able to absorb the atmosphere. Lizards sunning themselves on rocks darted into crevices among the stones and a couple of llamas cropped the grass in the largest flat spot between the buildings where one small tree grew. I passed flowers here and there, orchids, begonias and a bush with a purplish honey-scented blossom. I met the German couple from dinner the night before – or, more precisely I met Claire, who was sitting on a flat rock that overhung a sheer drop, and Klaus's boots, which sat alongside her. I reckoned that she'd just pushed him overboard. It would be very easy to do – the drop was breathtaking – but she insisted that he had gone for a walk. We watched as a swallow-like bird with a blue breast dived from the edge to swoop out over the depths of the valley. Standing there, I felt as though I was on top of the world and yet secluded from it. But the edge occurs so abruptly it made me uneasy to look down. Looking out was okay, but not down.

Watching the clouds rise up and out from the humid canyons below, I felt the permanence of this place. It will always be here, suspended in the mist, a shrouded apparition out of the past. They say that on nights of the full moon the shimmering light falling down on Machu Picchu is a majestic sight.

I had lunch at the cafe near the entrance and I found that the prices had gone up with the altitude. A Coke that cost one eighty in Cuzco was six sol here and a microscopic icecream was seven dollars fifty Australian. Fortified by these wild extravagances, I walked down the seven-hundred-metre-high mountain path that was part of the Inca trail and led back to Aqua Caliente. Now that I have seen this trail I find it amazing that the Incas mastered the mountains and jungle so competently. The trail mainly consisted of high, rough-hewn stone steps that went almost straight down and were hard on the legs, and it was shaded by forest trees and partly over-grown with ferns – maidenhair, sword and Boston – red, white, pink, yellow and blue orchids, impatiens and begonias, bamboos, and shrubs that had sweet-smelling mauve berries. I had been assured that snakes, bears and pumas lurked about in this humid jungle, but saw only birds and lizards, thank goodness.

The Inca boy rushed past me in his red knee-length tunic trimmed with gold. Leaping down the steps at breakneck speed he shouted 'Hola' at me and disappeared into the thick greenery. I heard him shout at the bus as it went by on the road, then another boy dressed identically passed me and, as I progressed further, another and another. One handed me a sprig of some fragrant herb as he flew by and another showed me where the path re-entered the jungle as he stood waiting for the bus.

Sometimes I had trouble finding the path again when it crossed the road. It occurred to me that I would not like to spend the night out here with the cold, not to mention the snakes and pumas. At length I reached the dirt road to Aqua Caliente. It was great to walk level again, although I still had a one-and-a-half-kilometre, mostly uphill hike to the village, crossing a suspension bridge over the boulder-strewn, wildly tumbling river on the way. Only the garbage littered everywhere spoiled the beauty of the walk along the quiet road.

At Aqua Caliente I rewarded myself with a cold beer, though I was almost a candidate for CPR and felt more like a nice lie down, a cup of tea and a Bex. A peddler came to my table and I bought some jewellery as a result of the beer. Then, as if I hadn't done enough walking for one day, I hiked up the main 'street', a flight of concrete steps up a steep hill lined with restaurants and shops. I invested in a pair of hand-knitted alpaca socks, so warm that once I put them on I only took them off to wash my feet.

Arriving early to board the train back to Cuzco that evening, I found it already packed almost full – and still mobs more passengers crushed on, filling the aisles and shoving bundles anywhere they could. An iron pick-axe came to roost under my feet and a Cyclopean Indian woman, clutching a massive bundle, squatted in the aisle next to me and almost obliterated me when she leaned across to bellow to friends outside the window. In the space between our carriage and the next a solid mass of people was squeezed, some of them hanging out over the sides of the train.

The journey back to Cuzco was mainly downhill and the train travelled fast, rattling frightfully on the hillsides, which had big drops beneath them. As the train lurched along I watched the people hanging on to the outside, and was terrified that they might fall. The conductor shoved his way through to the end of the carriage and, waiting for the train to stop, got out and sold the hangers-on tickets as though they had regular seats.

Soon it was dark. In the headlights of the train I saw the line curving away ahead. The Southern Cross appeared outside my window, shining brightly in the clear dark-blue night. After two hours of near asphyxiation in the pack of bodies, the train stopped at a village where many got off. Without all that body heat the train was suddenly cold, but my alpaca jumper, shawl and socks preserved me. I stretched out on two seats and went to sleep.

Then the lights of Cuzco appeared far below, lying like a diamond necklace in the valley, and the switching of the rails commenced. Each switch magically brought the lights closer until I could clearly see the square with its three massive churches. Five switches later we were at the railway station, where the red van that had brought me here waited to take me back to the Hotel Felice, just as Maria had promised, bless her. I was in bed by midnight.

The next day was Sunday. I declared a day of rest and did nothing except walk around Cuzco and the market. Once again the skies were blue and sunny, but it was still cold. Many of the streets, especially those with old walls, were redolent with the smell of urine. This was not surprising in a place where public toilets were as scarce as hen's teeth. Even when you did find one it cost twenty-five cents.

It was now time to move on to Bolivia. I was pleased to find that I could go part of the way by train – to Puno on the shores of Lake Titicaca, about half way to La Paz – so the next morning I was again forced out of bed early to catch it. It had been raining and the cobble-stoned streets were slippery but, undeterred by this, the taxi flew along skidding and skittering. Maria accompanied me to the train. She had arranged a hotel for me with a friend in Puno, and in return I'd given her a daggy cast-off bag. She was so thrilled that I wished I'd given her the new one I'd bought to replace it.

The train was very comfortable. Red plush seats were placed in pairs facing each other with a table between. I'd had many warnings of the dangers in South America, especially of robbery on trains, and I had been nervous about travelling here. However I read up well on how to avoid scams, dangers and annoyances and found that the fear of the unknown was worse than the reality. Once in South America I never thought about being afraid.

The passengers in this train carriage were mostly foreigners or South American tourists. As the train gathered speed it rocked a lot and ours, being the end carriage, was even more shaky. We almost took off on bends. Soon the food sellers started clambering onto the train and from then on for the South American travellers it was one long munch. I had lost my appetite days ago – yes, me! Altitude does that to you. I could eat but I wasn't hungry, a sensation totally new to me. I had also been drinking coca tea, which prevents altitude symptoms, but takes away your appetite. My only real trauma from the changes in altitude was that some of my sponge-bag contents leaked and I lost most of my deodorant. Physically I suffered no ill effects, except that I was a little breathless on climbing and had a slight headache at times.

Suddenly I was hungry again and set about making up for lost time. This train even ran to meal service. A waiter took my order for Pisco Sour, salad, bifsteak and fruit and delivered it to me at my table. The meal was okay but I was soon hungry again so I bought an item from a vendor that looked like a pasty. And it was. A delicious homemade pasty like Mum used to make. I had another. The seller's small girl stood by my side absorbing me for an hour, and never said a word.

The train trip took eleven hours but it was a pleasant ride. The track climbed only a little and there were no alarming drops over the side to contemplate. Even so, we were at a height of almost four thousand metres on the alti-plateau by the time we reached Puno, three hundred metres higher than Cuzco.

Leaving Cuzco with its appalling amount of rubbish by the tracks we had travelled, with mountains on either side of us, through small villages and plots of land that were now mostly fallow for the winter. The rain and cloud soon cleared as we continued to run south through valleys where snow-topped mountains sometimes formed the backdrop. Later the land opened up and there were large expanses of green grassland on which small flocks of sheep, cows, alpacas and llamas hoofed around. The train stood for a while at one of the wall-enclosed, thatch-roofed, mud-brick villages. Then, as a train from the opposite direction passed, I realised why we had been waiting. There was only one line. The meeting of the trains had been timed rather well as we had only been there for fifteen minutes. USA Rail eat your heart out – we would have been there all day with that company.

In the afternoon the mountains became more rounded and were covered in the same brownish-yellow grass as the pastures. More vendors got on and off the train. I felt sorry for one old man and, in a moment of folly, bought a white, fluffy alpaca fur hat. It suffered a sad fate when I got home. Unbeknown to me it was to appear to my cat, Josephine, who is also a white ball of fluff, as a deadly rival and at the first opportunity, in the middle of a dark night, she leaped up onto the cupboard where it sat, challenged it to mortal combat and attacked in deadly earnest. I heard the commotion and found the chewed remains of the alpaca on the floor.

At five exactly, as advertised, we reached Juliaco, where the train stops to connect with the train from the south, and then we continued on to Puno in the dark. I was met by Oscar, the hotel owner. He bundled me off the train, trundled me through the pack of sharks at the station gate, pushed me into a van and took me to his hotel.

Peruvians seemed very laissez-faire about payment. I had a scrappy note from Maria that told Oscar to take four dollars off my bill because the Hotel Felice owed it to me. It had been the same at Aqua Caliente, just a scrawl on an old scrap of paper to say that I had already paid. No one asked for cash in advance or tickets before you got onto transport. If shop-keepers needed change they would go off to find it, leaving you alone with all their goodies.

At the Hotel Baija my first-floor room was almost warm. It had an entire wall of windows that received full sun during the day. Oh, the bliss of lying in bed in the sunshine while taking my siesta after lunch. I was even given a feeble, one-bar electric heater, an item I had thought to be an unknown quantity in Peru. As usual I had asked for extra blankets and slept in my long-johns. You do some disgusting things when travelling. The shower, another of those frightening electric devices, produced water that was almost warm. The shower curtain rail was a piece of wire devoid of curtain, the toilet seat disintegrated under me, the wardrobe was a few pegs on the wall and the only furniture was a sturdy wooden chair and a bed, but everything was clean and the hotel staff were, as usual, friendly.

Dawn seemed to come earlier in Puno. By six it was fully light and at that time the spruiker at the small bus station directly opposite my room started shouting destinations. The station was merely a vacant block where drivers waited in ancient buses behind an old grotty wall. The buses slept here at night and started off very early in the morning.

Hotel Baija's exterior was utterly without charm and the lobby was a grim freezing hole, but I considered my warm room wonderful and I enjoyed the breakfast that was included in the price – egg rolls and delicious, freshly squeezed orange juice. This was provided in a room at the back of the building whose windows looked onto the rear of the hotel and the surrounding roofs. The view was, to put it mildly, uninspiring. The area looked derelict, like an abandoned slum. Electric wires protruded from the walls to swing in the air before re-entering the crumbling brickwork. Broken windows were edged with haphazard bits of tin and the roofs defied description. They were covered in a collection of battered, loose bits of tin thrown one on top of the other and held down with old planks of wood. The whole mess was overlaid with rubbish.

7 Gaol bird

Puno, which was founded in 1668, is on the Peruvian shore of Lake Titicaca and on the overland route that I had chosen to get to Bolivia. From there I could travel by bus to La Paz, and onwards north to Amazonia.

Oscar organised a trip on Lake Titicaca for me. A deep sapphire blue, the lake straddles the Peru–Bolivian border at an altitude of 3810 metres and is the highest navigable body of water in the world. It is also large, 233 kilometres long, 97 metres wide and 457 metres deep. The pre-Inca peoples believed that the sun and their god, Viracocha, arose from the waters of the lake. The Incas also believed it to be the birth-place of their civilisation. Life around the lake has not changed much since those days.

My excursion would take me to the floating islands of the Uros people, who began their aquatic existence centuries ago in an effort to escape the Incas. The islands, made of totora reeds that break free from the bottom of the lake and join other clumps of weed to form islands, have a population of approximately three hundred inhabitants. The Uros folk use totoro reed to make canoes, boats, furniture and as feed for animals. The *Ra Two* was built of this reed for the Norwegian explorer Thor Heyerdahl, on the island of Suriki in Lake Titicaca.

I joined a united nations of tourists that included a jolly pack of Israelis. We clambered into a crowded mini-bus to drive to the lake. Puno's streets and houses were run down and the town was crammed with so many tiny shops that I wondered how they all survived. Reaching the water's edge we climbed down onto a five-metre wooden boat with a half cabin. At first I sat up the top in the warm sun, but the wind quickly froze me and at the first stop I zipped inside the cabin.

As we moved slowly out onto the calm lake I was surprised to see birds perching on floating clumps of reeds. One narrow island that had been formed by dredging soil from the lake's bottom was a mere strip of land, but cows and sheep, as well as a reed house stood on it. Nearby a man harvested reeds in a reed boat. The other islands we saw were the floating kind made entirely of totora. We stopped at one and as I walked on the piles of reeds that constituted its surface, they sprung under my feet like sponges. This little island was only a few metres wide but it boasted not only a village of tiny reed houses, but also a miniature museum that had a collection of stuffed birds, native foxes, long-tailed rabbits and fish. One exhibit turned out to be merely asleep – in a small patch of sun that fell in the centre of the floor, a grey cat snoozed in a contented curl.

Back on terra firma I ate a set lunch in a nearby cafe. I found these set meals intriguing – you never knew what sort of a surprise was in store. This one produced a bowl the size of a bucket full of mushroom soup, an equally large plate of spaghetti and a glass of juice. All for five sol. But the biggest surprise was that *Hamlet* blared from the television set in the corner. That night I dined at the posh hotel in the main square. It even ran to fabric serviettes instead of the usual paper one cut into quarters. The meal cost five dollars more than my hotel room, but the Lake Titicaca trout with garlic was divine. Back in my room I put the one-candle-power heater on, survived a lukewarm shower, erected my emergency lighting system and, toasty warm, jumped into bed to read.

The bus to La Paz left at eight in the morning. And what a

swish beast it was. The collection point was only two blocks away so Oscar carried my bags to it. I was presented with a form I had to complete with my passport number and other details in order to get on the bus, but no one looked at my ticket.

The road to the border of Bolivia was fairly good. For a while it ran alongside Lake Titicaca's immense blue expanse, which had an occasional boat at its edge and looked as limitless as the sea. Then we were among rolling brown and yellow hills and fields dotted with animals and mud-brick villages. Potatoes, barley and fava beans grow here in land that is still ploughed by oxen. Women shepherds stood in the fields knitting and near one village a small boy played at bullfighting, waving a towel at two young steers. Occasionally we passed through a town. There were few vehicles on the road, but we did encounter a van that had three sheep sitting on top of it in the pack rack.

Then the lake was near again. Behind it, brown hills rose in front of another range of higher mountains whose tops were heavily laden with snow and ice.

At the Peru–Bolivia border I shuffled slowly forward in the long line that waited in the dusty street in front of the immigration office. I had read that the border officials were notorious for stamping passports with the wrong date, then tracking you down and fining you. But I encountered no such problems. Next I walked a couple of hundred yards up a hill and, passing through an old stone arched gate in the wall that divides the two countries, emerged the other side in Bolivia.

Soon after being reunited with the bus we came to Copacabana, a lovely little town set between two hills and nestling around a splendid bay. This place has been a site of pilgrimage since Inca times and now it is a religious sanctuary, famous for the Virgin of Copacabana, a black Madonna who is said to perform miracles. We stopped at Copacabana for lunch and in a tree-shaded garden I sat on a piece of chopped-up log thinly disguised as a chair, at a table of rough wood, and ate what was described as a 'send whitch', a whacking great lump of bread the size of a small loaf.

After lunch we were transposed onto a Bolivian bus that was old but horribly fast, especially on blind corners in the mountains we entered. The bus, top heavy with piles of luggage tied haphazardly high on its roof, swerved dreadfully along narrow dirt tracks below which five-hundred-metre drops fell terrifyingly close. The speed maniac of a driver roared up and down the mountains with his brakes screaming. By the time we reached La Paz they were making the horrible sound of grinding metal and pouring forth smoke like a train. To stop the bus on the steep downhill street of our final destination the driver had to jam its wheels into the kerb at an angle. But the view was superb from the sides of the heavily snow-capped mountains down to the beautiful blue lake with its sunny islands.

Halfway to La Paz we arrived at the isthmus of Lake Titicaca where we had to alight and get into motor boats while the bus crossed the lake all by itself on a barge. The barge was welcome to it. The boats were grossly overloaded and we were bobbing about on a freezing lake with no life jackets. But this was still hugely preferable to the bus. I can swim, but I can't, as yet, fly.

After a couple more petrifying hours in the mountains, the bus was running on flat ground in a valley of brown and yellow grass with soaring mountains in the background. The countryside looked much the same as Peru. We climbed again to negotiate the highest pass of 4200 metres and looked down on La Paz before descending to it at 3800 metres. The city appeared to radiate up from its centre at the bottom of a deep valley and, rising from the bottom of this bowl, it swarmed up the surrounding hills. The houses were all much the same brown colour as the hills, only the odd tree made a splash of green, while behind the enclosing arms of the brown hills a backdrop of jagged snow-covered mountains stood against a clear blue sky.

Almost four kilometres above sea level, La Paz is called the world's highest capital city (but it is only a de facto relationship – Sucre is the legal capital). Many visitors suffer soroche here – the city is so high that it doesn't need a fire brigade. It is hard to keep even a match burning in the oxygen-poor air, making it a depressing place for pyromaniacs.

When the Spanish marauder Pizarro swooped on this peaceful spot in 1531, a prosperous community lived here, irrigating crops and fruit and mining and working gold and silver. The Spaniards seized the mines and founded La Paz as a post on the trade route between the silver mines of Potosi in the south of Bolivia and the Peruvian ports. The Spanish extracted fortunes of gold and silver from the Potosi mines, making the miners work under atrocious conditions. The Potosi mines were the holocaust of Bolivia. The Indians died in droves, despite – or maybe because of – being given coca to keep them working harder without food. Black African slaves were also imported by the million and worked to death or killed by silicosis.

Bolivia, landlocked and isolated, is not only the highest but the second-poorest South American country. It has a predominantly indigenous population of 6.6 million, seventy per cent of whom live on the bleak alti-plateau west and north of La Paz. There are also a mixed bag of other nationalities – Europeans descended from Canadian Mennonites, escaped Nazi war criminals, missionaries and one per cent of the population is of African descent. Half the size of Western Australia, Bolivia shares borders with Peru, Brazil, Paraguay, Argentina and Chile and boasts some of the world's wildest frontiers, as well as the highest concentration of cosmic rays on earth. Perhaps that is what gives it its feeling of otherworldliness.

Since Simon Bolivar gained independence for Bolivia in 1824 there have been 189 governments – there is an abnormally high mortality rate among politicians. President Murillo was publicly lynched from a lamp post in the square named after him.

Agriculturally Bolivia is a subsistence nation that exports small amounts of coffee and timber and is the world's largest legal exporter of coca, earning US 1.5 billion dollars from its sale. But only half of this remains in the country. One-third of the Bolivian work force depend on coca for employment. There are 54,000 hectares under cultivation in the Chapare region alone, and they yield 100,000 kilos of coca per annum, all of which is exported. Although cocaine is illegal Bolivians chew coca leaves daily and make tea from them. Mama Coca is the daughter of the earth goddess and the earth cult revolves around the coca leaf, the use of which was a privilege originally reserved for Inca priests and the royal family but which eventually spread from Bolivia to Columbia. Cocaine is grown as coca leaf, then dried, soaked in kerosene, mashed into a pulp and treated with hydrochloric and sulphuric acid, then with ether, to produce white crystals.

From high above La Paz we began to descend through the poor and littered upper suburbs of tin or straw-covered adobe houses that flank the approach. The muddy, uncared-for roads were lined with downmarket auto repair shops and junkyards and Indian women washed laundry in the sewage-laden river. Then the earth dropped away and it all disappeared as La Paz lay four hundred metres beneath us, climbing the walls of the canyon that is almost five kilometres from rim to rim and gives the city in its arms protection from the fierce winds and weather.

Driving down the one major thoroughfare, whch follows the path of least resistance through the canyon and along the course of the Rio Choqueyapu, we reached the city centre. From the downtown skyscrapers of the main square everything zoomed steeply uphill to the rim, behind which the white-topped, seven-thousand-metre peak of Illimani loomed.

Happily I parted company with the bus. The sight of the

remains of several of its ilk, as well as the forests of little crosses beside the road commemorating other vehicles that had gone flying over the edge, had not endeared me to it. Putting my watch forward an hour made the time now five and already it was decidedly frigid. Winters in La Paz are very cold and dry and the temperature falls below freezing as soon as the sun sets.

I was taken for the proverbial ride by a taxi driver. I knew he was a villain when he let a kerb-side window washer clean his stationwagon's rear window and then refused to pay. And the poor fellow didn't even complain. Apart from this taxi driver, I liked all the Bolivian people with whom I had dealings and found them courteous and kind.

The hotel I finally found was in San Pedro, or Saint Peter's square, opposite the prison. While negotiating the price of the room the manager, a kind and gentle soul, joked that I could get free accommodation over there. Hooray! I now had enough Spanish to understand a joke. The hotel, a hulking two-storey stone edifice, was okay but very cold. My room didn't have a window, just a skylight recessed a million kilometres away in the lofty ceiling. Staring up at the grotty piece of plastic sheeting that covered the skylight and the bare light bulb that dangled beside it, I longed for my sunny room in Puno.

Begging another blanket, I doubled it over on my bed, but the air was still too cold to allow my hands out to hold a book. My room had a TV, which to my surprise featured the news from the BBC in English, the main item being a plane disaster in Paris. Nice comforting stuff to watch when you're travelling. Once again I very nearly electrocuted myself using the diabolical electric shower in the bleak Arctic bathroom with its perpetually wet floor. I would have gladly swapped the TV for a bath-mat or a heater. The electric socket by the bed light didn't work but instead of fixing it someone had roughly banged another into the wall alongside it. The hotel had wooden floors throughout and what sounded like herds of elephants passed along the corridor beside my door.

Abandoning my freezing room for the marginally colder streets, I walked downtown and found much activity and a busy night market. Hundreds of lantern-lit stalls lined the main street, and in the clear air lights glittered all over the slopes where the city crawled up the sides of the canyon. The main avenue, known as El Prado, was a promenade of trees, flowers, monuments and old homes with iron latticework and balustrades. Many small streets, mostly cobbled or unpaved, branched off the main drag. They were lined with tiny shops that sold leather, weavings, alpaca items, silver and antiques, while street vendors offered, among a variety of goods, irons heated by charcoal, stone carvings, and medicinal cures of the ancient Incan medicine men. A couple of beggars sat on the steps of the large San Francisco church in the main square and a man with no hands played a mouth organ. There is no welfare system in Bolivia.

With all the clothes I was wearing the cold was bearable, but I pitied the poor and homeless. Most women wore national dress – you couldn't fail to be warm in all those skirts and petticoats – but many were heavily laden, their backs bent almost double with bundles and babies. I resisted the offerings of unbottled drinks, cream cakes and other goodies, possibly featuring instant typhoid, and, meeting two English girls who had shared the horrors of the bus ride from Copacabana with me, went with them to a chifa, a Chinese restaurant and had a decent meal of fried rice, chop suey and local beer. The beer was good around here but it was impossible to find it cold. Fridges were sometimes used merely as storage and were either not turned on, or turned on so low that their contents were barely cool.

The chiming of the San Pedro church clock in the square woke me in the morning. The square had benches, photographers with old-fashioned boxed cameras draped with black cloths on stands, the ubiquitous pigeons and a few scrappy bushes. I couldn't find anywhere that served breakfast so I bought a couple of plain bread rolls from a street vendor and walked along munching. The bread was good enough to eat and cost only a quarter of a bol per roll – there are three bolivianos to an Australian dollar. It was a sharp climb up to my hotel from the main plaza but in the narrow streets that rose from it there was much less of the horrendous traffic that congested the centre and gassed you with exhaust fumes.

All that day until late afternoon I walked around La Paz with only half an hour off for lunch. It was a delight to wander aimlessly up and down the extremely steep but fascinating streets. I found La Paz was well endowed with elaborate churches. Ninety-five per cent of Bolivians profess to be Roman Catholic, but it is a hybrid Christianity incorporating the ancient folk religion, especially in rural areas. Ekeko, the little dwarf household god responsible for matchmaking, finding homes and success in business, still has a big following. Perpetually lost, I found the hechiceria, the witches' market, by mistake. Here women sat on the footpath selling potions and spells to kill, cure or get you a lover, as well as talismans to ward off evils arising from the aforementioned spells. Then there were incenses and fragrant woods to burn for all of the above reasons or just because you liked them – and dried llama foetuses that were so totally gruesome I couldn't imagine owning one no matter what it might do. Items used in white magic and animism, including grease, nuts, wool and concoctions, were on offer. Although I fancied some of the spells, I desisted, imagining the outrage of an Australian customs officer confronted with them.

Further on was the hurly-burly of the black market which sold everything – contraband, medicines, sulpha drugs, codeine containing analgesics, pots, pans, leatherware and food galore. Stall after stall, street after street, it continued on both sides of the road for kilometres. In my meanderings I came upon the hotel that a British boy on the bus had told me about and went in to inspect it. I was shown a big, sunny room that cost twenty bolivianos and booked it for the following day. Taking a short cut that led in the general direction of my present hotel, by some miracle I rounded a corner and was right at the door. Maybe one of the talismans rubbed off on me.

In my freezing room I scrunched down under the blankets to write, wearing my alpaca fur hat, three jumpers, long-johns, knitted socks, slacks, pantyhose, singlet, long-sleeved spencer, shirt and poncho. It was a major operation to get dressed and undressed. I went out to dine towards evening still wearing the big fluffy hat because it was so warm I couldn't bear to take it off.

La Paz at dusk as the sun settled on the surrounding valley was beautiful. A reddish glow enveloped Illimani and the surrounding high peaks of the Andes against the deep blue sky. In the street all the women goggled at my hat. I thought, Well, they should talk, what about their own stupid hats? I am sorry if this sounds uncharitable. I like hats, but those bowlers they wear look ridiculous and I wouldn't be caught dead in one. I read that the bowler hats and voluminous skirts worn by Indian women were imposed on them by the Spanish king in the eighteenth century and that the centre parting of their hair was the result of a decree by the viceroy of Toledo. Both these men obviously hated women.

I ate in the Cafe La Paz, a quaint old dive that is a hang-out for politicians and businessmen and was, until he was expelled in 1983, Nazi war criminal Klaus Barbie's favourite spot. After dark the entire canyon, up to where it met the alti-plateau, was ablaze with lights. And above the rim, the stars were brilliant in the clear night sky while the moon hovered over Illimani's eternal snows.

At nine o'clock the next morning I presented myself at the gates of the prison to try for the tour of the premises that the hotel manager had told me was possible. The prison building was very old and had one massive windowless stone wall about twelve metres high right on the street. The wall on the other side was the same height but high up in it were narrow slits of windows. In the middle of the front wall there was a large gateway with iron-reinforced, wooden doors. The outside of the prison was a grim, forbidding place that chilled me to look at but inside, what a contrast! Its exterior totally belied what lay beyond the wall.

I stood on one side of the great gate in the brilliant morning sun and tried to communicate to one of the guards with large guns who were stationed there that I wanted to go in. A couple of other foreigners who had also heard of this attraction joined me, and a large mob of locals who had come to visit relatives waited in a line on the other side.

Finally we tourists were allowed into the arched stone porch, where several more guards were posted at a desk. My handbag was checked for cakes containing files and weapons of destruction – well, it is big enough for a couple. At the back of the porch was an open-grilled but barred and pad-locked gate about two-and-a-half metres wide and through it I could see a sunny courtyard with trees and flowerbeds. A terrific clamour arose from the mobs of prisoners – this is an all-male prison – who were pressed against this gate. Pushing their arms through the grille they called out to me: 'Senora, senora!' This was a bit scary but I think they only wanted to sign on as my guide.

I was led away from the other tourists and shunted into a dark stone alleyway on one side where a woman guard sat at a desk. She took my passport and entered my particulars in an exercise book. Then she body-searched me and asked whom I wanted to see, 'amigo o marido', husband or friend? So much for being pleased that I looked like a local.

I realised now that I had ended up in the wrong place, having been separated from the herd who had been sent else-where. I was no longer an interested spectator, I belonged!

Help. Using all the Spanish at my command, I got out again as fast as I could. Now I had to walk through a corridor where crowds of prisoners pressed against a metal wall that had an iron grille from waist-height up. Women visitors who could not pay the price to go inside the grounds were allowed to stand here and talk to them. Nice – I looked like one of them. Not only the gun moll of some degenerate felon but a poor, unsuccessful one at that.

Back at the gate I started again. I gave my passport to the guard to guarantee my return – Lord, would you want to stay in there? – and, with a couple of Dutch men, was handed to a guide who greeted us cordially, shook hands and said his name was William. He warned us not to take any valuables with us. A bit late now, I thought. What should I do with any I did have – give them to another prisoner, hopefully merely a murderer and not a thief, to hold for safekeeping? 'Stay close to me,' William the Villain said, and three of his fellow miscreants fell in behind as the rearguard. I guess it would be terribly bad for business if one of us was murdered.

The prison was amazing. The accommodation consisted of ancient, tiny, stone rabbit-warrens that you had to buy for the duration of your stay. They cost from four hundred to twenty-five hundred dollars. Extra comforts could also be bought. You could sublet or sell your cell and I saw 'for sale' signs posted on walls. There were seven sections of cells. The best were 'safe'. Children could live with you and many tiny tots were in evidence. The bigger children went to school and rang the bell to get back in. Bizarre. Wives with money, though apparently not ones who looked like me, could visit, but only during the day. Once inside the gates, there were no guards. Not game I suppose.

Before we started our tour we first had to be presented to, and inspected by a man who was introduced to us as 'The Head Man' and his deputy. They were fascinated by Australian crocodiles and asked how big they grew and so on.

I impressed them no end by saying I had seen crocs in the wild. It was all very pleasant and convivial. The Head Man's room had a TV set and a phone. He said that he regretted not having the internet.

We visited the shop, various food stalls and a large old church decorated with murals. The priest came every day at ten to say mass. Pet dogs and cats wandered about and washing that included tiny clothes was hanging over balconies. Incongruously, a large pine tree that reached right up to the roof grew alongside one exterior wall. It looked as though it would be easy to shin up it and jump over. I was told that many prisoners carried on trades, making jewellery, doing carpentry and running businesses.

The kitchen looked awful and smelled worse. Joking, I asked if I could stay for lunch but was told the food was 'little and terrible'. It was a case of buy your own or starve. There were eighteen hundred men in this prison. Some were washing clothes outside in stone troughs, while many just sat in the sun. All smiled and said 'Hola'. I felt that we were their day's entertainment.

Back at the gate I shook William's hand, paid him the ten-dollar price of the tour and was let out. I heard later that he was a murderer.

My new hotel was the Dynastie. My octagonal third-floor room sat on a corner of the building and featured four large windows that looked down into the market on the street below. All day I heard the cries of pedlars but they quietened down at night. From early morning the windows allowed blissful sun into the room which kept it warm. The windows on one side framed a view of the belfry and cross of an old church that rose above the market. The church had a roof of ancient tiles, many of which were broken or haphazardly crooked with long grass growing out of them.

The Dynastie served breakfast on the sixth floor. I needed oxygen by the time I got there after starting my ascent at reception. The view of the mountain peaks that seemed close enough to touch made up for this, although it didn't quite make up for ordering eggs and getting cake – just when I thought my Spanish was coming along nicely.

From La Paz I planned to travel up north, firstly to Coroico, then to Rurrenabaque in the Bolivian lowlands. I read that the lowlands were hot, flat and sparsely populated. I couldn't wait, especially for the first two.

The part of Amazonia that covers most of Bolivia's north is less spoiled than that of Brazil and Peru. Amazonia, the basin of the River Amazon and its tributaries, covers a huge area encompassing tracts of Peru, northern Bolivia, Colombia and Brazil. There is only one road to it. It connects the alti-plateau, the high Andean plateau where I now was, to the yungas – the valleys beneath – and the level Amazon rainforest. It passes through Coroico, a village noted for its tranquillity and spectacular position. Perched at fifteen hundred metres on the shoulder of a mountain, Coroico has outstanding views of forested valleys, plantations, cloud-wreathed mountains and the peaks of the Cordillera Real, Bolivia's most prominent range of mountains and one of the Andes' highest and most impressive.

The road through the Andes was the major drawback. Considered the most dangerous road in the Americas, it takes two hours to drop three thousand metres, winds all the way to Coroico and features appalling rock overhangs, horrifying chasms and waterfalls eroding the narrow track that is flanked by near-vertical, thousand-metre precipices. An average of one vehicle per week goes over the edge. I thought I had seen it all on the way here and could not imagine any worse. I was already scared stiff, but was assured by my guide book that what I had traversed so far was a doddle compared to what lay ahead.

Enquiries I made at various tourist agents about onward travel towards the north elicited the information that minibuses were okay, but big buses and trucks were not safe. They were top heavy and 'fell over the side a lot'; jeeps did the same because they went too fast. No one denied that lots of both varieties did fall over. That didn't leave much to choose from. From my bus rides so far I had come to the conclusion that no vehicle driven by a local was safe.

I took a taxi to the minibus company, looked at the beat-up object that stood there with the top of its roof loaded up to the sky – and hired the taxi! At least I could, hopefully, control its driver. I asked him if he would take me to Coroico. He agreed. I inspected his vehicle's tyres and looked under the bonnet. We agreed on a price and that he would drive carefully and slowly. That night my taxi driver reneged on the deal. He brought his wife to tell me that she wouldn't let him go. Wise woman. Scouring the street, I found another taxi driver with a four-cylinder stationwagon who said he was willing to go. I bet he won't do it again. When he started asking directions of passers-by, I realised that it was his first time too. I wouldn't do it again either. The guide book described it as the most terrifying ride in the world and, for once, it was right.

At first the road consisted of two lanes of asphalt with steep declines surrounded by brown and barren mountains with little sign of habitation, just an occasional person with a few animals. Then we were way up at the top-most level of the range and the mountains right beside me were close enough to touch their bare black rock. They were topped with snow and looked like badly iced cakes or as though they had been dusted with talcum powder that had slid off untidily. Ice that had fallen down from their hillsides lay heaped beside the road.

All too soon we reached La Cumbre Pass. At 4600 metres it is the road's highest point and from here the ride descends to Coroico. Beside the big boom gate there was a sign that said that this was the start of the one-way road and that drivers were to go one way between certain hours and the opposite way at other times. This turned out to be a myth. No one observed the rule. At the point where drivers were about to start the horror of the road, mongrel dogs lined up to be fed for good luck and there was much ritual sprinkling of tyres with alcohol. Never mind the tyres, it was the passengers who should be sprinkled, inside and out. Then, horns blaring, brakes squealing, the vehicles set off suicidally, their loads lurching out over great abysses edged by the omnipresent white crosses. The worst tragedy had occurred a few years before when two trucks loaded with passengers collided, fell over the edge and killed more than one hundred people.

My driver, Miguel, who had long before taken down his taxi sign, paid the toll at a wonky wooden office, the gate was lifted and the narrow dirt road began. It was horrible, even worse than I had visualised. Rough and potholed and barely a few metres wide, it had ghastly elbow-bends with crumbling edges that hung over sheer space and a drop of a thousand metres. There was little room to get around these bends, and trucks and other vehicles that were coming the other way when they weren't supposed to be there had to back up to manoeuvre past. We almost crashed into several of them. Waterfalls fell on us from above and washed over the road making it slippery with mud. Despite the appalling conditions, everyone drove as fast as they could.

We had been stopped by customs men looking for drugs at a road block just before the bad road began. My bags had been searched, all my belongings played with and my passport examined. They asked me if I had marijuana or cocaine. Sure thing buddy, I'd be likely to tell you if I had. But now the road was so scary I longed for any sort of sedative. The only way to do this trip is unconscious. I sweated blood as I clutched the side of the car and the seat in front of me, and shrieked 'Despacio!' ('Slowly!') at Miguel. He drove far too fast with little care for the health of his car, not to mention his passenger.

Now the mountains and valleys below were greenish and so was I. Looking across to where the road snaked around the mountain opposite I saw wrecks and the scattered remains of vehicles sprinkled down the hillsides. It was sick-making. Later there were many rainforest trees, vines and shrubs, while towards Coroico bananas and palms grew. When we finally made it and passed the church in the plaza, Miguel crossed himself. I wanted to join him. Instead I fell into the dining room of the hotel calling for the strongest drink in the house.

I stayed at the Esmerelda, a quiet, secluded hotel built into the side of an almost perpendicular mountain eight hundred metres above the village. This mountain is said to be the home of Pachamama, the earth goddess. From here the view was sensational and Coroico, nestled on the mountainside, was utterly beautiful. Steps cut into the mountain led down almost vertically from the hotel to a lane cobbled in stones so rough they hurt my feet through my shoes. The lane finished in the plaza but was so steep that I was glad when I managed to hitch a ride back up it with the Esmerelda's four-wheel drive vehicle. In the plaza I booked a seat on the bus to Rurrenabaque the next day. I also needed to reserve space on the truck that takes you seven kilometres down the mountain to connect with the bus at Yolosi in the valley below Coroico.

That night I ate in the hotel dining room, which was lit by candles. It was a strange sensation to be dining on the edge of a dark precipice. Looking out I could see nothing except a few lights in the village. I talked to a Bolivian gent who said he came up here regularly to stay in his weekender, nineteen kilometres away, where, he said, there were many beautiful birds, including toucans. It would require more than a few feathered friends to get me to ride regularly over that hideous road. But Coroico was a delightfully peaceful spot and after extracting an extra blanket from the management and having a great hot shower in my huge bathroom, I slept warm. In the morning, when the sun reached over the mountains, the twittering birds got me up. I watched a tiny hummingbird sipping his breakfast from a banana flower.

The Esmeralda jeep took me down to the plaza, where I ate a huge breakfast of eggs, bacon, ham, tomato, bread and sheep's cheese. The plaza was a pleasant place that was lined with many small shops and had garden seats under huge palm trees. I talked to an itinerant trader from whom I bought a petrified shark's tooth. Don't ask me why, it must have been the altitude. When I asked him directions to a loo he took me by the hand and led me there. I also met a park ranger who told me that recently in the north an anaconda had been found that had a suspicious bulge in its middle. On investigation this turned out to be a twelve-year-old boy.

When it was time to truck it down to connect with the bus to Rurrenabaque, I saw, shock horror, that the truck was not only open and a stand-up-in-the-rear job, but that it was already packed solid and grossly overloaded. I refused to stand on the open tailgate, which was the only space left, and was squeezed into the front seat. Even though it was only a few kilometres, it was still a hideously steep road and I begged the driver to go slowly and, dear man, he did.

The village of Yolosi had a checkpoint where vehicles had to stop and pay a toll in order to pass. This was where you waited for the bus. Enterprising souls had set up stalls to sell warm cold drinks, mandarins and bananas to those forced to stop. Many vehicles went through, mostly buses and trucks. There were few private vehicles and all of these were four-wheel-drives. I had been given the number of the bus I was allegedly booked on and told that it would arrive at half-past-two. It came at half-past-five. There had been a landslide on the road. During the long wait I talked to other travellers or sat on my bag and read. Someone said that two trucks had gone over the edge close to Yolosi the week before and more than twenty people had died. Eight children had survived by being thrown off.

I walked down the road in search of a loo. All I had to do was follow my nose – I smelt it for ages before I got to it. When I reached the gate I found it securely locked. I questioned a nearby shopkeeper about the possibility of a key and was sent to the house of the man who was the Keeper of the Toilet. He opened the padlock on the gate, gave me a ration of rough, pink loo paper and charged me a third of a boliviano.

At last the bus arrived. It was a lumbering old brute whose top was heaped high with baggage – to which mine and eleven other people's was added. Two men who failed to win a seat had to stand in the aisle.

Then we were off. Steep, jungle-covered cliffs loomed above humid, cloud-filled gorges and the first hour and a half was a continuation of the same narrow, nefarious track that had brought me to Coroico, but now I was in an overcrowded, top-heavy vehicle that tipped and swayed as it lurched along the edges of precipices and around blind elbow-bends. At one stage I looked back at the road we had just traversed – a strip of dirt halfway up an incredibly high mountain, a mere wisp of white on the dark-green vegetation. It was so scary my stomach churned and my heart leapt into my mouth trying to escape.

The bus bumbled on, tilting and rocking, waiting on the blind corners for trucks to pass. I was sitting at the rear, which had five seats in a row across it. My companions were three Irish girls and one Bolivian gent. The girl nearest the window groaned in horror every now and then. I thanked heaven that, unlike her, I couldn't see what was, or was not, under the back wheel.

At six o'clock we stopped for a meal at an outdoor cafe. It was merely a few tables under a wooden verandah, but they fed me reasonable tucker for a tiny price.

It started to rain as we took off again. Terrific – now it was not only dark, but slippery to boot. Jolting along the edge of a precipice while slithering in mud in the pitch-dark convinced me that this would be my last mountain ride ever. Flat, flat terrain from now on, thank you.

At around nine we stopped for more food and at about four in the morning, when we were out of the mountains and in the yungas – a source of gold as well as the major area of coca production – we drove under a scaffold that enabled the police to search the top of the bus for drugs. Then they entered the bus to search us. It was a very perfunctory search – I could have had heaps of loot hidden under my feet. Sometime later we ground to a sudden halt and something seemed to have broken. Fortunately we were out of the mountains by then. The driver jacked up the bus and asked the passengers for a knife. Someone obliged and I saw the driver cutting up an old tyre tube. The repairs took an hour or so. I think it had something to do with the springs. We went on very carefully after that.

Dawn found us on a road that was almost flat. My relief was unbounded, but the road was still appalling. It took seventeen-and-a-half hours to travel three-hundred-and-fifty kilometres. When daylight came I could see that the country was very green, the vegetation consisting of rainforest thick with trees and vines. Now and then we passed a type of house that I had not seen before, made of wooden planks and with over-hanging thatched roofs. Chooks, pigs, small plots and banana trees surrounded the houses. Occasionally we would pass a man walking on the road, carrying a rifle and a machete.

Rurrenabaque is a real frontier town but it looked fine to me after the bus, the road and the Andes. Rurre, as it is known, lies on the Rio Beni – the 'river of wind' in the language of the Tacana, the original people of this place. They were one of the few lowland tribes to resist Christianity and western civilisation. Now only a few forest tribes continue a hunting and gathering existence in the country around Rurre, but along the jungle waterways there are tribes that have had minimal contact with modern civilisation and still roam the deep jungles as they did thousands of years ago. It is said sometimes that they are the remnants of the tribes who inhabited the lost Atlantis.

The Spanish came here looking for El Dorado, the Gilded City, in the mid 1600s. They gave up and moved on. Jesuit priests founded the first mission in 1675 and imposed Christianity where they could, but they also brought cattle and horses. Despite what some people think, northern Bolivia is not all cocaine and rainforest – there are large cattle ranches in the savannahs. Some of the cattle are descended from the Jesuit herds, but most are Asiatic Zebu imported from Brazil. The Jesuits also taught European trades like leatherwork, and established tropical agriculture, including the farming of bananas, coffee, tobacco, cotton, cacao and peanuts. The Jesuits were expelled in 1767. Other missionaries and settlers came later, but they only brought disease and slavery.

My luggage and I were transported from the bus station on a motorbike, for which dubious pleasure I was charged one-and-a-half bolivianos, forty-five cents, the price for any ride around town. From the several small hotels available I chose one situated on the River Beni that was named, not very originally, The Beni. Its outlook was not as picturesque as it sounds, as it only backed onto the river – the rest of it was in the main street. The Beni's design was pseudo-Spanish with balconies and a courtyard where hammocks were slung invitingly between pillars.

Rurre had rough dirt streets that were lined with shanty shops and rows of stalls, but the town was clean and the shops had limited supplies of cans and bottles on their small wooden shelves. A big cement curb separated the street from the area in front of the shops. Not good enough to call a footpath, it meandered haphazardly up and down and over planks that had been laid across the open drains to help pedestrians negotiate them.

I found breakfast down the road at the Rurre Club, a

pleasant outdoor spot overlooking the river under huge mango trees. While I ate I watched the coming and going of the motorised canoes that provide transport up, down and across the river. I had read that passengers were taken on the cargo vessels that ply the mighty rivers of Bolivia's north, and intended to try for one.

Then I slept for several hours. When I surfaced I indulged in a washing fest. This was the first place that had been warm enough to dry clothes. I had now thrown off my winter woollies. Bliss! The noisy air-conditioner in my room worked for a little while, then gave up the ghost. The hot water service did ditto but the TV was fine. However when I complained that I was not able to change channels I found the solution was simple. There *was* only one.

In a tour office in the main street I arranged to take a three-day trip into the jungle. The tour lady was a charming Slovenian with a lit-up face. A born-again Christian, she was reading the Bible when I rocked up. Bella told me that she had spent a year in a jungle village living off the land with a local tribe because 'God sent me'. She made a detailed note of my name and particulars – in case God lost me? Bella exclaimed in horror when I said that I had come by road and told me that she lost a friend that way when the jeep he was travelling in went over the side and eleven people were killed.

I ate dinner on the riverfront in a basic cafe that was half outdoors. There appeared to be no way to lock it up and the bottles on the bar were left out in the open when the place closed for the night. A handy spot to go for a free drink after hours, I thought. Long, sleek motor canoes put-putting by and boys on motorbikes doing wheelies on the foreshore provided the evening's entertainment as the sun set behind them and sent a blaze of fiery colour over the calm water of the river. Large birds that looked like jungle fowl but were a type of vulture zoomed in. They hovered gracefully like hawks, but landed like malfunctioning bulldozers, then waddled off like ruptured ducks. In a tree close by, a tiny monkey, who should still have been with his mother, was attached to a limb by a rope that was tied very tightly around his middle. A big green parrot, also securely fastened, kept him company. I watched a woman set up a rival cooking establishment outside the cafe, unpacking from her basket a small burner, cooking pots and other bits and pieces. As each customer finished eating, she rinsed his plate in a bucket and dried it on the edge of her apron.

I saw no cars in Rurre's streets, just a couple of four-wheel-drive vehicles and several motorbikes. There were, however, a multitude of placid dogs. I heard that sloths lived in the trees of the plaza but did not find one. I did see two toucans sitting on top of the wooden sign above a shop. They were so brightly coloured and larger than life that it took me a while to convince myself they were real.

Walking in the streets I passed many men who carried rifles and machetes. Everyone said 'Buenos dias'.

8 Road to ruin

Next morning I had the local breakfast of meat, egg, rice, tomato, coffee and bread. It was good and the coffee for which the yungas are noted was excellent. Seeking information about onward boat travel from Rurre, I was sent to the naval office, where a charming uniformed officer shook my hand and informed me that there were no boats at this time of the year as the water was too low. I would have to endure another bus ride. A road to the north had recently been completed but before this the river had been the only form of transport.

Great river systems drain this vast area – the Madre de Dios (Mother of God), the Beni, the Mamore and a score of others flow northwards towards Brazil, into the Amazon tributaries and eventually to the Atlantic. I motorbiked it to the bus station and bought a ticket to Riberteralta, five hundred kilometres further north, for a few days hence, when I was due to be back from my jungle trip.

The Beni Hotel was terribly rowdy. I moved to an upstairs room hoping it might be quieter. Getting rid of the air-conditioner was a good start but now I had an overhead fan that went around in the accepted manner but didn't send any air down where I needed it. Goodness knows how this was possible and what it did with all that air.

There was no electric power in Rurre from midnight to seven in the morning. I had a cold shower by torchlight at six, packed my bag in the dark, then presented myself at the tour office ready for the jungle. Three hand-carts piled with gear were pushed to the riverbank and loaded – along with a young Belgian couple, the guide, the cook, Bella as the interpreter because she couldn't find an English-speaking guide and me – into a huge canoe with a forty-five-horsepower motor. The canoe had been carved entirely from one big tree – its base was very narrow for its length and only just fitted two people across.

We motored over the river to San Buenaventura, which had no road into it. Its only access to the outside world is via the ferry from Rurre, as it was with all these towns before the road was built. In San Buenaventura we paid a tax and registered our names and passport numbers with the police. Then we set off on the wide, calm River Beni.

As soon as we left Rurre behind we were among dense jungle with few signs of inhabitants. Now and then there would be a small clearing and a native house with a canoe tied at its landing – a blissful idyllic scene. After a time the river occasionally broke into boiling rapids and whirlpools. I could see the terrific pull of the current and, thinking that this would be a dangerous river to fall into, realised that we had no life jackets. High-water marks and huge trees with massive trunks that had been uprooted like toothpicks lay where the river had dumped them on sandbanks.

The Beni was joined by a smaller river, into the channel of which we now turned. The water in this river was lower and sometimes the guide needed to take up a long pole and punt the canoe along. Occasionally he stopped the motor and jumped into the water with the cook to push us over a sand bar. At the shallowest places we all had to leap into the river and heave against the rushing current. Under my feet I felt the smooth stones that completely cover the river bed and much of its banks. The stones were lovely – round, smooth and flattish. I lusted after them for my garden.

The only traffic we had passed on the Beni had been a few canoes and a man fishing from a raft, but there was nothing on the second river. We made slow progress and now it was very hot, so I popped up my pink sunshade.

The camp we were going to was a steep climb up the river bank from the landing place, which was itself well hidden in the jungle. This tour company brought the only people who ever visited here. The camp consisted of two blue plastic tarpaulins that covered the cookhouse/dining area and the sleeping platforms. The latter had been constructed of slender trees that had been split in half and laid three inches off the ground and had poles at strategic places to which mosquito nets could be tied using strips of bamboo. The beds were thin slabs of foam rubber with one blanket on top. The dining table and benches were also constructed of split trees cut locally. The cook house, in which the cook performed miracles, was a primitive arrangement that incorporated a two-burner gas jet.

We all helped carry our supplies up from the canoe, and as a reward for this chore, were given tea, bikkies and fruit and told that it would be lunch time in forty minutes. The meal duly served was a local specialty called picante macho. It was delicious. Served with rice, salad and many side dishes, it was made of chopped vegetables and meat in a wonderful spicy sauce. The cook then made a speech which Bella translated. He said, 'If you get sick, come to me and I will make you better with local herbs and tea.' I wondered at his timing, telling us this during a meal he had prepared.

Then it was siesta. I slept soundly for two hours, after which we punted the canoe to the other side of the river and fished for piranha – without luck. It seems even piranha are frightened off by me. But we did see the marks of turtles and capybara – like an enormous guinea pig, it is the world's biggest rodent – on the sand banks. Dinner was another seven-plate feast, then we tripped out in single file for a night walk that lasted for hours and achieved the sum total sighting of one mouse. I hadn't expected much else with all the racket we made trooping through the undergrowth like a herd of rhinoceros.

I bathed at the river's edge, dippering water over me with one of the plastic soup-bowls from which we later ate breakfast. It was lovely lying under my mosquito net in bed watching the shadows behind the glow of light put out by the candle stuck on a post at the end of the bunks, listening to the frogs croaking and the monkeys hooting. In the distance thunder rumbled and lightning flashed. Toward morning the frogs stopped their racket and then it was beautifully quiet.

The cook, Santos, was a man of much nervous energy who took great pride in his work and was very eager to please. The guide, Enrico, was quiet, with a nice smile and kind eyes in his deeply lined face. After breakfast they took us for a four-hour walk in the jungle where they showed us plants that would fix anything that ailed you or were otherwise useful, like the sap of the ajo ajo tree that smells like garlic and is a good insect repellent. And just for fun, there was the Big Mac, a liana whose seed when germinating opens to look like a hamburger with mustard, ketchup and pickle in the right-sized bun.

They also told us tales of jungle animals. I was intrigued to learn that a small capybara-like animal and a poisonous snake are friends who sleep curled together in the base of tree trunks. In the case of snake bite, fluid from this animal's body will act as an antidote. Some stories were gruesome, especially the one about a certain kind of monkey, thousands of which fall out of huge trees at night and tear people to pieces. They also do this when it rains. At that moment it started to rain and I was seized with a perfectly understandable urgency to leave immediately the vicinity of the large tree under which we sat.

We partook of another ten-platter meal for lunch. This time there was fried rice and a potato salad like no other I've ever tasted, as well as fried chicken, fried banana chips, fruit and vegetables all attractively arranged. The rain, which had started so gently that it only hit the canopy and didn't reach further, fell stronger and steadier while we were eating, until it was wetting the ground. We were told that it was dangerous to walk in the jungle when it is raining as tree branches can fall on you. The others went fishing but, knowing this was a lost cause, I slept.

Dinner was once more very good – this time it was noodles added to all of the above. Afterward we paddled the canoe over to the opposite river bank again, lit a huge bonfire of driftwood on a sand-and-stone-covered spit of land and, sitting on logs, watched the yellow eyes of animals that came down to drink at the water's edge of the opposite bank. Now that the rain had stopped it was a lovely night and the Southern Cross and the Milky Way stood out in the dark velvety sky. Enrico and Santos told us tales of anacondas as thick as tree trunks and said that there was an example residing in a zoo in Riberteralta, the next town I was heading for. I resolved to see it.

I woke at dawn to the sounds of birds and monkeys and made my way down to the mist-shrouded river to wash. After breakfast of fritters, bananas and coffee we packed up the camp and trundled down to the canoe, then we proceeded to the opposite river bank to collect some big trunks of balsa wood to make a raft. Further down-river we stopped to chop off a couple of tree branches and strips of bamboo for ties. When completed, the raft consisted of seven large logs tied together with smaller ones that were a movable feast placed on top as seats. We tourists and Bella scrambled on board and Franz, the Belgian boy, took first turn at standing up front with a pole to punt and paddle us along.

Going along noiselessly with the flow was very peaceful and all went well until we hit the rapids. Then we were bumped and dragged over the stones on the bottom. It was great fun and we all took turns to drive in the two hours that elapsed before we reached the spot on the Beni where we met the canoe bearing Enrico and Santos. We stepped ashore here, and Enrico led us inland to visit a primitive village of Chimane Indians.

For half an hour we were marched briskly in single file through jungle so lush it totally covered us overhead, while underneath my feet the path was soft with damp fallen leaves.

The warm air, heavy with the sweet, dank scent of flowers, hung about us absolutely still and all was quiet except for the cries of birds. Enrico pointed out the tree that animals rub against when they are wounded to heal them, as well as the diarrhoea tree, the worm tree, and the chocolate tree with its livid red fruit that turns brown and smells like its name. We sloshed through a couple of muddy creeks and, crossing a stinking rivulet, climbed up its bank to where three families of Chimane lived.

At first I thought that they must sleep on the ground in their open-sided shelters of sticks under palm-frond roofs, but then I saw that there was a sleeping platform under the fronds. 'Away from the tigers,' Bella translated. A fat, exceedingly grubby, naked baby toddled about the flattened earth under the shelter. Almost everybody had a baby in Peru and Bolivia. One family consisted of a small woman with pleasant features, her husband, also very short, and two grimy children. They all wore vestiges of tattered clothing. We had brought our left-over food for them and it was fallen on instantly – even the two pet monkeys got a piece of biscuit. Their household goods included a geriatric rifle that had been mended with solder, a waist-high piece of tree trunk that was now a stand for pounding grain, a chopping-block also cut from a tree trunk, a table made from pieces of bamboo tied together, some woven reed mats, a fire on which a couple of turtle carcases smouldered, a bottle of yellow fluid that I discovered was urine used as medicine and for healing, and a bottle of filthy river water that looked even less appetising than the urine and was for drinking. No wonder they need the healing tree and the diarrhoea tree. Their only livestock were a couple of chooks and the two gorgeous pet monkeys. They said that the day before a jaguar had nearly made off with one of the monkeys. Looking around outside the shelter, my stomach heaved when I encountered the stench from chunks of meat that were drying on a bamboo rack and a bag of stinking rib cages standing under it.

When we left, one of the children, a small boy of about six who had trouble holding up his tattered pants, picked up a small bundle of this meat. His father took a bigger one and they slung them in the traditional manner on their backs, suspended by a band around their foreheads, then they followed us. The small boy, who was in front of me, kept looking around anxiously at his father behind me. He thinks I'm going to kidnap Dad, I thought. Or maybe he feared that he might be left with this weird woman. I tried to get Dad to pass me but no go. Maybe he was the rearguard defence against the tigers. I wouldn't have been a lot of use. A jaguar, when mature, can be nearly a metre tall at the shoulder, two metres long and one hundred and twenty kilograms of sheer power with its massive jaws and big, square head.

Back at the river Santos had set up his gas cooker in the narrow canoe and made us a delicious lunch, four platters of mixed goodies plus rice and fruit. He offered a share of this feast to a couple of other travellers who happened along, a pair of Israeli fellows who were about to set off into the jungle alone and on foot. Our guide said this was very dangerous. Aside from the snakes and tigers, there were evil bandits to avoid. He said that an American girl had left Rurre alone in a canoe and attempted to reach Riberteralta. She had been killed and her body found in the river. I had also read that women should not go into the jungle alone or in pairs with a guide. Bella said that kidnapping occurred often in La Paz and other cities but not much in the country. No, here they just murder and maybe eat you. She also said that the Indians kill much wildlife and the reason that we hadn't seen many animals was that there were numerous Indians living in this area. Now she tells us! Although we didn't see them, there were anacondas ten metres long, alligators of five metres and insects of twenty centimetres as well as jaguars, tapirs, peccarys, anteaters, monkeys, snakes, capybaras, giant river otters, armadillos, agoutis – a long-legged rodent – sloths, lizards, parrots and spectacled bear living nearby. And turtles, fish and pink dolphins were in the river. Not to mention zillions of bugs – I could vouch for them.

The small boy shared a seat with me in the canoe. He was dubious about this at first and kept looking nervously at his father in the rear, but finally I got him to smile. When I was not looking he studied me carefully and edged beneath my pink umbrella to see what life was like under there.

At Rurre two hours later I tipped the guide and the cook handsomely – well, by local standards anyway. It was the best food I'd had this trip. Bella found me a hotel that was quieter than the Beni. It had an interesting shaded courtyard that was paved with thousands of pieces of broken tile and had hammocks slung around its edges. After a quick clean-up I met Bella at five o'clock and we took motorbike taxis to see a friend of hers, a Swiss fellow who maintained an animal sanctuary for orphans and strays, as well as a very cheap backpackers' hostel. Judging from the specimens loitering in the garden this was also for orphans and strays. At the sanctuary I met a beautiful jaguar called Gaddafi, who had been orphaned as a baby, and a large, lithe enchantress of a black monkey named Monica Lewinsky. She was prettier than her namesake.

I ate chilli con carne in the cafe down the road, slept well and, cursing, rose by candlelight to be at the bus station at seven. The bus from La Paz was late so I had a 'brekfest compleat' – the usual gargantuan repast – in a nearby cafe. The station waiting area was a bench under the verandah. From here I watched a black pig foraging freely around the square in front of the station, while countless dogs sniffed by and a grazing horse wandered up and down. The seven o'clock bus finally arrived at half past nine and a man got off it carrying his fighting cock in a leather sling over his shoulder. It was the same bus that I had come up from Coroico on, very high in front like a truck (which made it difficult to get in and out of), as well as old, worn and already full. I talked to an English couple who got off here. They were definitely going to fly back. Apart from the terrors of the road, they'd had to stand for four hours despite having numbered tickets.

We rattled off with a huge load on top as well as inside. This bus was a veritable vegetable market. One man carried a large coconut palm, another a box of six sprouting trees, while another had a plastic bag with a growing fig tree in it which he hung from the window hook. I had a little trouble getting my reserved seat but the problem was resolved amicably in the end. I sat in the middle of the row of five back seats between four Bolivian men and put my feet up on my bag. We all snoozed.

The road was in even worse condition than the one this far had been, but at least it was flat. It stretched in front of the bus like a ragged ribbon of dust to the horizon. It was hot, so all the windows were open and the dust poured in mightily. When I got off I had filthy, uncombable hair, a dirty face and clothes that were stiff with dirt. By that time, however, I was long past caring about keeping up appearances.

The uneven, winding and deeply rutted road required first gear to negotiate the bad parts and the countless creeks. And this was the great new road! Then came even worse, many kilometres of boneshaking corrugations that were interspersed now and then by a pothole so bad it almost shook the teeth from my head, and sent me flying up off the seat.

The first stop we made at a bus station I rushed to the loo and joined a queue from another bus. While standing there I gazed upwards and a hole in the ceiling enabled me to see the manufacture of this establishment's interior. It was chicken wire with papier-mâché spread over it. While I was contemplating this marvel I heard our bus engine start and by the time I came flying out, waving and shouting, it had backed out and was moving off. But I wasn't as delinquent as the passenger who actually missed it. How can you miss a bus that is three hours late? A few kilometres from Rurre a motorbike roared alongside the bus and a passenger who'd been left behind got on covered with dust.

We encountered pampas country north of Rurre and after a while I saw cows, horses, large white storks and egrets, and, looking down as we passed over a bridge, several large crocodiles basking sinisterly on the riverbank. Later I saw many more on the marshy wet lands, paddy fields or creeks by the side of the road.

I was glad I did not see the appalling logging and deforestation that is taking place out from Rurre where once there was thick rainforest. Mahogany trees are cut down for only the bottom five metres – the rest is burned for charcoal and firewood. Less valuable trees are simply burned on site. The land is being stripped and sawmills and lumber yards have sprung up since the new road north was opened.

Lunch was provided in a ramshackle dump where I ate soup, meat and rice at a rough wooden table while fowls pecked in the dust around my feet. The Bolivian men who had shared my seat joined me, and I helped myself to a glass of their Cola by mistake. I thought the drink was communal as so much else was. When there were only two of us left on the wooden bench the other fellow got up, the bench catapulted me off and I went flying onto the dirt floor. The men hauled me to my feet, dusted me off and set me straight again. Then I went out the back to look for the ladies'. Stepping among the pigs and the plentiful mud, I came to a wooden outhouse that was used for washing, but there was no toilet. I used the ground as indicated by one of the ladies of the establishment while she stood in front of me to protect my modesty. Then I did the same for her. We are all sisters under the skin. I washed in a bucket of water drawn up from a round, brick-lined well. It was a pigpen of a place but the people were friendly. I asked what the name of this spot was and they told me it was Sheraton. The hotel chain would be pleased.

The dinner establishment was a lot better. In a neat riverside village flying a Bolivian flag, we crossed a wobbly pontoon bridge and stopped at a cafe surrounded by a white picket fence. Sitting at tables on its wooden-floored, semi-enclosed verandah, we were served decent fish and rice. Two big green parrots sat near me on top of the picket fence and carried on a noisy argument in Spanish while I ate. The waiter, a Quasimodo replica, one eye blinded by a cataract and with one shoulder up near his ear, lurched at me with a mad leer and a cackle. I didn't know whether to laugh or run, but as no one else seemed to notice anything odd, I stood my ground. This time I sat with some Bolivian ladies, one of whom had been sitting in front of me in the bus. She had the usual hairdo – two long pigtails – and lots of skirts and petticoats and she hung her precious bowler hat in a plastic bag from a hook by the window. A businessman with glasses, briefcase and watch sat beside her and soon they were in deep conversation. The young men nearby occasionally swigged chicha, an unappealing milky-coloured local hooch made from industrial strength maize, out of big, plastic bottles.

The bus had broken seats, missing armrests and smashed windows mended with tape, and became ever more littered and filthy. The conductor took off his shirt later in the day when it got hot and some passengers did the same. Night came with a glorious red-ball sunset followed by a fabulous, apricot-and-crimson sky.

During the night a bolt sheared off from somewhere underneath the bus. I was surprised the whole caboose hadn't shaken to bits long ago. The passengers climbed down to wander around on the road in the moonlight waiting for it to be fixed. Back on the road, this journey seemed as though it would go on forever – jolt, shake, bump, lurch, crash. Everything I had rattled, but, just when I had completely given up on ever arriving, we did. I fell off totally relieved to be on firm ground again. We should have arrived in Riberteralta at eight in the evening. It was now after six the next morning. It had taken more than twenty hours to travel five hundred kilometres.

9 Jungle juice

Motorbike taxi-ing to the Amazonia Hotel I found it all in darkness. I knocked on the massive, ancient wooden door until finally a light showed and a large, rumpled but friendly man gave me access to a bed, bless him. Badly needing a shower first I asked if there was hot water. 'No, aqua naturalle!' I didn't care. I fell on the bed and slept for hours. Today was Sunday the sixth of August and this was National Day in Bolivia. I heard church bells as I went to sleep.

The Amazonia Hotel, a stone, two-storey building of obvious great age, cost forty bolivianos per night. Lots of wood had been used in its construction. The lofty ceilings were all polished wooden planks and the walls were panelled to chest height. The entrance doors were like those of a fortress, great solid old barricades secured by padlocks. I saw no other type of lock in this town. The floors were lovely parquetry or ceramic tiles. Set into the tessellated yellow brown and green floor tiles of the entrance-lobby-cum-sitting room was one continuous plank, without joins, that must have been twelve metres long. It started at the front door and passed through into the kitchen to disappear under a 1920s' dresser. It was possibly mahogany and there were signs of wear in its middle. Although I puzzled over it I could not work out its use. The hotel owner, a laid-back man who had a Spanish look, had a great job, as two young Indian girls did all the work. He unselfconsciously wore a torn, creased shirt and had three-day old stubble on his face, but he was very kind to me.

My room boasted an overhead fan with only one speed – noisy – and a feebly inadequate fluoro light. The wooden plank door into the swampy bathroom was fastened by a plastic bag twisted to make a loop over a long nail and the shower rose was suffering from third-degree rust. The windows and the door panels had no glass, just fly screens. There were two huge double beds, an open rack for my clothes and a hideously incongruous, triple-seated brown vinyl couch. A wide verandah outside kept the big room cool. Palm trees and bushes grew in the courtyard and around the outdoor sitting area and somewhere in them lurked a pet parrot who was up early and very verbose. This was not a tourist town and I could not find a laundry, so I washed my filthy clothes outside in the yard sink.

Near the main square I had a great lunch of the famous Beni beef – in the form of barbecued shaslicks – with rice and lovely fresh apple juice. This was the first decent pile of meat I'd had since the *Atlanta*. The town was sleeping in the hot afternoon, so I went back to bed until evening when a smashing rainstorm came to cool things down.

Taking a walk at five o'clock all the people I passed greeted me with 'buenos tarde'. One small boy had a monkey on his shoulder and there were the now expected legion of dogs. The two main streets were brick-paved or cobbled and the other streets were dirt. The footpaths went crazily up and down over breaks, holes, deep ditches and open drains, lethal at night when the streets were unlit. Shops were very basic, but the streets were reasonably clean, helped no doubt by the pouring rain that soon had them awash. Boards placed conveniently over the deepest drains and gutters enabled them to be negotiated without drowning, but I still got very wet. (I don't mind this as long as it is not cold.) The market displayed the usual array of goods in a big covered shed. Near the hotel I passed a large second-hand-clothes shop and wondered where all the stock came from. Most people looked as though they were wearing their old clothes – as did I. The rain washed away the band and the celebrations for National Day were a total fizz. Shame. All that was left in the plaza was a lot of rubbish and a damp, forlorn seller of fairy floss.

Riberteralta is on banks of the River Beni near the confluence of the Madre de Dios. After the rubber boom collapsed around 1914 it resorted to its current mainstay of growing, producing and exporting oil from Brazil nuts. My guide book said that Riberteralta is 'paralysingly hot with a contaminated water supply and deadly open sewers'. The town's plaza was enormous and in its centre was a rotunda surrounded by gardens and seats under large trees that were neatly clipped into dense umbrella shapes. The edges of the square were colonnaded, or shaded by the verandahs of stone buildings, none of which were grand – indeed, some were rather tatty. The few cafes had their seating outside on the footpath. Nothing was fancy. The cathedral that fronted the plaza was a massive, new-looking pile of reddish brick, not at all conventional in style. When I looked inside at seven in the evening it was packed with worshippers. The pews all faced the altar in a fan shape and on one side was an almost open confessional – a pretty public place to be airing your sins and negligences.

Away from the square the buildings were mostly basic wood or clapboard and had divided swing doors that opened directly onto the street. The top half of each door was often open and I could see what family life was like inside. There seemed to be only the bare necessities – a bed, a table, a cot.

At the Social Club I waited an hour for some picante macho but when it arrived it was very good. I also had some delicious juice of unknown aetiology. The club was an attractive building outside but inside it was a monstrous, empty stone place with high ceilings, arches and columns and pale green walls. There were fancy metal chandeliers with glass shades, ceiling fans, and lots of white-cloth-topped tables with red artificial rose buds in glass vases. The kitchen was so far away I couldn't smell any cooking, which had me worried when my dinner took so long. And I had all this echoing emptiness completely to myself. Lunch seemed to be still the focus of the social scene.

Riberteralta traffic was motorbike or scooter, on which it was pleasant to ride pillion in a cool breeze. Discovering that there are no buses that travel further north, the next morning I went to a share taxi stand on the edge of town to negotiate a ride to the Brazilian border. After I had arranged to be collected at my hotel at twelve, I had a sumptuous breakfast of pawpaw juice in a milkshake, coffee, real French bread, two eggs and chicken salad – all for the usual five bolivianos. Then I tried to change some money and found that both banks were closed, possibly because of the holiday or just out of pure cussedness. I was saved by the hotel proprietor who sent one of his girls off to a moneychanger for me.

The taxi came for me three quarters of an hour late. The driver, who had a round jolly face, helped me with my bags and made the hundred kilometre trip in half the time that the book had alleged the mythical bus took. The beat-up old car made horrible noises and I never thought it would make the distance, but it zipped along over the dirt road at eighty kilometres per hour most of the time. This got exciting at corners but Jolly Face was a good driver. Soon after leaving Riberteralta we crossed a bridge over the wide river where an entire village was in the water washing clothes, pots, pans, kids and themselves. Long lines of poles supported by posts were festooned with dripping clothing. It was a washing-fest extraordinaire. But it *was* Monday!

The country we passed through was jungle so dense I couldn't see a metre past the side of the road. There was only a very occasional clearing occupied by a lone house or a tiny village. The houses were made of white-painted adobe or wooden sticks, with thatched roofs. We crossed another river, this time on a punt that was pushed by a canoe with a twenty-five horsepower Yamaha outboard. No fee was charged for this. At times there were roadworks and bridges in progress along the road. And once a man on horseback wielding a big, business-like whip chased a three-coloured – white, brown and black – bull down the road. Later I saw cleared and burned ground and herds of cows, mostly skinny white brahmins.

10 Across the river to Brazil

Guayaramerin, the terminus for the road from Riberteralta, is a small, dusty settlement with a frontier atmosphere. Situated on the alligator-infested Rio Mamore, opposite the Brazilian town of Guajara Mirim, it is a river port and, due to the impassable rapids further on, the end of the line for transport along the Mamore. It is also a rail town where the railway never arrived. The line was planned to transport rubber during the boom days by connecting Riberteralta to Porto Velho in Brazil and thence to Manaus, the Amazon and the Atlantic. The 364-kilometre line from Santo Antonio to Riberteralta, completed in 1912, cost six thousand lives thanks to malaria, yellow fever, gunfights and accidents. But the line to Porto Velho was never finished and no trains ever came. The world price of rubber plummeted and the railway became a white elephant while it was still under construction. Today the road goes across the railway bridges, but the railway line is used only occasionally for short tourist trips from Porto Velho.

My taxi driver helped me find a hotel, took my bags in and shook hands before departing. Everyone seemed happy to see you in Bolivia. A nice girl showed me a room that cost fifty bolivianos, sixteen Australian dollars. The hotel entrance was merely a corridor next to the pizza shop in the main square. The corridor led to a narrow garden with two rows of tile-roofed, stucco rooms either side of it. Guayaramerin was hot and there was no breeze, but my room had a good fan and was comfortable. The bathroom, however, was a fine example of DIY electrocution, with exposed wires hanging out from where the hot water switch had been. I presumed from this that there was no chance of a warm shower.

Lunching on terrible tough meat at a table on the footpath in the plaza, I took my Japanese lacquer fan from my bag to try to combat the heat. This fan has had a hard life and was partly broken. The cafe owner, lovely lady, saw this, went into the nether regions of her shop and, returning with a hot glue gun, fixed it. And she did this even after I had interrupted the siesta she had been enjoying on a mat on the floor behind the counter while her assistant minded the empty shop. The plaza was bigger and smarter than Riberteralta's and it was graced with many yellow flowering trees and ungraced by many cruising motorbikes ridden by girls and boys.

Guayaramerin was still celebrating National Day and the holiday parade started at half past six that evening. Unfortunately that meant that it was mostly too dark to see what was happening, but days were too hot for such strenuous celebrations. Groups dressed in the colourful traditional costumes of different Indian tribes danced exuberantly around the square to the music of brass bands. To my surprise I saw that they were still at it at eight the next morning, albeit looking more than a little frazzled and some of them drunk, or high on coca. Even when I left Guayaramerin at eleven there was lots of partying going on.

I ate dinner at another outdoor cafe on the plaza and continued to watch the parade. A man at the next table drank his coffee, poured down a glassful of a vicious-looking green concoction and soon after commenced an animated conversation with the empty chair opposite him. I wish I'd known how to say 'I'll have what he's having'.

In the morning I followed the road that leads from the plaza down to the riverfront and port offices. Atop high, wide stone steps there was a spacious area that housed a small cafe and several moneychangers who were seated at wooden desks. I had an excellent breakfast here for a few bolivianos then, at the port captain's office, made enquiries about a boat to Porto Velho. A sailor in a white uniform took me to the ticket office and showed me how to get to Porto Velho. This operation did not, darn it, entail the use of a boat except the river ferry that crossed from here to Brazil.

I transported myself and bags back to the waterfront with the local taxi system, a three-wheeled motorbike with a seat tacked on the rear. Many ferries, which were really only glorified canoes with a cover on top, lined the bottom of the steps waiting to fill with passengers who wanted to cross the wide river to Brazil. Other canoes constantly criss-crossed the water ferrying freight – including contraband, I was told.

A policeman took me to immigration to get my passport stamped. I'd never have found it alone. I don't think they expect a lot of foreigners. You could cross over and back without papers but if you were continuing on a visa was necessary. On the Brazil side I took a taxi – a car no less – to that country's immigration office and continued on to a hotel. It was strange to go from one side of the river to the other and find that everyone now spoke Portuguese.

So here I was in Brazil, the fifth-largest country in the world. It received its name from the hardwood that was its first export. Although Chris Columbus gets the kudos for inventing South America, he really had made a giant boo boo and thought he was in India. He only set foot on South America on his third voyage, in 1498, when he reached the mouth of the Oronoco in what is now Venezuela. Adventurers, pirates and crooks have followed him, and so have I. Brazil, which has taken immigrants from all over the world, won a bloodless independence from Portugal in 1822.

I'd found a decent room that was quite cheap. It had air-conditioning, hot water and the first shower screen that I had seen in a long time. And just because I had a shower screen and didn't really need it, I had the item I'd longed for – a bath mat. It was a limp dish-rag of a thing but it was for real.

After the boisterous gaiety of Bolivia, the Brazil side was deathly quiet. There was no fiesta here. The streets were deserted and by siesta time – one o'clock – everything was shut. I wondered if the locals had closed the town and run away to hide when they saw me coming. For lunch I tried the only cafe I could find open, a pay-by-the-kilo place. Its sign said 'Lanchonette', which wasn't too hard to work out. You helped yourself and then your plate was weighed – what a great idea. There was a good selection of dishes and a big feed could be had for five Australian dollars.

Later I sat by the riverbank waiting for the cool of evening to arrive. Boy, it was hot, humid and overcast, but it did not rain. I could not find a place to change some money. The bank refused to perform this service but a helpful teller came out from behind her cage to show me where the money-changer hid out.

I ate dinner in a restaurant alleged to be air-conditioned but this luxury had been turned so low it was cooler outside. Still, I had a great fish meal with an enormous selection of side dishes. I realised that I had ordered a two-person meal – that's the way most come in Brazil. A doggy bag was needed.

I found the internet office. The line was out of order but I met Jose Luiz there. A Brazilian who spoke English, he arranged to meet me the next morning and take me for a boat trip. Dead tired, I was asleep by nine o'clock. Next morning a good self-service breakfast was available in a neat dining area of the hotel. Included in the room price it offered crisp rolls, cheese, ham, juice and a pot of coffee, unfortunately heavily pre-sweetened.

I finally found the elusive anaconda the guide in Rurre had told me about. He had said that it was in the zoo in Riberteralta. In Riberteralta they had said it was in Guayaramerin and in

Guayaramerin they said Guajara Mirim. Everywhere I had asked, the zoo was supposedly in the next town. The anaconda was actually in this town, but it was in the museum not a zoo, and it was stuffed. Well and truly. But it *was* bloody big! Seven metres long at least and a tree trunk around, it stretched the length of the main salon. Other museum delights included such delicacies as a one-headed, two-bodied piglet in a glass jar and photographs of an Indian attack on the town in the 1960s. The museum was the wonderful old revamped railway station of Guajara Mirim, outside which stood two beautifully restored steam trains.

At last I discovered, after being given directions many times, that the moneychanger lurked behind an unmarked door in a side street. I knocked and the door was opened a crack by a man who let me in, but stayed to keep guard downstairs while I climbed some seedy stairs. A great place for a mugging, I was thinking, as I approached the hole in a wall through which the money exchange took place. Afterward, the man downstairs unlocked the door and let me out.

To meet John Luiz I did as I was told – sent him a message via the cashier at the ferry ticket office. After I waited three quarters of an hour, he appeared. He hadn't received the message but was just passing. We took off in one of the covered ferries with its driver and chugged up the Mamore River until it met the Beni. A lodge was being built here. It looked an abomination to me. Huge expanses of wooden walkways meant that more local trees had been cut down, but JL was immensely proud of it.

The river water was calm and dark green. Big white water hyacinths grew along its edge and yellow-brown-blue and black butterflies flitted among the dense jungle. Birds abounded – long-necked white egrets, black and white cranes, big black and white birds that were a kind of vulture and eat carrion, large black storks, small beautiful golden birds and tiny, glorious, blue hummingbirds. I heard dolphins blow but

157

saw none. And way out there in the wilderness there was a bar. Made of grey-brown wood, it was a derelict ramshackle riverboat, the good ship *Titanic*. After a while the driver of our boat got out his delicious Bolivian tucker and a Coke, while I was given a packet of imported dry cracker biscuits and a bottle of water. He did offer me some of his food, but he had a revolting habit of blowing his nose overboard with his fingers and the biscuits started to look better.

On the return trip we rounded the junction of the two rivers and, turning into the very wide Mamore which flows all the way from the Andes, the driver whizzed up the speed and put on his lifejacket. Nice captain – never mind about the passengers. Approaching the town I asked about the several riverboats that were apparently abandoned in a compound at the water's edge. JL said that the compound belonged to the drug control department and that the boats that lay there had been impounded for drug smuggling. There was much smuggling across the river from Bolivia as well as up and down it, he said.

JL told me that he had once gone to Coroico by road and had never been more frightened in his life. I was glad to hear that the locals felt that way too and not just us wimpy tourists. He took me to his office and showed me a postcard someone had sent him from Australia. He wanted to know what Uluru was. Then he gave me a letter to a friend in Porto Velho who, he said, would help me find a boat to Manaus.

JL said that the river from here to Porto Velho has twenty waterfalls and that the railway had been supposed to by-pass them. He reckoned that the town, which had been a short while ago a bustling, thriving place, was now on its uppers since recession hit and the road obliterated a lot of the river trade from the south. Walking around I noticed that half the buildings were derelict or empty. On the buildings in use, the evidence of slap-dash work was everywhere. Exposed live electric wires hung waving in the breeze from exterior walls on the street. The only traffic I saw on the road was an occasional bike. There was a queer, ghost-town feeling in the wide deserted streets, the middle of which had no median strips, merely a big tree every now and then with its base painted white to prevent cars climbing up it. Some of these trees bore massive, bright-yellow blooms that flowered on their bare branches and fell to make a golden carpet on the ground. To look up a street and see this dazzle of yellow at each end of it, as well as in the middle, was a beautiful sight.

A magnificent cathedral extended from one main street through to the other. In a style that was strange to me, it had twin white-painted belfries. Another church was painted blue and white and had a pointed tower like those depicted on Dutch Delft china. The cathedral's interior was a stark contrast to those of Bolivia and Peru. There was paint, not gold, behind the altar and simple plaster statues stood around.

The town was deserted at night and I couldn't find a place to eat apart from the fish restaurant where I had dined the night before. A drum band followed me home, banging up the street, and it continued to boom for hours. It sounded like the execution squad marching a prisoner to be shot at dawn against a wall. Some of the walls around town looked like they had been shot at, often. The back streets were lined with derelict dumps of houses and filth and rubbish, but rampant yellow flowers with black centres cascaded everywhere over the mess.

I took my bags to the bus depot in the main street and – on the riverfront where there was a slight breeze – filled in the time to departure drinking the milk from a coconut and eating the fleshy fibre. The bus arrived and what a shock it was – sleek and modern and no baggage on top. It even had seat belts, tinted windows, air-conditioning, beautiful seats that reclined way back, foot rests, leg room and a loo that flushed and had toilet paper. I struggled manfully with the door of this wonder for a good while before I realised that it pushed in not out.

We took off on a good bitumen road that later had metre-wide holes in it but was still okay. We progressed only six kilometres before stopping at a bus station where a crowd of people got on, but the bus was still only half-full. This was not much of a place but it was the forerunner of four more stops that we made in the five-hour trip. The purpose of these stops seemed to be mainly for passengers to gallop off the bus and get food. I bought a hot roll during one stop. It contained a fine sliver of a ham-like substance and was dead boring. At about the fifteen-kilometre mark we were pulled up at a check point – after all, this road *is* called the Trans-Coca Highway. Everyone was made to get out of the bus and our documents and baggage were minutely examined. The customs' men were greatly intrigued by the two stones I had souvenired from the Beni river and highly suspicious of my spray bottles of insect repellent, possibly because there were three of them. It was embarrassing to have all my clutter and paraphernalia spread out on a bench by the roadside for all to see.

The country we traversed looked sad and burned. It had been cleared to graze the large herds of mainly white cows that I saw on it. The occasional pocket of original, beautiful, dense shady forest only emphasised the bleakness of the spoiled land, which was spiked with dead sticks that had been trees. But behind the cleared areas the forest stood tall, as though it was waiting for a chance to march in again. An occasional grand hacienda and many palm trees dotted the cleared areas. The palms were shaped like half-opened umbrellas pointing upwards.

11 Afloat again

Porto Velho is a huge town. A taxi drove me through the soft warm air from the smart bus station to the Hotel Tia Carmen. Scrambling out of the taxi in the dark I stumbled over a live object that set up a great barking. I jumped backwards thinking I was under attack from a fierce guard dog, but started to laugh when I saw that the minuscule object going for my ankles was a tiny black Chihuahua. An old lady sitting on a stool outside the entrance called it off and saved my life.

The room I found was a dump but, although it smelled musty, it was clean. And for once the sheets stayed on the bed – even though the bed base was flattened cardboard cartons. The air-conditioner had its face off – a face lift extraordinaire – and made a shocking row. The bathroom was an afterthought that had been bunged in a corner of the room and was separated from it only by a curtain on one side. But this room had another of the attractive wooden ceilings, a pot of artificial flowers on a natty mat on a table and a TV that was showing a dubbed Australian film featuring none other than ex-footballer Jacko speaking Portuguese – a vast improvement on his English.

The agreeable hotel owner and her darkly beautiful daughter served a good breakfast outside on the sidewalk, where I luxuriated in the lovely morning. But I was given the terrible pre-sweetened coffee again and when I asked for it plain I received another just the same. I tried again and this time I got coffee with milk. Giving up, I fetched my own from my room.

Walking a long way to the river's edge to investigate the boat situation, I found there a pleasant area in which drinks were sold from huts with thatched roofs alongside the place where two smart riverboats were moored. This was not the commercial boat dock, though – I had to walk further to reach that. I bought a coconut to fortify myself and, among much rubbish and litter, hiked along the train track, passing a railway museum where many old steam engines sat rusting in open sheds. One restored steam train does run from here, but unfortunately not on this day. I noticed thankfully that there did not seem to be many dogs in this town. Apart from the hotel Chihuahua that I had almost exterminated, I saw only a couple.

I didn't need to look far for a boat. As soon as I appeared on the scene I was grabbed and hijacked by waiting riverside pirates. Taken to view a boat, I negotiated a price for a cabin at very reasonable rates. The cabin was coffin-sized but it was clean and it had an oscillating fan attached to one wall. The boat was loading cargo, which was either fired down a wooden chute or carried down very steep, narrow and slippery steps cut in the earth of the bank. I was apprehensive that I might fall as I picked my way down, and stepped gingerly with my parasol aloft. Don't laugh – my umbrella saved me from a box of bananas that fell off a truck and hit my brolly instead of my head.

It was hot as blazes on top of the riverbank and the workers were all barefoot and shirtless. I gravitated to a nearby stall, a narrow table covered overhead by a tattered blue tarpaulin, that sold drinks and snacks cooked on a brazier made from an old wheel-rim on a makeshift stand. I sat on the long wooden bench and ordered an orange juice. Six oranges were put through the juicer with ice and the results poured into two plastic bags with straws. Not being thirsty enough for two I gave one bag to the enterprising gent who was procuring my ticket. An old man sat on the other end of the bench munching a bowl of rice. I got up and tipped him off.

I transported my bags to the boat then walked back up to the main street for supplies. Porto Velho was the biggest town I had been in since Lima and it had many shops. Prices seemed about the same as in Australia but food in cafes was cheap. I ate lunch at a kilo place and, once I'd managed to put my card in the right way, extracted some money from a machine in the Bank of Brazil. When I put my hand in the slot to check that I had taken all the money, the machine grabbed my hand with its teeth. I shrieked and all the people standing nearby laughed.

By the time I returned to the boat rain was falling, and the steps down the bank were becoming increasingly slippery. I stood pondering the descent and wondering at the amount of rubbish that had been thrown down the riverbank and into the river. It took a while to muster the courage to tackle those steps, but eventually I made it down. Then the rain became heavier and four or five people slipped and fell. Shrieking and sliding, covered in mud, they provided great entertainment. I also watched as three large engines were manoeuvred down the mud steps to the boat next door. One escaped and slid away a distance before being recaptured. But the rain was a welcome relief as the weather then became refreshingly cool.

Departure time of six came and went; at eight o'clock cases of tomatoes were still being loaded down the chute. The boat already seemed to be full of tomatoes and bananas when a truck piled high with huge hands of green bananas arrived. Labourers took these on their shoulders four hands at a time and ran surefooted down the steps of the bank with them. These bananas were stacked on pallets on the lower deck – and very neatly too, considering that they were thrown in with a whump.

Half past eight was dinner time. Two huge aluminium cauldrons were boiling a nasty mess that looked like baby sick – and had been since six o'clock when I had first ventured down to the galley investigating the possibility of food. The cook was a cheerful young man but his off-sider was a cranky woman, the only person I encountered in South America who was not friendly and smiling. For all her ferociousness she was exceedingly tiny, like the hotel Chihuahua. She was youngish, with nut-brown curly hair, and she would have been pretty except that her mouth was set in a thin, lipless, turned-down line. For the entire trip she wore shorts and singlet and stomped about with her teeny feet in thongs. She snarled at me but finally let us at the food.

Passengers served themselves from communal plastic bowls that the snarly one dumped onto the long communal wooden table as though she was throwing the pigs their swill. The stuff of unappetising appearance that the cauldrons produced was a thickened soup containing a conglomeration of potato, carrots and beans. On closer inspection, it looked like poster glue. Splashing some into my glass plate with the army-sized aluminium serving ladle, I heavily disguised it with chilli and made it edible, but the cuisine of the QE2 it surely wasn't. The dining area consisted of the wooden table at which we sat on chairs perched near the clearance to the loos and showers that were behind on both sides. A sign warned that they were not to be used while a meal was in progress. It was mostly ignored.

The engines started at around nine, long ropes front and back were cast off, and we backed away from the bank. After starting the engines the captain, whose bare hairy chest was festooned with numerous gold medals and crucifixes, crossed himself on the breast and lips and kissed all the medals. Good grief! had he so little faith in his vessel? We chugged a couple of hundred metres, then turned back again. Cripes, I thought, he's forgotten something, probably forgot to kiss a medal. But it turned out that a yoo-hoo to the port authorities on the bank was necessary.

We finally began sailing upriver at ten. I watched the town lights disappear and then went for a shower. This was good timing as Snarling Dragon Woman had just finished sluicing them out with Omo and a bottle of bleach that she had spread liberally about.

Either side of the ablution areas stood caterpillar-green porcelain basins topped by containers of hand-wash lotion. These basins were scrubbed twice daily by a sailor, but the water that flowed into them was the same mud-brown colour as the river. Alongside the basins were coolers of clear, cold, drinking water. The shower was basic no-frills and the water was straight from the river, but the cubicle was big and clean and had hooks for your clothes. It even had a window, which fortunately opened onto the river not the deck. The toilets got smelly between cleaning because, although they had flushes, people didn't seem to use them often. The loos were very popular and constantly in demand and you had to guard the door once in situ, as the latches didn't work.

My tiny cabin was brown polished wood all around and situated at the prow of the boat, directly behind the wheel house. It was very dark inside with the door shut – the window was a small triangle that was covered with a plastic film that was a repellent shade of blue. Two narrow bunks, one on top of the other, filled the cabin from end to end, leaving a narrow space at the side. Apart from the wall fan, the room's only other accoutrement was an ornate brass light switch. This, however, didn't work and I had to hot-wire it. There was a power point, but the current was 110 volts – it took a long time to boil a cup of water for coffee with my 240-volt infusor. The bunks had a paper-thin mattress, one clean sheet and a pillow case. The lower bunk collapsed when the drawer underneath it was pulled out and remained with a definite list to one side.

Not long after we started off the engines slowed and there was a sickening crunch, then another and another, as we hit the river bottom. Looking out I saw a crew member hanging over the prow doing depth soundings with a big heavy piece of iron on a string. I recognised this as the implement that I had previously used to hammer some nails in my wall for a towel rack. Well, they shouldn't have left it so conveniently by my door.

Eventually we got off the sand bar and were on our way again. At four I got up to answer the call of nature and, opening my cabin door, was almost blown away by a cold, howling gale. I wrapped my all-purpose blanket/poncho around me and, clutching it tightly, made it down the deck and back. All the lights were on in the hammock area and people were moving about. It must have been very cold out there on the open deck. A fat man sat writing at the dining table – I guess it would have been difficult to fit him in a hammock.

There was a pounding on my door at seven in the morning and breakfast was announced. Not worth getting out of bed for, it consisted of dry biscuits, butter and the revolting sweet coffee. Rejecting this, I secured some boiled water from the cook, made my own and went back to bed.

The boat was made almost entirely of white-painted wood. Four wooden railings encompassed its decks and the cabin and wash-house doors were decorated with fancy carving. It was not very old and in much better condition than some I saw. The lowest deck contained the hatch for the hold and, looking down into it, I could see that it was filled with cargo. At the far end of this deck was the tiny galley where the cook presided over his two monstrous aluminium cooking pots on a black, iron stove. Cargo, mostly bananas, was stacked so high on this deck that you had to squeeze between it. At the front of the second deck were the wheel house and six cabins. The only instruments the wheelhouse contained were a speedometer the same as a car's and a large, silver-plated clock placed crookedly, and someone obviously thought artistically, in a wooden anchor on the wall. The captain – who apart from his medals, wore shorts and an open army camouflage jacket – had several assistants in the steering department. The only other crew were the cook, one sailor, and the Dragon Woman stewardess/cleaner.

Down the middle of the second deck about sixty hammocks swung from hooks in the wooden roof, crammed in so closely that they touched each other. The hammock-travellers' goods and baggage were piled under, in front and alongside them. To get past you had to duck underneath the hammocks and sidle past the bags, tricycles, bikes, pushers, kids and even a dog kennel. At the end of this deck were the showers, toilets, the dining area and a tiny servery. At the very rear, behind the dining area, two windows opened onto the river above a trap door in the floor which, when lifted, disclosed the galley below. Through this ingenious device the bowls of food that were held up by the cook were received by the Dragon Woman, who knelt on the floor. The top deck sported a satellite dish, for the soccer of course, and a massive stereo that blasted out non-stop, ear-splitting music. At the very front of the top deck were two more cabins, behind which was a bar and a small shop that sold large quantities of bikkies and beer. Then followed an open space with a few plastic tables and chairs and wooden benches attached to the sides of the boat. And at the very rear were an outdoor shower, a slide for the kids – not down into the river, unfortunately – and the water-storage tanks that contained brown river water.

Rain was still spitting down when I got up. It stopped by mid morning but the sky remained overcast. The river was not wide here and I could look out on the banks that were both covered in thick green jungle and rainforest. Now and then I saw, half-hidden among the jungle growth, a native house with a thatched roof.

We were now in Amazonia, the world's densest and greatest tropical rainforest. This three hundred and fifty million-hectare basin that encompasses West Brazil, East Peru, Ecuador, South Colombia and North Bolivia has been called 'a vast unspoiled tribute to the abundance of the Amazon River'. It is mostly a trackless jungle of fast-disappearing primary rainforest, where river steamers still sink or get lost on dead ends of the great rivers. Its natural resources are a vital reservoir for plants, animals and peoples that are found no where else on earth. The Spanish tried to conquer it, believing that it hid El Dorado, but their explorers ended up dead, insane or captured by Indians. Deep and mysterious, Amazonia is both a scarcely inhabited Eden and a green Hell, a frightening place of isolation and lawlessness that has long been a magnet for adventurers and dreamers.

The word Amazon, evocative of mystery, means 'breast-less' and was the name given to the fictional female warriors of Greek legend who cut off their right breasts to help them in shooting bows or throwing spears. In 1541 a Spanish expedition entered the jungle. At one stage it was attacked by a tribe whose women fought with the men, and they were told by other Indians that there was a tribe of women warriors nearby, hence the name Amazonia was given to this region.

The boat stopped, then spent an hour outmanoeuvring a sandbar and some shallows. We had left Porto Velho accompanied by a dinghy with an outboard motor and now I learned its main purpose. The dinghy went ahead to lead the way over the shallows. A few more grinds and bumps and swinging around with the engine off and eventually we were over the sandbar. At midday we came to a town where wide concrete steps led up to a miserable collection of stone and adobe buildings and an imposing pink church that looked down-river. Ten or more people with baggage – including an air-conditioner – came aboard. We departed with the usual three long blasts of the boat's horn.

Lunch was great considering the cooking facilities. You had to wait for a seat at meals. Children were fed first, then the adults lined up for several sittings of sixteen to the table. There seemed to be a shortage of utensils and plates and each sitting had to wait while they were washed by the grumpy Dragon Woman. This meal was meat, beans, spaghetti, rice and salad, which I mixed together and loaded with chilli. It was difficult to linger at the table when other hungry passengers stood hopefully behind your chair willing you to finish.

Small children pounded constantly about the decks. There were a great many in this predominantly Catholic country. Two handsome, devilish little boys in the cabin next to mine played hide-and-seek and peek-a-boo with me around the cabin door. Mum looked very young. Another very young mother did embroidery sitting up in her hammock with a baby at her breast.

Late afternoon saw us again slowed down by shallow water. A very smart, blue-and-white pilot boat, its bridge topped with a satellite dish, came out from a town and guided us through. We passed two barges, each one pushed by a tug. They carried semi-trailers, one of which had refrigeration units on it, and a couple of other barges passed bearing tarpaulin-covered cargoes. We pulled to the riverbank where there was not much to see except the usual high, steep steps of mud and here we took on another big load of bananas. At the water's edge wallowed a large old semi-sunk wooden outrigger canoe with a thatched roofed cabin. It had been there so long it had plants growing out of its wood.

Dinner was good – spaghetti, salad and fried chicken. The motor boat was launched at about ten and I was aware of the boat feeling its way through more shallows. A terrific grinding crunch woke me at two. The boat had pulled into the bank. I had no idea why – was the captain asleep and had we run aground? Apparently there was no harm done, as we soon continued on and at first light we came up to Manicore, almost halfway to Manaus, and a sizeable town. Passengers got on and off here and I pinched some bananas for breakfast – it wasn't difficult and there sure were plenty.

At Manicore a big, red-and-white church with twin towers overlooked the river and there were dolphins in the water as there had been at most places. The weather was warm when we were in port, though the sky was still grey. Out on the river it was cool again. The banks looked much the same and so did the river – it was still a dirty brown.

Later that day I noticed that some of the banks and surrounding country had been cleared, but this didn't last for long. A huge barge with a massive pile of logs passed and another followed with more semi-trailers and containers.

The weather became warmer, even out on the river, and there was a pleasant breeze, but I didn't see a patch of blue sky until after four o'clock that day when we left Novo Arequipa. This was a well-kept town with a neat landing of stone steps with blue-and-white railings and a row of blue-and-white buildings on top of the riverbank. Many river boats were tied up here and kids and dolphins were swimming in the water that was now greyish-green and looked much cleaner.

About this time I created havoc in the toilet. I pulled the cord for the flush and the whole damn kit and caboodle fell down off the wall on top of me. The pipe broke and water shot everywhere. Dragon Woman was not amused – she knew I was a trouble-maker.

During the evening the boat slowed and the dinghy, loaded with boxes, roared to the shore to make a delivery at an isolated hacienda. The boat sped off and the dinghy caught us later. Finally the weather was brighter, and there was a beautiful sunset of gold and amethyst painted on the dark retreating clouds. On the other side of the river a full moon, bright white like a hundred-watt globe, rose in the fading blue sky. Later the moon re-appeared from behind the black clouds that had covered it and painted their edges silver.

The Brazilian flag fluttered in the breeze from the rear of the boat and the moonlight lay on the ripples of the water, turning them into silver fish scales. The dinghy, bobbing on its rope, chased along behind us on the foaming wake. Markers winked at us from the bank, red on the port side, green on the starboard. Children played on the slide and rode tricycles round the deck, while thirty or so adults were glued to the soccer on the TV.

On the morning of the third day, the river was boot-polish brown and very wide as we came to the point where the Mamore River meets the Amazon. Then we turned around and went up the Amazon towards Manaus, the heart of the province of Amazonia. At last I was on the legendary, 6700-kilometre long Amazon, the most famous of the three huge river systems that make up this area. The Amazon was first sighted in 1541 by Francisco de Orellana, a Spanish conquistador. He called it the 'Rio Mar', River Sea. It has seventeen tributaries, each over fifteen hundred kilometres long, plus eighty thousand kilometres of navigable trunk rivers that ocean-going ships can travel as far as Iquitos in Colombia, 4300 kilometres further upstream from Manaus. One-third of the world's oxygen is produced by the vegetation of this area, which is also rich in gold, diamonds, lumber, rubber, oil and jute.

Now the river banks were low, flat and very green. Buffalo, brahmins and cows of mixed ancestry – a motley lot – grazed on the sodden land. We passed a couple of wooden houses on stilts, then the banks became higher and covered with even lusher jungle. We drifted by a stone house that appeared deserted, then a similarly lonely church; it was blotched with mould and had jungle encroaching on it. More wooden houses, each with a canoe or two tied up at their banks, came into view. One canoe held a fisherman who was hauling in a good catch of silver fish that shone in the glistening net. Stone steps ascended from a two-storeyed wooden boathouse and jetty at the river's edge to the top of a neat green bank, where a village of white, wooden houses and a church nestled.

Then the middle of the Amazon river was strewn for many kilometres with islands covered by almost drowned trees. Now that the boat had swung around, the current was bucking us and we pitched and rolled as we battled upstream. Waking from my siesta, I found the river again wide and open ahead and the banks no longer close together. But we rode close in to one bank and I could see that the foliage was impenetrable and brooding. The Amazon had an air of watchfulness, a tense stillness. The trees were mahogany, cedar, palo sangres – so heavy it won't float and with blood red wood, huacapus – so hard that nails won't penetrate it, giant sumaumas, tall lupanas, called the river lighthouse because boats use them as landmarks, rubber trees and chonta palms, whose long hardwood shafts are good for bows and arrows. There were also bromeliads, vines, mosses and mushrooms.

Now instead of an occasional house and a few cows, I could see buffalo dotted on the land and in the water. Steep, beige-yellow cliffs came down to the river's edge, broken now and then by a little sandy beach with palms, and occasionally there appeared wooden houses on stilts with glassless windows, some of them right on the beach.

We arrived in Manaus just as it was getting dark. Following a brilliant sunset, the milk-white full moon had sat for a while in a lone patch of icy green-blue sky before the night enveloped it. The water rushed at us, demonstrating the strong pull of the current. Passing many lights on the bank, a big refinery and many ships, some ocean-going, the captain negotiated through a tight space and squeezed his boat between two other riverboats. He nosed the prow up to the dock and the passengers had to alight up and over it, no mean feat while clutching your baggage.

I took a taxi through the seedy-looking area around the docks to the hotel I had selected. Near the wharf I saw a hotel displaying a big sign that said, 'One hour, Five Reals. Two hours, Ten.' Happily, my hotel was in a more salubrious area, near the centre and the main streets. It was not a nice hotel, though. A lady who was more interested in the soaps on the TV sent me to my room with her young assistant. I was led out the back, down stairs, up stairs, along corridors and outside again. The place looked like a bomb site. It was actually a construction site. The hotel was being extended at the rear and I had the very end room. I could live with the bomb site but it was a grubby room and the only window opened onto the walkway outside and had no flyscreen on it. There was no furniture apart from two beds, a rowdy air-conditioner and a metal rack, of no use whatsoever, that was completely covered in grit. So was the floor. The builders were still welding and hammering at half past nine at night. The bathroom was filthy, there were old pieces of soap on the floor of the shower and the bin was full.

As I went out to eat, I told the television fan at the front desk that the room was dirty. This had no effect. No one came to clean the room, so I did what I could myself with toilet paper. The good free breakfast in the morning atoned somewhat for the proprietors' sins of omission, but immediately after eating I moved two doors down to the Paradise, which it wasn't, but it was better and cleaner than my previous digs, even though there was still no hot water. This was not too hard to bear as Manaus was very hot, around forty degrees Celsius at this time of the year.

The Paradise's desk was presided over by a cheerful little man who was round all over, even to his smiling round eyes. My room had three beds and a chest – this was getting better – and a window that opened all the way along the room. There were still no screens, but at least the window had bars. I eventually worked out that the sign above it said, 'Don't throw your rubbish out of the window.' Nice sort of people they expected here. The evidence proved that guests heeded this sign – they threw the rubbish under the chest. There was a waste bin in the bathroom but I presumed it was only for toilet paper. The sewers were obviously still unable to cope with it.

I went out to see Manaus town, the splendours of which I had read so much about. Here, isolated in the densest part of the jungle, the wealth from the rubber boom had provided a customs building and lighthouse that had been imported piece by piece from England, stately mansions, the first street-cars in Latin America, and docks built on hollow iron tanks eight metres in diameter that float up and down with the flood. A scale built into the escarpment of the harbour shows variations of fifteen metres in level between wet and dry seasons. Then there is the famous opera house, the gem that I most wanted to see.

Manaus, the capital of Brazil's Amazonia, was a rubber-boom town that became unboomed due to a shifty piece of work by a sly fellow who, early in the twentieth century, smuggled some rubber seeds out to Malayan growers who were soon competing with Brazil.

Walking down the street from the hotel I came to the commercial centre and main shopping area, where lots of tourist rubbish was on offer. Further on, backing onto the wharf where dozens of riverboats bobbed on the water in a row and near where I had alighted the night before, was the marvellous market. This was more to my taste. In a fabulous nineteenth-century building of cast iron I found seeds, spices and exotic food. I needed fluids by then, so I tried the local drink, guarana, which seemed to perk me up. I wondered what was in it – probably something highly illegal.

I made it back to the hotel at four, having walked my feet off. Near my hotel I had passed a new building with a sign that quoted, I thought, a ridiculously low price to stay in such an illustrious-looking establishment, so on my evening foray out for food I wandered in its door for a look. It was a very posh building with little balconies protruding from the face and sides of its eight storeys. A charming young Brazilian man struggled with my limited Portuguese and took me to see a room, assuring me, I think, that it was twenty real – about twenty Australian dollars – a day for as many people as I chose to pack into it. I still wasn't terribly sure this was correct but I booked a room for the next day.

I walked a long way that evening looking for a place to eat. Once again it seemed to be usual only to eat out for lunch. The outdoor cafes were all drinking or hamburger places.

The next morning was Sunday and a huge street market was in progress in the main street. I strolled down through the hundreds of stalls to the port and the wharves, which were piled sky-high with containers. Accosted by a tour tout at the port I negotiated a four-hour trip to the Meeting of the Waters, the place where the Rio Negro, whose billions of decaying leaves turn it into black tea, meets the milk coffee of the Amazon.

The Meeting of the Waters was just as advertised, yellow on one side and black on the other, with no mixture of the two. It took an hour to get there on the *Claudia*, a canoe with an awning and an outboard. We passed much shipping on the way, including big tankers, container ships and small ferries. After the Meeting of the Waters, the *Claudia* took me on to an island national park where I cuddled an anaconda – and I have a photo to prove it. But the anaconda owner wouldn't let me hold its head. I also came across a three-toed sloth whose baby clutched Mama endearingly. I even cuddled an alligator with a taped-mouth – the alligator's not mine – and saw some wonderful bright macaws and more sloths. True to name, they hung about in attitudes of complete idleness, even munching their leaves slowly. Among all this lot toddled a fat, naked Indian baby chortling over his plastic rattle.

The boat detoured into a small tributary that was completely covered by a green umbrella of giant trees and vines. I glided in the *Claudia* along waterways that flowed through flooded trees in a cool green light, while over us floated the scent from the flowers of a tree whose yellow blossoms hung in bunches like wisteria and smelt like a subtle mixture of jasmine and honeysuckle. Yellow and black birds flitted among the white flowers of the water hyacinth.

Viewed from the river by daylight Manaus was huge and ugly. Wooden shanties and industrial horrors spread along the waterside for kilometres. The boat pulled up for petrol at a gas station floating on a steel platform. Nearby eight tugs were tied to another dock that was made from several anchored steel barges. Walking back to town I felt the floating dock moving under my feet as the traffic passed along it. Manaus was dead this Sunday afternoon. Nothing was open except one cafe, where I had a pizza for lunch.

12 Amazons and anacondas

Next morning my hotel provided breakfast on a teeny table in a room off the foyer. There were great crispy rolls but the coffee was that frightful heavily sugared muck. I said I couldn't drink it, so the cheerful desk person obligingly brought me a cup from the competition two doors away, the hotel I'd left in a huff the day before.

Moving camp again, I walked to the new hotel with only one bag in case I'd got it wrong and they were selling the apartments, or something had been lost in my translation of their sign. This time the manager, who spoke English, was there. He told me that because the hotel was still being finished they were offering cheap accommodation to cover a few expenses. There was no TV or phone. This suited me. I couldn't understand the TV and I had no one to phone locally. The hotel was so new it didn't even have a name. The next day I decided that it had been named. Something new had been painted on the front wall. But this turned out to be a sign saying that some rooms also came complete with a kitchen.

It was great to stay in a room that no one else had used. The doors hadn't had a second coat of paint yet and the electric plugs were not finished, but I had a good air-conditioner, a new bed and new sheets, towels and mattress. A glass door on one side led to a dear little balcony and big windows made the room light and bright, unlike some of the dungeons I'd been incarcerated in lately – and this room was even cheaper than they were. But although it was a big room with plenty of space, the skimpy bathroom was silly – it had no shower alcove or curtain and water splashed over everything, especially the loo, whose seat was always wet. High up in one wall there was an oblong window and, to my delight, I saw framed in it the gloriously pretty dome of the opera house, the spire of the ancient church next to it and the flashing red light on the radio tower. And through the other open windows I could hear the church clock striking.

The hotel was in President Varga Street. President Varga was a strongman who took over Brazil by a military coup in 1930. He was deposed in 1945 but got legally elected in 1951. After a long series of fights with the military, who opposed him, he shot himself and became a national hero.

The following day I thought it would be easy to take a bus back to my hotel from the market. I had seen them whizzing up the road past it and, thinking why not, jumped on one labelled Centro. I did not realise that these buses didn't stop unless you rang the bell. I couldn't see a bell anyway. It was way up on the ceiling. The bus rocketed past my stop and, by the time I knew it, I was kilometres away.

Ah well, I thought, it's a central bus. It will go around the block and come back to this spot again. I sat there waiting for this to happen. I went all over the town, and out into the country. For seventy cents I had a sixty-dollar tour of Manaus. But I doubt that a tour would have provided the excitement of a local bus-driver's antics. These certifiable lunatics scream around corners and roar up tiny lanes, bumping, swaying and flinging passengers off their seats.

Finally, after an interminable time, the bus came to a screeching halt at the terminus, where I laughingly told the conductor and driver that I was lost. Producing my map, I showed them where I wanted to go and they said the bus would return there in ten minutes. Bloody mad tourist, they were thinking, no doubt. I hate to disappoint people so I usually oblige with a superlative mad-tourist performance.

When I climbed back on the bus I tried to pay again, but they would have none of that. In the end I rode this beastly bus for an hour and a half. They could have charged me rent.

In town again at last, the driver stopped the bus and, while the other passengers patiently waited, read my map and indicated that I should get off here and walk through to the next street. By this time my bladder was up to my eyebrows and I was heat stressed. I reached my room and collapsed on the bed.

In the evening I actually found a restaurant that my guide book had featured. A ruddy miracle – I didn't usually find anything that the authors had written about. They would write that something was 'near' something else and leave you wondering where the something else was, or that it was 'close to' a square that was a hundred kilometres around. I was disgusted with them and vowed to sue them when I got back. What was truly infuriating was that they would give you the name of the best restaurant in the whole region and then make no mention of its whereabouts. What am I – psychic? They expected me, a new arrival in town, to find a place without directions. Sometimes they would say it was 'around the corner' from some other place. I would go far from this other place, getting madder and madder. Why not say it's in a certain street? I'd be better off without these suggestions, thank you. Boo, hiss, guide book.

But I did find this fantastic restaurant that served wonderful meat. Although the meal was a set price for as much as you could eat, you didn't help yourself – waiters ran around with the meat on hot trays, or trolleys, or skewered on hot pokers, and they chopped off bits for you. I counted fifteen staff. There was every kind and cut of meat imaginable – roast, barbecued, fried or grilled steak, beef, lamb, liver, kidneys, chicken. As well as this, ten dishes of rice and other goodies were put on your table and all kinds of salads were offered to you on trays. A nice waiter, who tried to teach me some Portuguese, was assigned to me. Just when I was getting used to the peculiarities of Spanish, now I had Portuguese to contend with. They don't say 'h' but 'r' so Rio is Hio and 'd' is pronounced 'j'.

In the shopping area near the river I found some incredible bargains, but walking about in the sweltering humidity was debilitating. Trying to return to the hotel by taking a short cut, yet again I got utterly lost. I ended up far from the city centre in a shanty town down by the river where there were no footpaths, just dirt and grass among shacks made from planks of wood sticking out of the mud on sticks. I thought they appeared to be about to fall down. Deciding that I didn't like the look of this place, I hot-footed it out and walked more kilometres round in circles until I was back where I had started. This exertion was not advisable in the middle of a baking day and I returned to my hotel in a state of yuk. But a cold shower and the air-conditioner soon restored me.

The next day I took a short cut again and actually passed one place for the third time before I realised that I was going around in circles like you do when lost in the bush. The locals must have been wondering about me. Goodness, there she goes again, that woman with the pink umbrella – and again, and again. I'll have to change my umbrella and get a disguise. Then I thought it seemed a good idea to take the bus back from the market now that I knew how to ring the bell. All went well until we came to the first major corner. Instead of going straight up the road to my hotel, the bus driver whizzed around the corner and zoomed off in the opposite direction. I said to the young conductress, 'Will it come round again?' 'Oh yes,' she said. Okay, I'd take a ride. I sure did. The bus did come around again – about an hour later.

A girl student sat next to me and she and the conductress tried to talk to me. They asked if I was an Americana. I said, 'No. Australiana.' They found this entertaining and seemed to think it was a great deal more interesting.

On my protracted ride, I had plenty of time to ponder why

I like short cuts and why I persist in trying to use buses. I think it's because I get such a kick out of it when I do get one right. Or is it because when you have enough time on your hands, getting lost really doesn't matter? You meet a lot of people and see different places.

But this day's odyssey went on a little too long. I went round and round the town and outskirts even further than I had before. I went out into the country where there were goats and shacks on hillsides. I went everywhere. And just when I thought I was never going to get off this bus, it pulled into its terminal, a shanty out in the boonies.

The young conductress spoke to an inspector-type man who looked grim. I grasped enough of the conversation to understand what she told him: 'No, no, no. Not American. Australian.' I don't think he liked Americans. He wasn't all that keen on me either. He probably thought I was stupid, whatever I was. But this was fair enough – sometimes I am.

The pair of them shooed me off the bus and said, 'Wait five minutes.' The girl then took me by the arm and put me on another bus, handing me over like a parcel to an older lady conductress. Brazilian buses have a little turnstile at the rear end where you get on and when you have paid you are permitted to pass through it to a seat. You get off at the front. When I tried to pay and go through the turnstile the conductress wouldn't let me. She signalled for me to sit behind the turnstile where there were a couple of seats. The driver possessed the obligatory lead foot and back there I had nothing to hold on to. He shot around the first corner on two wheels and my umbrella went flying – and I nearly did too. Then he screeched to a halt in a cloud of dust and the conductress indicated that I should get off. Standing in the middle of a dirt road in the back of nowhere I thought, Charming, now I have been abandoned here for the vultures. Then I realised that the driver was tooting and waving at me to get back on the bus through the front door. I did so and then the penny dropped. They had done this so that I wouldn't have to pay and they hadn't wanted the inspector to witness it. It was very sweet of them. I sat on this next bus for what seemed forever, but it eventually returned to the main street and dropped me right outside my hotel. Fantastic. Four hours for a quick visit to the shops.

That night at a nearby cafe I had a delicious whole baked fish in scrumptious sauce and on the way back to the hotel I walked past the icecream parlour. Well, not quite all the way past. I had to go inside to inspect it. What a pig's paradise. You buy icecream by weight, including trimmings. You choose a glass bowl, a dish made from edible stuff, a cone or a plastic cup and shovel into it as much of any of the dozens of flavoured icecream as you like – and then you add hundreds and thousands, chocolate sprinkles, flavoured topping, cream, wafer biscuits and jubes. Wonderful. I had a colossal pile of this stuff and it cost just two dollars. I deserved to be sick the next day.

That night I noticed that the dome of the opera house was unlit and the next day, when I finally visited it, I was told that the lights were only on when there was a performance. They would be on tonight as an orchestra was performing there. The opera house, Teatro Amazonas, is stupendous. I hadn't realised until I stood gaping before it just how huge it was. Set high up off the street and approached by wide sweeping steps, it was completely surrounded by an imposing stone wall. Nothing like I had imagined it would be, it was still fabulous. The building was Greco-Roman in style, coloured dusky-pink and white, and crowned by a large dome that was entirely covered in a bright, many-hued mosaic.

If the exterior of the building was marvellous, its interior almost defied description. But I was not let loose in all this splendour alone. I had to be chaperoned by a young lady guide. White Carrara marble plinths and great beige-coloured Corinthian columns reached all the way to the ceiling. And that was just the entry hall, where I counted the lights in the three colossal metal chandeliers – forty in each and every one covered by a little glass shade. I entered the theatre by a flight of red-carpeted stairs and found seven hundred red-velvet upholstered chairs that flowed down a gradual slope to the stage and four tiers of ornate boxes with red-velvet and gilded metal fronts. The boxes got plusher the higher they went until the governor's box, the last gasp in plush, was reached. This exquisite theatre, completed in 1910, was built for the private use of the one hundred local rubber barons – or did she say robber barons? – and their friends. This little lot, as you can imagine, were unbelievably wealthy. They imported mega stars like Jenny Lind to sing and the Ballet Russe to dance.

The entire ceiling was painted to appear as though you were standing under the four legs of the Eiffel Tower and each of the four segments was painted to represent a different form of art – ballet, music, drama and opera. All around the side walls there were lights in glass shades and immense paintings that had been created in Italy by a famous painter, who later came to Manaus to hang them. Everything except the wood for the beautiful floors, which were made from highly polished boards of brazil wood and jacaranda, had been brought from Europe.

From the level of the top box it was just a short walk across to the ballroom, which was also absolutely fabulous. It had an upstairs orchestral gallery with a front that was decorated in the same way as the boxes in the theatre and Carrara marble featured around the walls and doorways. The lights were Venetian Murano glass, mammoth great specimens two-and-half metres across with masses of bulbs and shades in several colours. The ceiling paintings had also been executed in Italy and shipped out later. In the centre was an angel who, as you walked across the room, actually appeared to follow you. Weird. By the time you had reached the other end of the room she had turned around and was facing you. I don't know how it was done but she actually moved. On one side of the painting a nude reclined with one arm outstretched and, as you crossed the room, she lifted herself onto her elbow. Amazing. These paintings were vividly colourful affairs but I wouldn't want to live with them. I have enough trouble with the cat following me about.

From the outside balcony you could look down on the town, but I was disappointed that I couldn't go up into the dome. When I said I would have liked to look at what appeared to be its stained glass, I was told that it was not glass, but tiles, which completely cover the dome's exterior. Although it was strikingly colourful and attractive I wondered, Why the dome? It looked strange sticking out of this classical building. It belonged on a mosque. But the dome certainly was a landmark – not only could I see it from my room, but it loomed large from many vantage points in the city.

Afterward my guide told me that I could stay and listen to the Amazonian 'sympathy' orchestra, who were practising for their concert. What good luck. I placed myself in the plushest box and revelled in the wonderful opportunity I was given to absorb the ambience of this enchanting building, said to be one of the best opera houses in the world.

I strolled downtown and bought a bath mat, fed up with not having one any longer. Then I went on to the post office. (No short cuts. No buses. I'd learned.) But the post office, which lurked in a dowdy modern building – I had been expecting something elegant, old and classical – shut at five. Surprisingly there was no siesta here. It was so hot during the day that shopping would have been much more agreeable at night. There were all manner of amazing goods to buy. Ever felt the need for a stuffed piranha? The number of staff employed by shops staggered me. I wondered if it was just to give more people work that three employees did one job.

The intricate method of paying was amusing. When you bought something you were served by one person who gave you a piece of paper, but smacked your hand when you made the normal grab for the goods. No such unseemly haste here! This piece of paper merely stated the price of the goods. You had to take this to the cashier and no matter how small the shop was, they would have a cashier, usually encased in glass. You paid the cashier, were rewarded with a receipt and then you proceeded with the goods to yet another person who wrapped them for you. You should not be in a hurry when shopping in Brazil. Even in a small juice bar or buying buns from a baker, the ritual was the same. At restaurants you paid the cashier, then another person seated at a table by the exit collected your receipt as you left. For what reason? Even outside shops that had only a few feet of frontage six assistants might be stationed whose job it was to lure customers in. At the supermarket in the main street I counted eighteen assistants manning the checkouts, as well as a staff member who was posted at the entrance to them and whose mission was to direct customers to the next vacant counter. This supermarket was massive but unfortunately it was not air-conditioned, and it was always packed solid with crowds of people. You stood sweating for ages in long queues just to pay or to get your veggies weighed.

When I finally managed to broach the doors of the post office I found that downstairs, where no one but a platoon of security staff hung out, it was beautifully air-conditioned. But air-conditioning doesn't climb steps and I nearly died of heat exhaustion upstairs where all the business was done. Ten tellers fenced in wire cages were stationed in a row behind a long, polished wooden counter, while in front of them stamp seekers stood dripping sweat in a line a kilometre long.

The cathedral was more interesting than the post office but it was very grotty outside. The grounds were strewn with rubbish and people slept on the steps, or reclined in the shade of its walls. It was not an attractive building but it sure was huge. I probed all the way around it seeking a way in and eventually found a big rusty gate that squealed ominously as I wrestled it open. Inside the cathedral I was alone, except for a couple of young women who were restoring part of the murals. Then it was afternoon, so I did what all sensible people in South America do. I had a lie down.

Early mornings in Manaus were cool, and redolent with the damp scent of the tropics. The woman in the high-rise apartment building across the way hung her washing out on her verandah. I hung mine on my tiny balcony and it waved companionably at hers. There's nothing like hanging out the washing to make you feel you belong.

I saw few beggars in the streets of Manaus and they were mostly cripples, but once a respectable-looking woman came up to me in the supermarket with a child on one arm and a can of milk in her hand. I only realised afterwards that she had been asking me for a contribution to the milk. In the streets I noticed that most people were quite dark-skinned. Brazilians are a symphony of colours as a result of the intermingling of whites, black slaves and Indians. The women wore such sexy clothes that at first I had thought that there were an awful lot of prostitutes in this place. Their clothes suited the tropical climate but I never before saw so much skin exposed on the street. Even older women, on some of whom such garb was not entirely suitable, wore tight and revealing get-ups.

At the port, looking for a boat onwards to Belem, the town fifteen hundred kilometres away that sits at the mouth of the Amazon, I asked a policeman the whereabouts of the ticket office. A young girl who spoke English was allocated to help me find a cabin. She sent me to view one with a jaunty fellow in a red knitted beanie cap who looked like a pirate. The boat was called the *Santarem* and appeared very new. My shiny clean cabin had its own bathroom and the entire boat was air-conditioned. I was told that the boat sailed the day after this but I could live aboard as soon as I had a ticket.

I paid for one and the young lady cashier who had helped me passed her hand under the glass shield to shake mine and wish me 'bon voyage'.

Next morning I woke to hear great claps of thunder and rain falling. It had looked like rain for days but had chosen to wait until I was about to move house to do so. I sloshed to the wharf and collected my cabin key. The first time I had gone to the boat to inspect the cabin the captain, who was Portuguese in looks, had appeared and shown me to it. This time he popped up like a cockroach out of the woodwork, stowed my bags, pointed out that my lifejacket was stored in a little slot at the end of the bunk, led me to his cabin and told me that I should just call him if I wanted anything. He didn't say what.

A couple of hammocks had already been slung in the open part of the deck, but so far I was the only occupant aboard. The boat's air-conditioning was not on yet and it was too hot to stay in my cabin, so I walked up-town and took refuge in the library. Another glorious building, the exterior was a classical design painted in two shades of pink and white. Inside it had either black and white mosaic tiled floors or wooden parquet ones. Silver wrought-iron banisters with brass-plated stairs curved from both sides of the foyer up to the second floor. At the base of the staircase were four beautiful metal lamps with multiple shades of fluted amber glass. The polished wooden counter stood between them and an epic painting hung at the top of the stairs. In the reading room three people were asleep at desks. I thought this was fitting as, in contrast to the elegant foyer, this was a horribly functional room.

Returning to the *Santarem*, I sat on the deck watching as men loaded it and other boats docked so closely together that they were almost touching. An enormous amount of shunting, shoving and shouting was taking place. Cases of beer shot down a plank to land in our boat. Bags of flour were loaded from the back of a truck – one man pulled the bag to the edge of the tray while another hoisted it onto his shoulders and then humped it down to someone else who took it into the hold. All the labourers were covered in flour. The one who was taking the bag onto his back wore a flour bag tied around his head like an Arab gutera.

In the evening I walked to the town to make a phone call home. I had thought that it might be dangerous on the wharf in the dark of night, but the place was crowded with people out enjoying the cool air. I finally found a phone that worked and, after buying some more guarana drinks – maybe it *was* addictive – I came back without any problems. During the day you needed your ticket to check onto the wharf through a turnstile. Fortunately this wasn't manned at night – I'd forgotten my ticket. The boat's air-conditioning was now on, and with a vengeance. Freezing, I stuck up the vents with sticking plaster from my first-aid kit, read a book and then had a very good night's sleep despite the partying of the folk in hammocks on the boat next door.

The *Santarem* appeared to be constructed mostly of metal. The sides and roof of my cabin were tin. I had two portholes that opened onto the deck, two bunks, one on top of the other, and enough room to walk beside them. There were plenty of hooks, a power point – and even a phone. The minute bathroom was spotless and everything worked. The toilet even accepted loo paper without throwing a tantrum. However, the water that flushed the toilet came directly from the river, and was almost black.

The *Santarem* had three decks. The top housed six two-roomed suites, as well as a sitting room and a bar that I never managed to find open. On the deck outside, two open-air showers and seats were at the rear and the captain's cabin and the bridge were at the front. On the second deck, ten cabins, including mine, and the purser's office were in the front and the central open area was crammed with dozens of swinging hammocks.

At each town many passengers got on and off, but this

boat was nowhere near as full as the last had been. I found two other foreign travellers, a young Austrian couple, on board. Behind the hammock space was the dining room, once again in close proximity to the ablutions that the hammock-dwellers used, although this time the dining room was enclosed. Cargo was stored on the deck below this one as well as in the hold underneath.

The activity in the port woke me early in the morning. I got up and did my washing in the minute bathroom, made coffee with my invaluable immersion heater then sat on deck watching the wooden boats bobbing up and down all around. The *Santarem* didn't seem to move as much as they did, probably because it was made of steel.

While it was still cool I walked downtown, picking my way among the bustle on the wharf. It was much hotter there. I lunched in a kilo restaurant where the food was upstairs but you entered downstairs. After eating I paid, went to the loo and threw the receipt in the bin. When I came out of the toilet I found two ladies examining my receipt. I took it and threw it in the bin again. They looked at me in horror and the penny dropped. I needed that receipt to get past the guard downstairs – it was equivalent to throwing money in the bin. I explained to the ladies that I was just an ignorant tourist and thanked them profusely. They saved me a lot of embarrassment at the exit.

Back at the boat I found the action had stepped up even more. Labourers zipped everywhere off-loading cargo from many trucks, while vendors sold drinks and bags of fruit. I bought some delicious little apples. I would have liked oranges too, but they came already peeled and hawking them around in a naked state in string bags leaves a lot to be desired in the hygiene field. One ingenious fellow had his peeling machine mounted on the handlebars of his bike.

The sailing time posted for the *Santarem* was four. We sailed at about five, not too bad for this part of the world. The captain and crew appeared on deck for this occasion looking spiffy in white shoes and white uniforms with gold epaulettes on their shoulders – they were a far cry from the bare chests and grotty T-shirts of my last boat's crew, and I was suitably impressed.

The captain blew three long blasts on the whistle and we backed very slowly away from the wharf – an interesting procedure in that crowd of boats. Leaving the busy harbour we passed among a congestion of huge tankers and container ships that had sailed all the way from the Atlantic, as well as canoes, navy boats and the ubiquitous wooden riverboats. As soon as we left our mooring another boat immediately pulled into the space and three others also departed heading downriver at about the same time as we did.

For a long time we sailed past Manaus, which was strung untidily along the river's edge, then we crossed the Meeting of the Waters, where a fat man told me all about it in Portuguese, none of which I understood. Looking down into the water of the inky black Rio Negro where it frothed away from the prow, I decided that the foam was about the colour of the head on a glass of stout. As I leaned on the rail the captain walked past, patted my arm and smiled at me. I hoped someone else was now steering the boat. I found a shaded chair on the top deck and watched the sun set in the cool breeze as we rode along the river. There were only about twenty passengers on the *Santarem*'s top deck. A wooden boat passed us with music blaring and I was glad to be missing that.

One of the crew came to tell me that I should eat. He took me down to the dining room, where a uniformed officer collected one of the meal tickets that had been issued to me. Very impressive. Unfortunately the meal was not. It consisted of the same ill-flavoured soup that I'd reluctantly consumed the first night on the previous boat. But it was edible and I ate a large bowl of it. Then I sat waiting hopefully for the next course. When it didn't arrive, I had another bowl of soup. No problem. I had my bag of apples. I'd survive.

Early in the morning I woke to the sight of the Amazon, a grey river beneath a grey sky divided by a strip of green bank. The phone on the wall beside my bunk rang and I was summoned to breakfast, I think. This repast was a pleasant surprise – pawpaw, rolls and coffee, albeit ghastly pre-sweetened stuff. A few hours later we stopped at a town that boasted a large church commanding the riverbank. It had a big white cross in front of it, a U-shaped building behind it that appeared to be a convent, and a two-storeyed school alongside. Even before we pulled to the wharf to tie up, a huge crowd of people had gathered and were cheering and calling out to us to buy their goods. They boarded the *Santarem* like a swarm of pirates and I bought some really delicious fried banana chips and a big hand of fresh bananas for a dollar.

We pulled out into the stream again. It was wide but I could still see the banks clearly on both sides – unlike on the Yangtse in China, where I saw nothing but water. The river was now brown, its surface bumpy with wavelets that occasionally produced a white cap. Later the waves grew bigger and we rolled with their movement. We were heading downstream and therefore going with the flow and the tide.

Every so often we came in close to the riverbank and, twenty-four hours from Manaus, I could see that the jungle was less dense. I thought it prettier – there were big trees and more variation in the undergrowth and occasional palms or a little house by the water's edge.

Late in the afternoon we approached a hamlet. This time the church stood high at the rear of the town at the end of a broad avenue. There was a wooden wharf, but our boat tied up to a metal, flat-topped landing barge that was attached to the wharf by a wooden walkway consisting of two broad planks. Across from where the boat was moored squatted the usual boring adobe buildings with flat roofs and open fronts. In a gesture that was meant to be enticing, one was labelled 'Bar'. On the landing another greeting committee of vendors waited to offer us iced lollies from their fridge boxes, banana chips and other munchies, but none sold drinks. They must have thought that we had drinks aboard. I hadn't found the ship's bar open yet, although I'd certainly been looking.

The sellers did a roaring trade. Everybody bought. Everyone also hung over the side munching and throwing their lolly papers and wrappers into the water. To pay you just threw the money down to the landing and your change was thrown back up. I saw a couple of salesmen using an ingenious device to make this operation safer. A long stick had been secured in the neck of a small green plastic bottle with its bottom cut off, and people place their money in this. A great deal of other trading went on. The meat supply for the boat was bought here. I watched six sides of beef dragged aboard over the grubby tyres that edged the wharf as buffers. Then the meat was manhandled onto the dirty deck. This was a marginally better place than its previous position in the sun on the wooden boards of the landing. Fish was also being traded from the boat. One man had come aboard in Manaus with several boxes full. A small boy walked about trying to sell a pretty parrot that perched on his finger. It had a bright yellow head, light green body and darker green wings.

As we arrived at this town a wooden riverboat was leaving. This boat, the *Boa Vinda Viagem*, had left Manaus at the same time as we had. We'd raced it up the river and had been having a contest with it ever since, mostly following behind it, tripping over its wake, a wobbly cream-coloured trail of what looked like chopped up vanilla icecream bubbling on top of the water. Now the *Viagra* pulled out and tootled off as we came in.

We continued on, still sailing close to the riverbank. What I could see was very beautiful. The sun was shining and even though the water was a muddy brown, the verdant foliage was lush and through gaps in the trees I could see green, green grass.

I was sitting on deck watching the sun going down as we

pulled to the wharf at the next town and slotted into a space alongside the *Viagra*. After going neck and neck with her all the way from Manaus, now I actually touched her side rails and made contact with the people on her. The gangplank was not lowered at short stops – passengers who wanted to embark or disembark had to sling their goods over the side and jump after them onto the wharf. Customs officers came aboard here and searched my cabin. They looked in my bathroom, under the bunks and studied my passport. I wondered what they imagined I could have hidden under the bed.

On deck this balmy night, absorbing the peace and the damp smell, I watched the bow of the *Viagra* as she took off into the total blackness of the river. All three of her decks were well lit and she made a cheery sight as she slid away into the night, the sound of her engines puttering fainter and fainter.

The captain sat down with me for a while and tried to converse. We managed, but it was pretty garbled. He said he had been on the river for thirty years. He was a nice man with fine, grey-blue eyes in a genial face. It must have been my night to exude pheromones, as later my amiable, fat, little drunk admirer chased me around the deck. He had spotted me soon after we sailed from Manaus and kept trying to renew an imagined friendship. He seemed to be saying that he had seen me in Porto Velho. Waving his ever-present can and spraying me with beer in the process, he would shout, 'Porto Velho. Porto Velho,' chortling wildly. This night, he waddled his round face, curly hair and lop-sided grin alongside me at the bar, peered closely into my face, and shouted, 'Oi!' It sounded like an accusation. Taken aback, I stared at him. He grinned and, sprinkling me with saliva, said even louder: 'Oi!' Suddenly it dawned on me that he was merely saying hello. 'Oi,' I replied.

During the night we stopped and, with a great deal of crunching, came alongside a wharf. I could see nothing except a few lights ashore, but from dawn onward there was activity outside and when I got up I discovered that we were at Santarem, the namesake of our boat and a big town that is halfway to Belem. We were docked not in the main part of town but at a wharf in a backwater where the embankment was old and rustic. The riverbank was a wall of soil three metres high fortified by planks held up by posts. On one side of us was a muddy foreshore and on the other a steel landing barge containing a couple of trucks, one of which was off-loading bags of rice and flour. At the end of the wharf a small boy, oblivious to all the action around him, fished with a hand-line.

A pair of housemaids now materialised in my cabin and set to with vigour, vacuuming, emptying the bin, putting cleaner in the loo and spraying the air with smelly stuff. This Herculean task ocupied them all the time I was at breakfast. I had already dubbed one of the cleaners The Voice. I had heard her screaming and shouting ever since I came on board. A formidable lady built like a small tank with grey hair, she was really quite agreeable, but I was heartily sick of the sound of her.

It was hot and humid tied to the wharf at Santarem, in contrast to the lovely coolness out on the river. The sun was still shining, but black clouds hung about and spat rain every now and then. We lunched on the daggy-looking meat that I had witnessed being dragged aboard the day before. Tarted up and disguised as a stew, it was quite tasty, but I knew it, I recognised the rib cages. In the late afternoon we were still waiting to sail. The sinking sun hitting the water turned all the wavelets into flickers of light that danced toward me like tiny stars shimmering across the river in constantly changing formations. Then a small boy, cleaving the water like a dolphin, dived into the middle of that sheet of glittering light and scattered its hypnotic illusion.

We sailed from Santarem into a lovely evening and were fanned by a welcome breeze as soon as we left the wharf. Vendors and visitors packed the landing to wave goodbye. One of the people who had come aboard here was a large bearded gent with an American accent. He saw the book I was reading and asked me if I was English. 'Wash your mouth,' I said. 'I'm Australian.'

James was an interesting chap and I talked to him for quite a while. He said he had lived for twenty-eight years in Germany. We were joined by the young Austrian couple I had met previously in the dining room. James told a story about three young German boys he had encountered recently. These lads, who had been born no more than twenty years ago, had flown to South America with an American airline that shall remain nameless, and were told that they needed to fill out a seven-question document and sign it. This paper related to 'the war'. In all truth these kids could have said, 'Which war?' The first question was, 'Were you involved in the persecution of the Jews?' I mean, were you likely to say, 'Sure I was,' even if you were? And these boys were not born until thirty years after the event.

Before dark fell we passed over the confluence of the Amazon and the Tapajos, the wide river that joins the Amazon at Santarem seven hundred kilometres from the mouth of the Amazon. The muddy one on the outside was the Amazon and the clean, faintly bluish one on the inside was the Tapajos. Sixty kilometres from Santarem lie the remains of Henry Ford's Folly, Fordlandia, a plantation and town he built that was supposed to supply him with rubber for his car tyres. Millions of dollars later it failed. Santarem was originally settled by former soldiers of the confederacy after the US civil war and still has families named Higgins and McDonald and such like.

Then we were chugging along pleasantly in the dark, the captain playing his searchlight from one bank to another following the buoy markers. A bag of mandarins I had bought in Santarem proved to be empty of juice and as wooden as the floor. I had been conned by a small boy who had been walking around trying to sell them without success and looking doleful.

I was a sucker for these little kids. Diminutive girls of five or six would wander up to me late at night while I was eating at an outdoor cafe in Manaus and want me to buy chewing gum. I would buy – at an inflated price of course, but I always bought. I could usually resist the adults who approached me while eating or walking in the street. They would try to sell a torch, a watch, a clock or some trinket but they didn't pester. If I said, 'No, thank you,' they went away.

We stopped once during the night. I was woken by the three long blasts on the horn. At six in the morning they were repeated and after a short stop we were off again. I was still in bed but through the window I could see that we now seemed to be on a sea – no riverbanks were visible. I was called for breakfast at a time that I considered too early so I didn't go until I was ready. That was a big mistake. The dining room was shut – there had been a time change in the night.

Out on deck I encountered a howling gale but the river banks had come into view again. The water had white caps and we got up quite a rock and roll on the swell. We passed barges bearing containers on wheels, other riverboats, large, floating clumps of weed and the odd floating log.

I had not seen any sign of habitation for a long time. The jungle here was different too – thicker, and it grew right down to the water's edge. Later there were many islands in the middle of the river again, all of them tree-covered. Still later we ran even closer to the bank and then I could see that the country was very pretty. Occasionally I spied a small primitive house with a rustic landing nuzzled by a canoe. A couple of times a few houses were huddled together next to a small church. Sitting in a comfortable chair on the shady side of the boat, I put my feet on the rail and watched it all slide by.

At certain places on the river small canoes paddled by young children came out to meet the boat. Watching these flimsy wooden crafts skimmed along the mighty Amazon by tiny tots, I marvelled that they were not afraid. The canoes

196

appeared so fragile and insignificant, a mere speck on the river's face. Some boys, no more than eight or ten years old, played a game with the boat. They would come alongside and throw a rope at the boat until it caught fast, then climb aboard and try to sell you palm hearts in jars or small live turtles. Some didn't bring anything, they did it just for fun. After riding on the boat for a while they would leave and I wondered how they would get back home again – they had to paddle upstream against the current.

The last light of the setting sun lay on the river behind the *Santarem*. The water in front of it was already gun-metal grey, but the waves behind had silver-foil crests and gold slopes. The river here was reasonably narrow and we finally passed the *Viagra*. But I cheered too soon. She had slowed down to turn off into a side channel. The cook told me that she was going to another town.

Searching for a cold drink down on the third deck where a snack bar was secreted among the hammocks, I was again bailed up by the boat drunk, my Brazilian admirer. He was smashed again, or still, and I took a while to disentangle myself from him. Still looking for a drink I went up a deck and a small boy took me by the hand and led me into the bar. He put on the lights, fished a Coke out of the fridge and gave it to me. And just then the captain appeared and caught us red-handed. He did not look at all pleased with my delinquent accomplice, but he chatted congenially to me while holding me by the arm – a citizen's arrest?

Sometime during that night we came across some wild water. The boat gave terrific bumps as it went up, up and then – bang, bang – down again. It was like being on the open sea. By morning, however, we were on more sheltered and calmer waters. The green gloom of the jungle on the river bank was very close and in places there was no bank at all, just submerged jungle, the trees marching right into the water.

13 Where the Amazon meets the Atlantic

We reached Belem and pulled up to a wharf on the outskirts of the town. Belem, the first centre of European colonisation in the Amazon area, was settled by the Portuguese in 1616. One hundred and forty kilometres from the open sea on one of the arms of the Amazon delta, it remains a trading centre and the gateway to the interior. Strongly influenced by the Amazon and the jungle, it depends on the river for contact with the outside world as the highway to the south is only open in the dry season.

At the landing in Belem there was not much to see except a few vehicles parked on a piece of dusty ground. Getting transport was no problem. Two taxi drivers came aboard to negotiate with the four foreigners – James, the Austrian couple and me – who seemed the only passengers requiring this service. Comparing notes with James I found that he had the same hotel's address that I did. We lobbed at the desk, where a charming young man, who seemed delighted to be able to practise his English, asked me how long I was staying.

'Not very long.'

'Is this your husband?'

'No,' I replied.

He then gave us a list of prices by the hour. I looked around and suddenly it dawned on me. Charming. I was in a brothel. But it was reasonably cheap, right in the main street, it looked clean and the staff appeared respectable. I managed to get through to the desk clerk that I wanted a room all to myself, thank you very much, and another gorgeous smiling young man, a Ricky Martin clone, shooed me into the antiquated lift, clanged the metal grille shut and up we creaked.

I dumped my bags and zoomed on up to the roof-top dining room to partake of breakfast. The Hotel Central, built around 1920, is classical art deco in design and must once have been quite grand. It would have been great up here on the roof in the hotel's heyday and even now, in its declining years, with all its glass doors open and a cooling breeze blowing through, it was a pleasant spot.

I was sorry to hear that it only catered for breakfast. A beer garden would once have graced the roof either side of the dining room, but now it was vacant except for some litter and a few pigeons. I sat in a cane chair that looked an original 1920s' model while a courtly older man served me. The coffee had no sugar. Ah, civilisation at last – the sugar bowl was on the table, not in my cup. James joined me and I think my breakfast went on his tab. It seemed to be unusual for a woman to be running about loose. The taxi driver and I had conducted a long conversation, all of which I managed to work out, concerning the whereabouts of my husband, if this wasn't he in the cab with me. This place was beginning to sound like Saudi Arabia, where the first and last words spoken to me had been: 'Where is your husband?'

Hotel Central was four floors high and it presented to the street a facade of pale-green and white tiles. Its foyer opened right onto the footpath and the tiles continued on the walls in there. Black and white tiles marched across the floor to the back wall, where a well-worn grey marble staircase with an old brass hand-rail ascended to the rooms alongside the venerable lift. All the stairways and corridors were covered to a fair height with off-white-with-age tiles topped by a black-and-white-tile frieze.

Each floor had a sitting area on the landing at the top of the stairs in front of tall French doors that opened on to a small balcony over the main street. This space was tiled in a bilious shade of mustard, patterned in an attempt to convince you that it was marble. None of the exterior windows or doors possessed glass, just green wooden shutters to close against the rain. A three-piece lounge suite, classically square-shaped but re-covered in an excruciatingly ugly maroon vinyl, sat on a threadbare carpet in the sitting area near my room. The carpets all looked as though they had been in situ since the year one – and in the darker recesses of the passages, a faint whiff of old socks came off them. They were so worn that in places no carpet at all was left, just the threads that it had been woven on.

This establishment didn't run to a vacuum cleaner. The housemaids swept the carpets with a broom. During my sojourn in the Central I used to read in the sitting area, as there the light was good, and here I met the odd short-term tenant, each of whom was very agreeable.

On an exploration foray, ambling along the main street under the huge old mango trees that line it, I came to the town square, the Praca de Republica. In a large, leafy park, a pre-election rally, as well as the usual Sunday market, was in full swing. Stalls that sold crafts, clothes, and food covered the walkways alongside the lawns.

Searching for lunch, I discovered that Belem shuts down more tightly than my home town of Adelaide used to on a Sunday. Nothing was open. I walked all the way down to the riverside, where a swish new building housed many exclusive shops and galleries. Beside this enormous edifice, the ram-shackle stalls of the market wandered a great distance along the waterfront. Fish were sold in a lovely old building but the rest, mostly fruit, vegetables and foodstuffs, was outdoors in lean-tos and shaded benches. Near the end, the market degenerated and became sleazy.

It was siesta time and, except for a few stallholders snoozing alongside their goods, there were few people about. A man and woman approached and the man spoke to me. 'Senora,' he said. And went on earnestly in rapid Portuguese. I think he was telling me that it wasn't safe to walk in the street now. It certainly looked seedy and the area was deserted except for some strange-looking people lying about in doorways. I beat a hasty retreat back to the safety of the town, passing many closed cafes on the way. By the time I finally found one open, I was desperate for food and, taking a wild stab at the menu, ordered a meal. Then I waited an hour to discover that the cook had barbecued a whole chicken for me. The chook was delicious, but so would have been fried running-shoes in my famished state. Even so I could still only eat half of the fowl. Yes, truly. Only half. I asked for a doggie bag.

Restored, I went to stock up on guarana drinks. I entered a doorway that I thought led into a shop, but actually went into the next building. Inside, in a foyer, I encountered two smart-looking young men dressed in white shirts and ties, who were handing out metre-long, gold-coloured plastic trumpets. I thought that this must be some kind of sales promotion. I didn't want a trumpet but the smiling young man forced it on me, as well as a sheet of paper covered in Portuguese. I followed some other people down a hallway and entered, to my very great surprise, not a shop, but a large auditorium full of seats that sloped down, row after row, like a picture theatre. At the bottom was a stage with a central dais above which hung a massive banner proclaiming, 'Jesus es me Senor' – Jesus is my Lord. Good heavens, I had bumbled into a revival meeting. I would be expected to blow my trumpet, stamp my feet and shout 'Halleluiah'. Apart from the fact that the show would all be in Portuguese, it wouldn't be much use to me – I am way past saving. The young men guarding the exit were most reluctant to let me go and tried hard to persuade me to stay. 'No, no, no!' they said, 'You'll really enjoy this show.' Or words to that effect. I pushed the trumpet back at them and bolted. I knew I'd enjoy getting a guarana fix from the shop much more.

It had been hot, thirsty work walking about Belem and when I reached my room in the late afternoon, I had a shower and zonked. James came to see if I wanted to go out to eat but I said I would rather continue with the siesta. When I woke it was dark, so I gave up on this day and, doing a Scarlett O'Hara, told myself I'd take up life again tomorrow.

I got up at the crack of dawn for a very satisfactory breakfast. Elegantly presented, it included cheese and ham slices, crispy French rolls, a huge slice of watermelon, fruit juice and really good strong coffee. The constantly beaming waiter was the only elderly person I had seen so far in Brazil. A dear old man, he looked a hundred, but probably was not a day over ninety-five. I sat by the open doors and fed the pigeons on the roof my watermelon seeds and bread crumbs. They were big, fat, glossy-plumed birds, one of whom wore white, 1920s' spats that make him look heavy-footed but were in keeping with the era of the hotel. Two pigeons were behaving themselves nicely with a couple of bread crumbs when a smaller pigeon flew in. One immediately stopped what he was doing and started posturing in front of her. From past observations I have come to the conclusion that pigeons seem to be utterly and totally obsessed with sex. This female was just trying to get a feed and was probably saying, 'Oh, just get out of my way will you,' like any sensible woman would when food was on offer, but the idiot male continued to bob up and down around her like a thing demented.

At the tourist office, which was set in lovely gardens, an agreeable young man listened intently and tried hard to understand me. He spoke English but his accent was so excruciating I scarcely comprehended a word. But he did his best to find me a boat down the coast to Rio De Janeiro, roughly four thousand kilometres away. I had achieved my goal – crossing the continent overland. Now it was time to go home and the logical place to get a flight back to Australia seemed to be Rio.

It was all to no avail. I could see that the young fellow

thought I was quite mad – tourists are supposed to fly, and that was such a simple operation. Why did I persist in making trouble for poor travel agents with my eccentric ideas? At one stage he interrupted the phone call he was making to a shipping company to ask me: 'Will you be on this ship on your own?'

'Yes,' I said, not wanting to confuse the issue, but privately I really had hoped there might be a couple of sailors to drive the thing.

Parting friends, he shook my hand and gave me a fine map and a special price of only $5500 to fly back to Sydney from Belem, which I declined gracefully. I didn't want to buy the bloody aeroplane, just rent a small space on it for a short while.

It was still early morning and reasonably cool if you kept out of the sun, so I walked up the shady side of the main street and entered several airline offices where various young ladies tried to find me a better fare without success. Finally one took me by the hand and led me a couple of doors down to meet someone she said might be able to help. They offered me a fare for four thousand. I nearly had a fit and asked if I could whittle it down a bit by taking the bus to Rio and flying from there. This reduced it to $2200. Then I discovered that all flights to Australia were fully booked. The first available seat was three-and-a-half weeks away. I put myself down for wait listing, or 'weight lifting' as it was put to me. It sounded as though I might as well be doing that.

After an enormous by-the-kilo lunch I racked out for a two-hour siesta. It was terribly hot in the middle of the day and by that time I always felt so hot and sweaty that I longed for a cold shower. That was lucky – there was no hot water in this hotel.

In the evenings I promenaded around the square on the lawns and under the trees with the rest of the populace. Wandering about at night among the food stalls and flood-lit statues seemed reasonably safe and was very pleasant. But, as there was no breeze, it was still not really cool. I imagined that it would be cooler down on the waterfront but from what I heard this would be madness. Big strong men don't walk by the river alone at night, let alone medium-sized women.

My spacious and spotlessly clean room had a beautiful parquet wooden floor. I was intrigued by the extreme height of the ceilings and doors throughout the building. I estimated the distance to the deco-style ceiling cornice in my room to be at least four metres. The door into the corridor was three-and-a-half metres high, the top metre being patterned glass in a wooden frame. A second door in one wall connected me to the next room. The door handle had been removed on my side – I hoped it had been on the other side too.

I possessed two windows, both of which were innocent of glass and opened into the corridor. But they did have louvred wooden shutters, the top half of which could be opened for air – and to allow people passing by in the corridor a sight of the top of your head. All the woodwork, doors, frames and shutters were painted the nauseous shade of green that had been popular in the twenties and they didn't look as though they'd had a touch-up since then. The furniture was also original 1920s, a classic oak dressing table with a black-marble top and a big oak wardrobe commodious enough to secrete a lover when your husband came home unexpectedly. And there was a little sink that was surrounded by hectares of white tiles edged with a black border and had an intriguing brass lever instead of a tap. A light swung from a cord in the ceiling a hundred kilometres away and a pedestal fan was plugged into a powerpoint that had been added as an after-thought. Well, a ceiling fan would have been useless way up there. The room was completed by a reminder of the good old days when there were rafts of servants at your beck and call – an ornate service bell of porcelain surrounded by brass was positioned in the wall by the door.

Each floor of the hotel had a huge ablution block that was

entirely covered in tiles – floor, walls and even the corridor leading to it. First you entered a great room that was no longer used, but still contained a row of cement laundry troughs under the windows on the far wall. Some guest-room windows opened into this area and I wondered how this set-up worked back in the days when the maids would have been out there washing by hand in the early morning. Progressing through the laundry you came to the bathrooms. Segregated into male and female sides, they contained not only showers and bidets, but colossal cast-iron baths, big enough to wash a baby hippopotamus in.

The main streets were extremely crowded. I have never seen as many buses as I did in Brazilian cities, and there were thousands and thousands of taxis. I had seen no street people in Manaus but sadly there were a few, as well as a couple of beggars, near my hotel. One was a woman who didn't look to be quite all there mentally but none of them was old. Street living is not an occupation conducive to longevity, I guess. The beggar to whom I invariably gave money was plonked right in the middle of the busy footpath of the main street, where people had to walk around him. He had no arms or legs, just a trunk with stumps on it, but he sat in the hot sun and smiled at the passers-by.

One day I solved two mysteries that had puzzled me – bingo halls and polished coconut shells. The former were actually places to play the pokies, but had large 'Bingo' signs outside. I investigated one and didn't have a clue what I was doing but the machine spat ten dollars at me, so I didn't complain. And the polished coconut shell halves that I had seen stacked on counters at small cafes or street food stalls, I discovered, were for soup. One evening I saw a woman deposit a few plastic chairs on the footpath, set up a tiny stall and start serving soup into these coconut shells. Nobody seemed to mind the sudden appearance of this obstacle, they just walked around the chairs. Multitudes of other tiny stalls sold similar items – belts, hair ornaments, wallets and so on. Some people merely stood on the footpath and held out items for sale.

I saw the marvellous church of Our Lady of Nazare. Built by rubber barons, it bristles with Victorian statues, Carrara marble and gold. The real church for masses of Brazilians is still the church of the spirits. The Africans who were imported as slaves by the Portuguese brought their gods with them and many times all they did was re-name their deity with a Christian name. The old voodoo religion, now called candombie, persists.

Having several weeks to fill in before my flight home, I decided that I'd love to see the mighty Amazon meet the Atlantic. I could do this by taking a boat out to spend a few days on the island of Marajo. As big as Switzerland, Marajo lies in the wide mouth of the Amazon and has forests, grassy plains, river beaches and big herds of water buffalo. The smart, new boat-terminal building seemed the logical place to start enquiring for a boat ticket to Marajo. It wasn't. I was given directions to the place that was alleged to be the one. Hours later, cheesed off from hiking about in the heat, I came back to where I had started and was given direction elsewhere. Then they said that this office would now be closed for siesta. Typical. These boat offices shut at eleven for lunch and then go on to siesta. A good life already, but that's not enough for them. They don't open again in the evening, as respectable people who have had a siesta should do. They only open from three till five. I considered this pretty stupid – not for the office workers, perhaps, but certainly from a poor traveller's point of view.

There was nothing else to do except imitate the supine staff, so I had lunch and a lie down before setting off again. This time I looked up my guide book. It swore that the boat office was 'at the junction' of the two streets it named but omitted to mention that from there you had to walk at least two kilometres. After asking for help many times I finally found the place, a big tin wharfside shed that housed several small ticket booths. From one of them, with my less-than-adequate Portuguese, I managed to extract a ticket for a boat to Surre, the only town on Marajo, in two days' time.

The next day I used seven buses – and only once wound up on the wrong one. I found a bus going to the main bus station and asked the driver to tell me when we came to it. In the very modern bus depot, which was more like a train station thanks to its flight of stairs down to the departure bays, a helpful man struggled with my hybrid Spanish/Portuguese and I booked a seat on a bus to Rio de Janeiro in a week's time. The journey would take fifty-two hours. 'A good bus with a toilet,' he promised. 'Hopefully,' I said. At first I had asked for a seat at the back of the bus but the ticket-seller indicated that this wasn't such a good idea. 'Pooh,' he said holding his nose. 'Toilet there.' After fifty-two hours I guess they *would* get a bit whiffy.

Catching another bus, I set out for Icari, a village famed for its pottery, on the outskirts of Belem. The journey took a very long hour. Although I did see the odd horse-drawn cart and quite a few donkeys, we didn't travel out into the country-side but through interminable suburbs of ugly, squat buildings. When we finally reached the bus terminus, I asked the driver for directions to Icari. He said that I should have got off earlier. The driver of another bus, which was about to return to Belem, kindly waited until I had finished the drink I'd bought at a dump of a nearby roadside stall and off I went again. About ten kilometres later he put me off. Standing in the dirt road, I thought, Crikey, this is a village? 'Don't miss it. It's wonderful,' the guide book's authors had said. I thought that they needed to examine their values – not to mention their eyes. It might have been wonderful if you were mad keen on pottery, lots of it and mostly the same, but I'm not. I don't care for it at all. I came to see the interesting village in the countryside that I had visualised. Instead I stood in a hot, dusty street lined with rows of dreary shacks, which were fronted by open drains full of sewerage.

I waited for the next bus alongside an evil-smelling butcher's 'shop', an open-air roadside stand with slabs of meat arrayed on a grotty bench. It was a long wait in the heat, and my mood wasn't helped by the devoted attention of hordes of flies. When a bus came I jumped on it – I didn't care where it was going. As luck had it, it went to the bus depot from where I caught another bus right to the door of my hotel. Fantastic.

Never daunted, lunch and a siesta later, I set off again on a bus, this time with the museum in my sights. Belem's botanical gardens, museum and zoo are combined in a wonderful park. I felt as though I was in the real jungle again. Beautiful, big trees and overhanging creepers completely shaded the paths I walked along in this magical green world that was dotted with picturesque old buildings and quaint stone edifices. The botanical gardens are built around a couple of huge trees that must be hundreds, maybe thousands, of years old. Bigger than any I saw out in the jungle, they were so enormous I found it hard to grasp their size. There were also many flowering trees and a blue creeper, like wisteria, that I had seen growing elsewhere. Quite a few bushes and trees had blue flowers and another had great pink blossoms. And there were many specimens of the tree that I saw everywhere in the streets and parks and was just now coming into beautiful blossom. I call it the 'golden shower tree' because all its yellow blooms hang down in a cascade like rain.

The live exhibits were housed among the trees and garden in natural surroundings. My favourites were a couple of massive anacondas, one beautiful spotted jaguar and another sleekly sinuous and as black as the night, who padded sinisterly about his enclosure. Gorgeous black monkeys swung languidly from branch to branch in their tree-filled enclosure and the biggest bird I've ever seen perched on a log. Much bigger than a wedge-tailed eagle, it looked like a huge, black-

and-white owl. There were also ravishing pink flamingoes and gigantic, rainbow-hued macaws. I was taken aback by the intensity of their glorious colours – screaming blues, aquas and reds. There was a good aquarium with many flowing fish in well-lit glass cases. The museum looked interesting too, but there were no English subtitles so I couldn't work out what most of it was all about. I could have spent much more time in this enjoyable place but, although there were plenty of seats along the shaded paths, the afternoon became hot and steamy and my feet wore out.

As soon as I made it back to the hotel I had a cold shower. I never thought I'd see the time when a cold shower would be the delight of my day but it was great to wash off the grime.

Later I forayed out to the Belem opera house, the Teatro la Paz. It was nowhere near the treasure that Manaus's was – the paintings and decoration were not as spectacular – but it was still lovely and it *was* bigger. One sweeping, curved stair-case was made entirely of white Carrara marble and another was wood and brass. The ballroom, entrance hall and upstairs foyer each featured three chandeliers, the central chandelier in each room being a mass of thousands of crystal drops and prisms. If it had fallen on you, you would never have got up again or lived to complain about it, but you surely would have gone out with a jangle. In this theatre I was allowed to stand on the stage and, looking out over the seating, I could appreciate that it must be something else to perform here. The rows of plush seats, the gilded decorations and the grand, three-tiered boxes made quite an impression.

Leaving the opera house I continued walking and, miracles do happen, actually found something I had been looking for. But I don't know why the locals were so proud of their shopping centre. It was as dreary as any of these monstrosities anywhere.

Later, sitting in the airline office watching the crowds walk past, I realised that apart from the hotel waiter, I hadn't seen many old people in Brazil. Statistics tell you about the massive

209

number of youngsters in this country, but where do they keep their oldies? I did see a couple in the park on Sunday – maybe they only bring them out then. Was something sinister going on, or was it simply that people wore out fast in the heat?

One day I saw a sign on a shop advertising 'tartlets', and pondered whether they trained young tarts inside. If you judged purely by the manner of female dress, you'd say every second woman was a tart. The clothing here was even more risque than it had been in Manaus. You'd be arrested by the vice squad if you went out dressed like that in some places.

My trip to the island of Marejo started out innocuously. I taxied to the gate of the terminal, from where it was only a short walk into the departure shed and a doddle from there to the boat that was tied up at the wharf outside. The shed contained rows of long, wooden seats and in one corner a tiny cafe. The boat was scheduled to leave at twelve, but at that time passengers were still nonchalantly strolling down to it, so it was obviously not expected to depart punctually. The boat was a smaller version of the wooden riverboats fitted with rows of benches that could accommodate six passengers. The first row of seats were grabbed immediately, and I realised that this was because they were smack in front of the television set – not that you could hear it once the engine started. The day was overcast and the brown-grey water of the river was flat calm as we took off from the wharf. In the bow of the boat the crew's lunch table was gracefully arranged between the two toilets. I sat near the back and can vouch for the fact that they get smelly after a while. Nothing new there.

Once we were under way, the security guard slung his hammock across the bow and went to sleep. A couple of passengers did the same. What a good idea.

For a while the trip was uneventful. At first we ran alongside the riverbank, then, skirting a couple of small islands in the middle of the river, came to what looked like the open sea but was really still the wide river mouth. The colour of the water changed to an impressive yellowish-green and after a short while a few white caps appeared. As the weather grew rougher the white caps metamorphosed into thumping great waves and the sea became very disorderly, lurching the boat about. The passengers shrieked and held on tightly to the sides of the benches. Water came pouring in over the sides of the boat while the crew rushed to pull down tarpaulins to stop it. Waves splashed over my bags so I moved them to a drier spot. Attempting to get out of range of the spraying water, I inched along the bench from my spot on its end, encroaching on a fellow who was siesta-ing on the rest of it. It was about this time that I realised that this boat had no lifeboats or jackets.

Despite the tarpaulins, water poured in the boat with each wave and soon the decks were awash. Later a Brazilian man asked me, 'Were you worried?' I said, 'No,' but I think he had been. Still, I was glad not to be further out at the pororoca, the spot where the Atlantic's incoming tide crashes against the out-flowing river waters. Here the waves are five metres high and the noise they make sounds like a jet plane. Eight trillion gallons of fresh water a day pour into the Atlantic Ocean, many times the water needs of the entire United States. In discharge and drainage the Amazon easily surpasses all other rivers and equals the total of the world's next eight largest.

After three-and-a-half hours we came in to port on the island and, once we were in sight of the shore, the water calmed. Everyone stampeded off the boat – so I did too. It had been raining and there were muddy puddles underfoot, but the ascent to the top of the high bank was facilitated by a duckwalk of planks. At the top I was surprised to find just a patch of uninviting mud. I thought I'd been supposed to arrive at the town of Surre.

A couple of young Brazilian men I had seen on the boat asked me if I wanted a car. No wonder I'd noticed them. They were both gorgeous blokes, and one was exceptionally beautiful. I said that I wanted to go to the hotel in Surre, so they took me in tow and shunted me into one of the beat-up old vans that were lurking about waiting for customers. Another woman joined us and we drove for a long time until it began to dawn on me that I hadn't got off the boat anywhere near Surre. And finally it clicked that I had actually alighted on the other side of the island. I discovered later that the boat only went all the way to Surre on certain days. And this, naturally enough for a persistent victim of Murphy, was not one of those days.

On this day I had to go overland, making the total journey longer than five hours. Jolting along on a shocking dirt track we crossed the entire island, passing through dull country dotted with a few small primitive settlements, at one of which we cast off the other woman passenger. Then our progress was halted by a wide river. The luscious Brazilian boys, who had by now decided to adopt me, paid the van driver and refused to allow me to contribute.

We teetered into a midget-sized, wobbly dinghy and were ferried across to the elusive Surre on the opposite bank. I discovered that my friends worked for the Brazilian phone company, Embratel, and had come to Surre to perform mysterious deeds with satellites and phones. They had a lot of equipment and baggage, which they paid porters to carry. Then they carried my luggage up and down steep inclines. They found a car, one of the few in Surre, whose driver was willing to use it as a taxi. He took me to the Surre Hotel, led me inside and negotiated a room for me before warmly shaking my hand, bowing and departing.

On first sight of Surre I thought, What a drab hole. It looked like a place that time forgot. It didn't even run to a phone to the outside world. But the people were sociable, if slightly bemused by me. When I first arrived it was almost dark and I couldn't work out whether the hotel was dreadfully old, or just dreadful. In the cold light of day, I saw that it was in fact very old, so its decrepitude was forgivable. Built of white-painted adobe in the Mexican-fort style, it had flimsy, home-made wooden doors with cracks in them through which you could see daylight. The wide front, with its huge expanse of tiled floor, opened directly onto the street. There was no way to close it against marauders, burglars and the like – I hoped that someone sat up and guarded the place at night. In one corner of the foyer was a small desk, on which lay a school exercise book in which the person in charge wrote your name. Nothing else seemed to interest her.

Various doors opened off the foyer, as well as a tiled verandah that led to the rooms that were ranged around a U-shaped, litter-filled, dirt courtyard out the back. My room was basic but had everything I needed. The rough walls were painted a brilliant cheery blue. The narrow bush-carpentered door had a lock that only worked if you heaved the door up a foot. Fortunately a piece of wire was provided to perform this manoeuvre – there was no handle. Above the door was a square of fly wire that served as a window. It had no glass. A coconut palm in the courtyard waved its fronds at me through the wire. I had a comfy bed and a dressing table with a fly-specked mirror that would have been nice if only it had possessed more than one drawer knob. Anyway, putting your belongings in drawers in hotels is a no no, a fatal mistake, as I have learned to my great cost.

I even had a bathroom. I handled the plastic tap with care as it was more than a little insecure and I was afraid that I might pull it off and start a major flood.

My room, one of a long row in the back part of the U, was fronted by a tiled verandah that was a high step up from the courtyard. As in Mexico, steps had been made this height on footpaths or verandahs so that folk could alight from their carriages or carts straight onto them. To my delight, there were three beautiful, young horses grazing in the courtyard.

I thought that they must belong to the hotel but later I saw these and other horses free-ranging around the town. They go home unbidden to where they belong at night.

The only meal available at the hotel was breakfast and, as I arrived ravenously hungry just before six in the evening, I had to forage elsewhere for dinner. I was directed to a cafe down the street and near the river, where I sat in the breeze off the water at a small metal table on the footpath. I managed to convince the proprietor that I wanted food and in time I received a huge plate of the most delicious fish cooked in coconut milk. It was accompanied by rice, salad and fresh fijoa juice, cost just six real fifty centavos, and was really satisfying.

Although the church clock had read five when I passed it on the way to the cafe, as I sat down the church bells started tolling for the six o'clock angelus. An old man drinking beer at a nearby table on the sidewalk crossed himself repeatedly and said his prayers. Then I witnessed the home delivery service of this 'pub' in operation. The proprietor, who was also the cook and very likely the washer-up as well, issued an order to the old man, who took a wheelbarrow that was handy in the gutter, heaved a box of beer into it and wheeled it off. Returning later he pushed the wheelbarrow back into its regular parking spot in the gutter. Meanwhile a buffalo cart piled high with bags of produce plodded slowly by. Then I heard clip clop clip, and out of the dark came two untended horses. They wandered up the street, then meandered past again. They were like the three I had seen outside my door at the hotel – not ponies, but small, fine-boned horses in very good condition.

After I had eaten I walked around the town. A crowd of young men hung around one shop front. I thought that it must be a disco or a game shop, but it turned out to be the butcher's. Apparently the butcher shop was the place to be. There were only a few shops but they were all open, in every sense, as they had no walls on three sides in order to allow air through. They had shutters that could be pulled down when the shop closed. All the buildings were constructed of mud-brick and looked antiquated, the way structures can do in the tropics even when they are not. Down the centre of the town's two main streets, and all around the waterfront, grew the most massive and beautiful mango trees that I have ever seen. I had previously thought that northern Australian mango trees were pretty big, but these rainforest giants in their natural environment made Aussie trees look like dwarfs. From their trunks, which were four-and-a-half metres around the girth, they climbed heavenwards to a great height, culminating in an extensive spread of foliage. The bottom part of the trees had been painted white and I wondered if this was to stop insects attacking them or motorbikes running into them. Coconut palms and other big trees also grew along the water-front. I thought it was sensible to grow trees that provided food as well as shade. Lets hope they don't have animals that pinch the fruit like the possums do in Darwin.

Walking back to the hotel up a dark street, I felt no danger. But in one particularly sinister spot I heard a footfall behind me and thought, Muggers! The footsteps were followed by a soft whinny and I decided that, unless the mugger was doing animal imitations, I was about to be coshed by a horse. I was in far more danger from the deep drains that ran alongside the broken dirt tracks masquerading as footpaths.

Passing the front of a Protestant meeting hall that was wide open to the street, I saw a group of worshippers seated in a circle on hard chairs. They were making a lot of noise. It seemed to me that they were doing this to show off. Despite Brazil's predominantly Catholic population, I saw many of these Halleluiah Hall meetings being conducted at all hours of the day and night. Almost next door to the Protestant hall was the big Catholic church with its unobtrusive side entrance and screened front door. I went in, mainly in defiance of the other lot – I object to having opinions thrust upon me. Far from lavish, the old church had peeling, painted walls, but was brightened by gaily decorated statues, flowers and the odd splash of gold paint. A novena was in progress in Portuguese, and even I could follow it. Then the congregation sang. Swaying to and fro to the up-beat music, the worshippers held out their arms and clapped, a bloke in the back row bopping from one hip to the other. It was almost Latin salsa! But it was nice – a real church, in contrast to the bare place next door.

The night was deliciously cool. I slept under a sheet with the fan on full-bore and in the morning woke to the sound of a rooster crowing. It seemed a long time since I had heard that sound – it took me back to the happy year I had spent working in an Indonesian village. I emerged from my room at eight o'clock to find a girl mopping the large expanse of tiled walkways and floors. When I returned at twelve, she was still at it. Breakfast, which was included in my room price, was served in the back portion of the open-fronted foyer under a ceiling that must have been at least six metres high. To my great excitement, I was presented with the first egg I'd had for ages. Unfortunately it had been fried in coconut oil with a barrel of salt and smacked until it was dead flat, but nevertheless it was an egg and I enjoyed it. I also delighted in the sugarless coffee. How easily I was pleased these days. The tiny breakfast table was covered by a bread box, a big jug of hot milk, a large tub of butter and an enormous, battered, aluminium sugar-basin.

Large groups of local lads congregated opposite my hotel in a large netted enclosure that was used for basketball games. A video machine lived in the office at the side of the court and from here some hideous, but hilarious, singing emanated, executed – in the full sense of the word – on that machine from hell, the karaoke.

After breakfast I explored Surre. The waterfront where I had been ferried across the river on my arrival was not far from the hotel. Sitting on a stone seat I watched the ferry as it chugged back and forth. A cool morning breeze blew off the water and rustled through the stands of trees that shaded the lawns between them. Unfortunately, this beautiful spot was hideously marred by a thick layer of papers, plastic cups and food wrappings.

Moving on, I followed the path that wandered pleasantly along the riverfront, stopping now and then to lean on the wooden railing and look at life on the river. Presently I came to a big landing, the sign on top of which said 'Surre', and in the building on the riverbank above it was the ticket office for the boat that I now knew was the only one that came all the way to Surre. It arrived on Friday and left on Sunday evening. I decided to take it back to Belem on Sunday.

The office was an old adobe-and-stone affair and in its wall was a half-round, wooden-edged hole, fronted by a tiny crescent-shaped, wooden counter where you bought your ticket. Outside the office were stone benches that were shaded by a tiled roof and supported by stone pillars, and from there a long, tile-roofed walkway went down in steps and stages to the water.

There was much activity here. Groups of teenage boys rode about on bikes and other young men frolicked in the river. I watched some of these strong swimmers travel long distances. Others were bathing and washing their shirts. I saw few girls, but there were children everywhere. Fishing boats and other small craft chugged around and a wooden, two-tiered boat, similar to the one I had come from Belem on, pushed a barge laden with cars and trucks to another landing across the river. I was approached by a small boy who should have been in school. He asked me if I wanted a drink. I looked over to see that he carried a beat-up esky full of water and a bottle half-filled with cordial; a tin cup swung on a string around his neck. I said, 'No thanks,' but he continued to stand in front of me, regarding me solemnly with great, soulful brown eyes. Sadly I said, 'No thank you,' again. I thought it would be utterly foolhardy, health-wise, to drink river water from his communal cup.

A few dogs wandered around, hopeful of something to eat, but they were not as many, or as tatty, as those I had seen in other places. There had been many street dogs in Belem. I had noticed two in particular that lived right on the main drag. One was an old dog who always lay on the spot that was the coolest at that time of the day, such as the marble step of a building. I don't know whether the shop people fed it but it didn't look in bad nick. It was still sleeping there at night, so I presumed that was its only home.

A blot on the peace of the Surre waterfront were the loud speakers that, attached to poles here and there, spewed forth a blaring radio station. Brazilians don't seem to be able to tolerate a soundless vacuum, they have to fill it with noise of some description. Similarly, they were amazed to discover that I was alone. They couldn't comprehend the pleasure of travelling by yourself and they didn't think it was at all a good idea.

Unfettered livestock roamed Surre. As I walked around I saw six horses cropping the thick grass down the centre of the main street under the shade of the mango trees, and half-a-dozen buffalo grazed unattended on the street verges. Scraggy chooks of motley colours free-ranged everywhere. As I neared the hotel a man, bareback on a beautiful grey horse, rode expertly past me. With all these loose animals you had to be careful where you stepped, even on the footpaths, but I preferred that to human rubbish – at least animal droppings help the grass to grow. Vultures scratched among the mounds of rubbish in the streets. What a shame they don't eat plastic.

Surre's streets were rough and ready and only the two main ones were asphalt-paved, but all of them were wide and spacious and divided by large expanses of grass and trees down the middle into one-way traffic. The reason for this precaution eluded me as there was practically no traffic – just one bike, motorbike or horse cart passed me every ten minutes.

The market had a large meat, fish and veggie section in a

covered building, while stalls outside sold mostly food, snacks and drinks. Further on was another large, white adobe building sporting a sign that said 'Turisma' and in which various handcrafts were for sale. I bought a postcard of Surre's mounted police – they were on buffaloes. There were a few hole-in-the-wall cafes and bars, or that's what they said they were. In the couple of general stores I found the merchandise to be dearer than on the mainland; bottled water, for example, was twice the price. Freight costs I guess.

Surre was not only much quieter than Belem, it was also, thanks to its beautiful sea breezes, much cooler, especially in the evenings and mornings. But walking about in the sun in the middle of the day became too hot, so then I would return to my room for siesta. One evening I decided to try a meal at the other hotel, the Marejo. It was more up-market than my hotel; it included a good-looking pool beside two thatched-roofed gazebos that overlooked the inlet. You could sit in the pool and watch the buffalo grazing along its rubbish-strewn sides. A pretty row of Madagascan periwinkle bushes smothered in white flowers matched the low, fenestrated white wall that surrounded the hotel's perimeter.

I found horse meat on the menu and hoped that was not why there were horses grazing around the town. I can't imagine killing an animal as beautiful as a horse just to eat it – not when there are really ugly sheep, cows and chooks that can serve the same purpose. I looked up the word for horse meat in my dictionary. I had guessed right. The only thing I could have mistaken it for was cavaleiro – horseman – and I was pretty sure that they didn't still practice cannibalism here. It was hard to concentrate on my food because six black-and-white vultures hung over me from a convenient palm tree.

At lunch time the next day I returned to the cafe near the market and the river. For three reals I had fresh juice and a 'plato dias', plate of the day – it was actually several plates of tasty fried fish. I know it was fresh because I saw the cafe owner return from the market carrying huge silver fish strung on a wire.

National elections were to be held this month and, in all the towns from Pôrto Velho onwards, I had seen walls plastered with slogans and the names of candidates. A terrible assault on the eardrums had been following me from vans that crept along the gutters blasting out propaganda. In Surre I saw one of these vans with a bullet hole through its windscreen. Courtesy of a rival? Surre even staged a rally. Attended mainly by dogs and small boys on bicycles, a van paraded through the town; the racket from its loudspeakers was enhanced by exploding firecrackers.

On another beautiful morning a rooster and cheeping chickens woke me. Outside, a cool breeze was gently moving the fronds of the palm tree and in the courtyard a mare with foal at foot quietly cropped the grass. The courtyard gate was shut so the horses must have used the guests' entrance, clattering in over the tiled floor.

Deciding to take a ride out to a beach I had heard about I walked to the market corner where the motorbike taxis wait for custom. The riders all wore red waistcoats as well as helmets, the first I'd seen so far. There was even a spare one on the handlebars for the passenger. I didn't see the helmet at first and wasn't offered it, so I felt that I might look a wimp if I insisted on wearing it later. I hired a woman rider, hoping for a more sedate journey. I'd ridden with men who should have been doing car chases in movies. This girl was a big, butch female – she would have fitted right in at Hell's Angels – but she drove exceedingly carefully.

The bitumen that graced a small strip of the main road soon ended, then we were riding on a one-wheel dirt track that wound round lanes and among village houses until it came to open country. Here we passed horses, goats, chooks and lots of water that lay about in the fields – buffalo wallowed here and white egrets fossicked. We glided through glades of trees and acres of thick grass. Then we came to a wider dirt road and, going through a big wooden gate and many water puddles, slid to a stop at a river beside the remains of a wooden bridge. Behind a spit of land I could see the beach I had come to visit. A ferryman paddled me across the river in a canoe. He told me that I could pay on the way back. That figured – after all, I had no other way to return. The bikie had asked me when she should come back for me and, finding myself on a beautiful, sandy, but utterly deserted beach, I was now glad that I had arranged a time.

I walked around the corner of this beach that I had been left abandoned on. A long, empty shoreline stretched as far as I could see. It seemed like a good spot to get robbed and murdered in. Waves pounded onto the sand on which I saw horse and buffalo prints as well as those of one man and one dog. Mangroves stood sentinel behind the beach so tall and thick that I was unable to see into them. There wasn't much shade and I wondered what on earth I could do to amuse myself for the three hours until the bike returned. I started to read my book, and then I felt a presence. Looking up I saw a barefoot man who wore only shorts, as many men did in Surre. He had passed by me a few metres away but utterly soundlessly. He disappeared into the mangroves after telling me, I think, that there was something further up the beach. I decamped and, walking a kilometre or so, found five rough, thatched huts on stilts on the sand. The biggest one had an open verandah that faced the sea and looked to be offering some kind of hospitality. There was no sign of life around it except for an enormous black dog that allowed me to ascend the four steps up to the verandah before it got up to inspect the beach out the front. I sat in a chair and looked around – there was no one in sight.

Immediately behind the huts grew thick jungle, mostly very tall mangrove trees. No sign of land was visible across the other side of the sea of river. A boat chugged past away in the distance, leaving only the sound of the waves hitting the shore. The cool breeze was great but what was better was that I had this beach all to myself. I watched the vultures and other birds wading and an old work-horse of a boat with a blue sail come in close to shore. Further out a sailing boat showed only as a dark triangle of sail against the horizon.

A man arrived from the opposite direction that I had come from. He carried a large sack of ice, which he put in the freezer. I guessed that there was no electricity. Another man carried in two big, shining fish. This was a stroke of luck for both me and the cat that had come to look me over. This beast was a perfect miniature of the jaguar that I had been enraptured of in the Belem zoo. It had short, dense, jet-black fur and a square head with large, yellow-green eyes. A man with a gun walked past and the dog barked at him frantically. 'Bom dia,' he called to me.

In the meantime the owner of the hut had appeared and provided me with a drink and I had ordered fish for lunch. It arrived, and I was monumentally disappointed. He had turned that beautiful, silver fish into four slabs of tastelessness coated with sawdust. My second mistake had been making friends with the cat. Now I felt a tap on my knee. I could tell from the firmness of it that there would be no argument. Never mind, there was plenty to share.

I left to meet my motorbike after using the toilet. At least I hope that's what it was. A topless square wooden box on stilts nearby, it had a hole cut in one corner of its wooden floor that seemed to be suitable for the purpose.

Walking back along the shore I thought that the water seemed higher. Could this be a tidal beach? You bet your bippy it was. I arrived at the beach to find it had disappeared. No sandy crescent remained where I had left it – it had done a bunk.

As I stood there wondering what to do, a man came up behind me. 'This way, follow me,' he said, and headed off into the jungle. I followed. The foliage of the trees met over-head, shading the path, which was hung about with lianas and vines. The ground was carpeted with white convolvulus flowers. A trail led through to the other side and there was the river, now running a torrent with the tide pouring in. The man kept walking and I tagged along. We continued along the river's edge until we came to where the canoe was anchored out from the bank. The ferryman appeared and waded out chest-high to retrieve the canoe and paddle it around the bend where the waves were not so strong and it was possible to beach it. On the other side of the river Ms Hell's Angel waited. I had no small money, so she paid the ferryman for me and we had a pleasant ride back to the town past the wallowing buffalo.

During my two-hour siesta that day I dreamed that I was in a sinking ship. I hoped it wasn't an omen – I still had to get back to the mainland from here. At sundown I ambled along the esplanade to look over the weekly boat from Belem that had already arrived and would now wait at the wharf until departure on Sunday. It was not too flash, but it did have lifeboats.

I sat on a garden bench that overlooked the river and, fanned by a zephyr, watched the sun go down. Small boats pot-tered about their business and the car ferry clanged its iron maw shut and chugged across and back again. Lights gradually came on as the river darkened and the clouds turned grey. The sky reddened and then was dark enough to show the sickle moon. People came to occupy other seats or rode horses into the river for their daily bath from the landing barge's ramp.

The next morning, Sunday, I bought my ticket for the evening boat back to Belem. As I was the first customer, the ticket-seller allocated me pride of place directly in front of the TV and was amazed to hear I didn't want it. Then I took a motorbike taxi out to see Surre's other beach, which was thirteen kilometres away on a track that consisted entirely of potholes. But the scenery was idyllic. After leaving the edge of town, we passed through a series of villages with houses of mud-brick or wooden planks and straw roofs. Later there were goats and buffaloes wallowing in mud. I decided that this looked a thoroughly enjoyable occupation and that I should try it one hot day. The vegetation cascading onto the track was lush – creepers with big blue or white flowers like convolvulus, bushes with clusters of dark pink blossoms and crowded palm trees that gave way to mangroves as we reached the beach.

This beach was also deserted; only the waves breaking on the shore disturbed the long white stretch of sand. Open-sided, round, wooden huts with conical thatched roofs paraded in a line along the shore. Behind them was a shack that offered beer and sustenance. I ordered lunch, I thought. It never came, so maybe I didn't. But after an hour my taxi did, so I left still hungry. Back at the edge of town my driver, a lithe and handsome young fellow, stopped and looked both ways, twice. Beats me why. I hadn't seen a vehicle the whole thirteen kilometres out or back. As this was Sunday, the traffic, except for an occasional bike, was nil.

14 Rolling down to Rio

Boarding the boat for the trip back to Belem I paid two real extra and this princely sum bought me the privilege of riding in the air-conditioned saloon on the top deck. But at first I sat outside with the hoi polloi, because I could see better and the breeze was refreshing. After we left the shelter of the island, however, the weather became cold and I retreated inside. On a lower deck you could buy toasted sandwiches from the galley, outside which a girl stood with a tray of lollies for sale. It was an agreeable four-and-a-half hour trip. The trauma lay in dismounting. Our boat tied up alongside another, across which I had to fight, dragging my bag through a shoving crowd, and then negotiate my way up a steep metal ladder and leap across onto the wharf.

At the Hotel Central I was reunited with the desk clerk, who greeted me effusively and gave me a bright, spacious room that overlooked the main street from the second floor. On a corner of the building and triangular shaped, it had French doors that opened onto a balcony that was engulfed by one of the huge mango trees that lined the street. I slept with the shutters open and in the morning was awakened by thousands of birds. Padding barefoot on the wooden parquet floor between the wash basin and marble-topped dressing table, I prepared for the marathon bus ride to Rio that commenced at eleven.

Ready early, I decided I might as well rock on out to the bus station. I had been having trouble with my door lock, which,

225

each time I had used it, had become more recalcitrant and now utterly refused to budge. I wrestled with it, banged it and swore at it. Then I had a moment of panic. Several actually. I could miss my bus. My room was on the extreme end of the building and pretty isolated. I could go out onto the balcony and scream blue murder and no one would hear me for the traffic. Even if they did hear me, they probably wouldn't understand what I was carrying on about. Eyeing the three-and-a-half metre high door into the corridor, I decided that to be heard through it I would have to climb up onto the wardrobe and break its glass top – and a leg or two into the bargain, most likely. There was no one out there anyway. Struggling with the door again, I shouted and banged, sweating and swearing something shocking. After about twenty minutes more of this unseemly behaviour, the bloody door finally flew open. What a relief.

The bus left an obligatory ten minutes late – did the bus companies adhere to dinner party rules around here? But I was delighted with this vehicle. At its rear there was a decent loo and a cooler containing cold drinks and chocolate milk. And there was no video or music blaring. The bus had only one flaw. The metal armrests between the seats wouldn't completely retract, so that even though the bus was only partly filled and I got two seats to myself, the armrest stuck in my back if I tried to lie down.

We drove out of Belem, heading more or less due south, on a one-car-wide strip of potholed, bumpy bitumen. The country either side was covered in thick jungle, scarred every so often by a patch of cleared land. I saw few villages. They were widely spaced and plainer and poorer the further we got from Belem. Although Brazil occupies almost half the South American continent, its interior is largely undeveloped.

Later there were massive expanses of cleared land. In places nothing had been left, not even the odd tree, and it seemed to me that soon there would be no rainforest at all. But some

226

of the undulating expanses of green sward, dotted with white cows, looked very pretty. Then there were occasional big faciendas – coffee plantations – where kilometres of coffee trees marched in formation to the horizon. And sometimes I spied a grand house surrounded by workers' cottages and coffee-drying kilns belching smoke. Brazil is still the world's biggest coffee grower.

A few hours further south we stopped for a meal. I had been waiting for this for some time, as it was by then half past three. The cafe provided a well-stocked buffet for five real, and I did it justice, thinking that it might be the last food I got my hands on for some time. After this, however, we stopped frequently. The Brazilians all charged off the bus clutching towels and toothbrushes and washed and showered at every opportunity, but there was litter absolutely everywhere I looked in the villages and around the roadhouses.

The bus company had placed a plastic bag on every seat. Laboriously I translated the Portuguese that was written on it. It said, 'Put your rubbish in this bag, please, instead of throwing it out the window.' The next day I saw a well-dressed man and woman, who had diligently obeyed these instructions, get off the bus. They held a bulging plastic bag chock-a-block full of garbage. The man stepped down from the bus and immediately flung the bag into the grass at the side of the road. There are 160 million Brazilians. The litter will be up to their knees soon.

I slept, having imbibed a beer with my toasted cheese and ham sandwich at the last stop of the evening. I woke with a bright light flashing in my face and sat up wondering what it was. It was sheet lightning – we were passing through a terrific storm. Despite the pelting rain the driver was still throwing the bus at the bumpy road as fast as he could. Suddenly there was a tremendous bang and, whump, all the drink bottles crashed from the cooler behind me. We had plunged into a whacking great pothole. The driver crunched out of it and thereafter drove more cautiously.

227

At first light we stopped at a roadhouse and I tottered out for something to eat. At half past eleven we stopped again, this time for lunch, and while we ate the bus and the toilet were cleaned. Amazing. Our rubbish bags were removed and replaced with fresh ones so that we could throw them in the grass.

About half way to Rio the villages and towns became progressively smarter. The roadhouses we stopped at were large, impressive affairs surrounded by attractive gardens and incorporating gift shops and rows of clean showers and toilets. But the use of most toilets incurred a fee and a woman attendant would demand the outrageous sum of fifty cents for the privilege.

The other passengers on the bus were a cheerful and friendly lot. Two young lads occupied the seat in front of me and a charming, handsome man sat behind me. The passengers and I attempted conversations, but there was not a word of English on the whole bus and not many words of Portuguese came from me, so we were handicapped in our efforts.

In the morning the woman across the aisle put her hair up in fat orange curlers, covered the whole mess with a scarf and left it like that all day. The next morning she put it up again. Until then I had thought that all South Americans had minimal-care crowning glories. Their wonderful thick hair, which made me ill with jealousy, never looked as though they did anything at all to it. Another woman, an attractive middle-aged blonde, wore her long hair in a swathe wrapped tightly around her head and secured every few centimetres with a long bobby pin. It looked like her hair was nailed to her head.

One bloke got on the bus, took off almost all his clothes and lay down to sleep across four seats. You had to climb over his body to get to the back of the bus. When he finally woke up, he turned out to be a barrel of fun. He performed animal imitations – first a dog, then a cat, then a cat and a dog fighting. Then he crowed like a rooster. He was quite a good performer and all the middle-aged ladies had fits of giggling at each performance. Then he'd imitate their giggles and have them in hysterics.

On the third morning it was cold and raining. I found it hard to believe that I was shivering again. The air-conditioning on the bus had been arctic all along, but I had prepared for this by bringing my woolly socks and jumper. The driver, who had charge of the air-conditioning control knob, was locked in his little cocoon. The weather remained overcast as we climbed through rolling elevations that were rather like the pleasing Adelaide Hills. Down in the valleys we passed an occasional village, or a man walking on the road with a rifle in his hand. Then we were in the highlands, among beautiful towering mountains that were completely covered with thick woods. I read that the Brazilian highlands are some of the oldest geological formations on earth and produce quantities of gold, diamonds, aquamarines, amethysts and other gems. The road was now a good, well-built highway of several lanes. There were no ghastly precipitous drops over the side and we zipped around the mountains and through long tunnels. No worries.

After breakfast there were no more stops and we arrived in Rio in the early afternoon. Although Rio is called the most beautiful city in the world, it has its darker side. Coming into the sprawling metropolis, for a long time we passed through slums of matchbox houses, multi-storey tenements and dreadful makeshift shanties and tents that clung to the mountain-sides. One-sixth of Rio's population live in slums where sometimes there is only one water-pump for hundreds of people.

Politically Brazil has had a chequered history. Since the military coup in 1889 that established it as a republic, it has been ruled – with varying degrees of success – by a steady stream of military and civilian presidents. Rebellion by the

229

poor was brutally put down and poverty and corruption remain major problems.

Reading my guide book in the Rio bus depot I was assured by its author that if I approached the tourist information centre the staff there would obtain for me a big discount at a hotel. What they offered me was not my idea of a bargain. 'No way, Jose,' I said, and looking up a hotel in my book, asked the tourist person if it was acceptable. 'Yes, yes,' he said, and tried to phone. The phone was not working so he wrote a note to the manager instead. He also told me that I must use a radio taxi to get there, as other taxis were not safe. The radio taxi was safe but it was also a lot dearer. The hotel manager, a charming young woman who smiled all the time, even while I was telling her I didn't want to pay her first price, accommodated me even if she did think that I was as mean as cat's poo.

My new home, the Hotel Turistico, was a big old building halfway up a steep hill. It sat opposite the subway, main road and bus route in the Gloria district. The Turistico had the usual faults, but the bathroom had been modernised – badly – and supplied lovely hot water all the time. The toilet-roll holder had been positioned, obviously by someone with a warped sense of humour, directly under the shower.

By six in the evening I was settled into my small room and listening to the homely sounds of church bells and someone in the throes of a music lesson singing lustily across the way. My room had a TV fixed on a stand high up near the ceiling. It didn't matter that I couldn't understand it because it had no remote control – if I had wanted to turn it on, I would have had to climb up to the top of the wardrobe to do so. There was also an air-conditioner that I didn't use, a fridge and a comfy bed that was also good for ironing my jeans, as it had a good flat board under the mattress. Not recommended if your memory is failing – there's a pair of my jeans still under a mattress in Penang.

I breakfasted in the first-floor dining room where the open

windows looked down the hill and into the trees of the park in the middle of the highway. The clanging of the church bell wafted across from a hill that rose on the other side of the road. Gazing at this pleasant scene and drinking excellent coffee was a great way to start the day. A light breeze came through the open window, and I noticed that it was glazed. I had rarely seen glass in windows in the north.

I shared my table with a young German girl who was a bit of a know-all. But at least she saved me from a fruitless trip downtown to the airline office. She told me that, this being Independence Day, everything would be shut.

I decided to take the subway to Copacabana Beach instead. The subway was fast, efficient and not too crowded, but to get out of its clutches you had to walk a very long way, then ride up an escalator, walk more and ride up more – and again and again. At first I went through a big cavern designed to look like a cave, then I was in a series of semi-circular, long tunnels with walls that were lined with lighted panels of all the graduating shades of the rainbow.

Rio is famous for its long stretches of soft, sandy beaches fringed by rows of tall palm trees and Copacabana was very beautiful. But I had enjoyed Surre's beach much more. There was no shade here. You had to take your own umbrella or sit baking on the hot sand. Still, today was a heavenly spring day and a wonderful day for a walk. I knew the temperature because every so often I came across a big clock and a temperature gauge in the street.

I ambled along the edge of the long white beach where grass-green coconut palms waved against a glorious stretch of blue sea and sky. Small, thatched stalls that sold drinks and snacks were dotted along the sand, while the other side of the road was lined with outdoor cafes and restaurants. As this was a public holiday there were people everywhere and the atmosphere was festive. In Copacabana you would never know that there were any poor people in Brazil. They were not visible here. Copacabana seemed to be for the rich and tourists. In the residential streets people walked expensive-looking dogs under big shady trees on the black-and-white-mosaic-tiled footpaths.

Coming into Rio I had seen the poverty of the slums, but I saw poverty close up around Gloria, where a number of people lived on the streets. Yet I was glad that I had chosen to stay in Gloria – it was close to the city centre and easy to get around from once I got my bearings. To return there from Copacabana I caught a bus marked Central to downtown Rio, thinking that I could get back to my hotel via the subway from there. But that subway had shut for the holiday. Empty streets fronted the masses of huge buildings, as though the human population had fled some cataclysmic event. Then, in a small square, I came upon a crowd of street people who were having a party. I guess the city was theirs when everyone else disappeared. I backed up and went around another way. But I was not generally afraid of street people. Most that I saw around Gloria would smile at me and say 'Bom dia', and not all of them begged.

A driver at the bus station told me which bus to take to Gloria. As the bus passed a grandiose building decorated by life-sized, bronze sculptures of horses and chariots, I saw a man in rags sitting on the stone seat in front of it. He crouched with his head on his knees, asleep in the sun.

The ride back to Gloria revealed to me that Rio bus drivers drove with just as much wild abandon as those of the north. Even Rio's dense traffic did not slow them down. It was as though they considered the journey some kind of a contest. You had to hang on to the back of the seat in front of you for grim death and you could still be thrown from one side of the bus to the other. And the long distances between bus stops gave drivers the chance to go like the clappers and get up steam.

I never saw any old people on buses. Just as well – they'd all have broken legs or arms. Anyway, an age-challenged person could never get onto a bus – the turnstile that had to be negotiated after you had paid your money could get you in a killer grip and do a death roll. But at least the buses came every couple of minutes, and even though they were dearer in Rio than in the north, tickets still cost just ninety cents. You didn't get much of a chance to see the sights from a bus as you flew past at a thousand kilometres an hour, but I did glimpse the famous Sugar Loaf, a high, skinny, bare-rock-topped mountain that sticks up on the edge of the bay like a pointing finger and has a cable car that swings up to its peak on wires strung across the sky. From where I was the cable car looked as big as an ant and horribly scary. I'll need some valium in order to ride that, I thought.

When I returned from Copacabana, I found a weekend market in the back streets around my hotel. The market sold mainly fruit and veggies and some trash and treasure. I saw no treasure, mostly trash, but I pounced on a book in English, *The Life of Winston Churchill* – I'll read anything – and collected some bananas, pawpaws, mandarins and bread rolls. I was about to reform and eat healthy, having scoffed so much junk food lately that I couldn't do up my pants. In the gutters half a dozen children and several street people were picking through the vegetables that had been discarded by the stalls. Later I saw children fossicking in rubbish bins and I was reminded that Rio and Sao Paulo are reputed to have vigilante groups who round up street kids and shoot them like rats.

That night I couldn't sleep for thinking about those poor people in the streets and the wretched dog that had followed me back to the hotel. I wondered if dogs pick up vibes from susceptible people. This dog followed me from the vegetable market all the way across two busy highways, up the hill and right to the hotel door. It was a big dog, part Alsatian, but it was so thin that its hip bones and collar bones protruded like knobs. It looked so pathetic I gave it a couple of my bread rolls. Then I thought that it seemed wrong to feed a dog when there were people in worse condition.

Rio was just as littered as the other parts of Brazil that I had seen. Rubbish lay thick in the streets and often my nostrils were assaulted by the unmistakable smell of urine, especially near walls or telephone stands. In fact, almost all public spaces ponged of ammonia. I wondered why, if women are able to wait until they reach home or a loo, men can't do the same. I reckon it is a macho show-off thing. Look at me, I've got a doodle! Thank goodness telephones were not enclosed in booths. They would have become public toilets. Instead phones, called big ears, were perched on posts and were partly shaded by a perspex hood, some of which in Belem had been shaped like giant parrots. It felt curious ducking under one.

I had been surprised when I first saw 'Bom Jesus' scrawled on a wall. I wondered if a terrorist who couldn't spell had passed that way, but later I discovered that Bom means good in Portuguese and you see it written everywhere. I noticed also that among the many buildings that had their names written on them, the name Ed featured often. There was Ed Franco, Ed da Silva etc. I thought that this Ed fellow was a very popular bloke, until I got to Rio and there were so many Eds that it finally clicked that Ed meant edifico, building.

One day I saw an unusually squeaky-clean beggar. At five o'clock in the evening she was settling herself down on the pavement in the city. With beautiful, clear skin and a sweet face, she was neatly dressed in a bright, freshly washed woollie and, only a child herself, she held a wee baby, not nine months old, who was also immaculately dressed in a white jumpsuit and a white knitted beanie with a pompom on top. The girl wasn't soliciting for money. She merely sat on a blanket with a few coins in her hand, looking so sad. I gave her all my change and grieved for the fact that someone of her age had come to this.

I found the office of the airline who had 'wait-listed' me in

Belem, but not easily, because the street it is in runs off another and the powers that be had not seen fit to put its name on it. A sulky young man with a bad cold, who didn't seem terribly enamoured of me at first, finally searched the computer and said that he could confirm a booking for me on that day but would keep trying for an earlier one. This was a start.

I tried to obtain money from a machine at the bank but it informed me coldly that I didn't have enough loot in my account for it to give me a sample. I have learned that there is no point arguing with a machine that has a fixation about something, no matter how big a black lie it is telling. I tried my other card and was told that the pin number was wrong. To my chagrin I discovered that, after you have inserted three wrong pin numbers, the machine refuses to play with you anymore. I moved to another bank where I eventually persuaded the machine to give me a few real and then moved on to the Great Phone Search. Embratel, the alleged phone company, had a huge building, but no telephones. I found only offices where people were paying bills. At one office I sought help and found an exceptionally obliging receptionist who spoke English. I explained the whole sad story to her and, leaving her post, she came out into the street with me and dialled my number on a public phone. To no avail. It continued to be cut off each time it rang. She said, 'I see the problem. I'll get my supervisor.' After a long consultation, the two ladies decided that I should go to the place that connected calls by an operator, and the supervisor led me down the street, around the corner and pointed me in the right direction. Lovely lady.

I never found the joint. Everyone I asked for help directed me elsewhere. I went round and round and up and down until my feet gave out. I tried again in the evening and, wouldn't you know, I had been walking past this blasted office all the time. Steps led up to it from the street but, more discreet than a house of ill repute, it displayed no outward sign that even hinted to the passing world what its function might be. Something had finally registered when the gate man of a big office block nearby, who took a lot of trouble to help me, told me that it was next to the police station.

People in Rio were generally very kind to me. But I also saw Cariocas, as Rio folk call themselves because that is the name of the central downtown district, do strange things. When driving around in traffic it seemed to be the passenger's job to stick his arm out of the window and give rude signs while screaming abuse at other motorists and pedestrians who got in the way. It appeared to be mainly good-natured reproachment and most of the time I found it highly amusing. Cars would actually stop for you at crossings and give you a beep to tell you to go ahead. Not buses, however. You had to jump back mighty smartly onto the pavement to escape them. They practically came up there to get you. At times buses swerved so close to the gutter that, if your nose had been protruding, you'd have been gone.

Downtown again on another beautiful spring morning, I walked about the parks and squares enjoying myself. With a 'Bom dia', I sat down next to a man on one of the seats that were dotted around under the trees. My companion turned out to be one of the many homeless who frequented the downtown area. Later I wandered into the large church that dominated one side of the square. I had recently sworn off churches, but I got sucked in again like I do every time. I like the look of church interiors and I love the feeling of peace that they generate. Besides, churches are good for a sit-down when you are tired of the tourist traipse. It is a pity, however, that they don't run to toilets.

This church's interior differed greatly from what its exterior promised. Outside, it was a peculiar mix of Grecian and Georgian styles but inside it was as though I had entered a long, narrow, lofty cave made entirely of elaborately carved wood. Down the cave's sides were interspersed glass-fronted niches that contained statues of saints and deities. And high up were wonderful carved wooden boxes, like those of a theatre, where the landed gentry must sit – very handy places to snooze through the sermon. The cave culminated at the altar, which was also all wood and rose, carving on carving, up to the far distant roof. Later I saw another church that was also entirely made of wood and had huge polished wooden columns that marched in a line all the way down to the altar.

In the evening I took the subway to Catete, the next stop down from Gloria. There was a museum here that was alive at night with people visiting, studying and eating at the snack bar in the grounds of the fabulous old building that had bronze vultures perched on its top. I took a chair and waited in the warm evening air for a turn on the internet and then sent a rocket to the phone-card pixies.

On Saturday mornings Rio has a wonderful antique market. I took the subway to near where I estimated it to be. On one of the main city streets I passed a corner niche of a building where a street person had cosily established himself on a ground sheet covered by a big cuddly blanket. A trolley that contained his belongings was parked alongside him and five healthy-looking dogs curled around his body – a five-dog night for real! The market had been set up underneath the freeway fly-overs and bridges near the waterfront where the ferries docked, and the stalls extended for kilometres. It took me four hours at a hard trot to get around this market. The merchandise was mostly good, nineteenth-century, European decorative items, such as lamps and vases in porcelain, silver and glass, as well as heaps of old costume jewellery. Some of the goods on offer were very highly priced but others were bargains. I bought a couple of small Chinese figurines that I reckoned I could manage to squeeze into my bag. But I sorely regretted having to leave behind the marvellous, but extremely clunky and highly breakable, oriental pieces that I coveted.

I continued walking on from the end of the market and came to the domestic airport, where I unearthed an accommodating cash machine and, at last, a phone that was willing to connect me to Australia. Halleluiah! But I couldn't use it unless I was prepared to haul someone out of bed at three in the morning. I figured that was stretching the bonds of family and friendship too far.

On reflection, I came to the conclusion that most of the people in South America were just as lost as I was most of the time. No matter where I went, at least one person would accost me and ask for directions. In Spanish or Portuguese. I took it as a compliment – obviously I didn't look like a foreign tourist. Believe me, you wouldn't want to look like most of the ones I saw. Although in the north I came across no western tourists except the three backpackers on the boat to Belem, they were thick on the ground in parts of Rio. I think tourists get mugged because they advertise the fact that they are just that. In Rio I found that I was dressed much the same as most other women of my age – slacks or jeans and a shirt. Rio is reputed to have the loveliest women in South America – but what about the men? A very unfair proportion of them are drop-dead gorgeous. On several occasions I was asked if I was Argentinian. I haven't worked out if that was good or bad yet.

On Sunday morning I headed for the weekly North East Fair at Cristobello, which was said to be a lively show. I nutted out how to get there by the subway but then found it shuts on Sunday. So I took a bus to Central, where I asked directions of a conductor who put me on the right bus. When I saw a police station labelled Cristobello, I asked the driver if I was there. He said, 'No, you've come too far. Sit down and I'll get you there.' I thought he intended to drop me off on the way back but after we had continued on for a long time I discovered that he was looking for another bus that was going to Cristobello. Finally he stopped his bus in the middle of the street and, hailing a bus that was heading in the opposite direction, chatted to its driver. I was then told to get on this other bus, around the front so that I didn't have to pay. The next driver took me right to where the fair was held, under overhead tarpaulins all the way around the outside walls of a massive stadium. The numerous stalls were interspersed, now and then, by bandstands and portable wooden dance floors that were surrounded by hundreds of tin tables and chairs and crowded with people who danced to the very loud samba music, sang, drank beer and had a ball. There was beer on all the tables. Wherever I went in Brazil, at any time of the day, I saw people drinking beer.

I walked around kilometres of clothes and all kinds of goods, but discovered to my surprise that all the big stalls sold hectares of plumbing supplies. This should have been called the Plumber's Picnic, not the North East Fair. There was food galore. You could eat barbecued corn on sticks, beef or chicken shasliks, grilled cubes of white buffalo cheese on skewers and many other goodies. One area was devoted to trash and treasure and mountains of it was laid out on the ground.

I was standing in a crowd watching some dancers, when a fellow in front of me turned around, took a look at me, then looked again quickly. I was not deluded that he had been stunned by my ravishing beauty. I knew instantly that he was a bad lot who had decided that I was an easy mark. Like the poor dog, I have a sixth sense about people sometimes. Sure enough, when I moved off, he immediately followed me. I stopped and let him pass and made certain that he was not able to get behind me again until I lost him. I read once that a well-known thief declared, 'You can't rob someone who is on to you.'

Back in the city I was making for a place where the Gloria bus stopped when I came to the entrance of a building that I guessed to be Rio's cathedral, the Catedral Metropolitana, but only because there was something to indicate this printed on the front doormat. There was no sign. A couple of hulking stone statues stood guard outside looking faintly Egyptian. This building, the last gasp in ugliness, looked more like a museum than a church. I had noticed it before but had resisted a visit, but now curiosity got the better of me. The flat-topped monstrosity looked nearer to Doctor Who's daleks than anything that belonged on this planet. I believe its design was a copy of an ancient temple. Totally circular in shape, its rough concrete sides went up in steps and stages to a great height. Once inside I saw that the steps were actually slot-shaped windows and then I could also see the four huge stained-glass panels that quartered the walls from the floor thousands of metres up to the top. The stained glass was impressively patterned with random, abstract designs and the sliced-off top was inset with a clear-glass square cross. There was no conventional altar, but hanging in the centre of the building, suspended from somewhere way up in the gods, was a big wooden crucifix, underneath which crouched a circular dais and a set of steps to mount it. Several wooden statues stood about. The temple/church/darlek didn't look any more Christian inside than it did out, but it sure was big. It could have seated the biblical five thousand on the backless, polished-wood benches that encircled the walls and came down to encroach on the dais. It was spectacular but it had no atmosphere. It was not the sort of place in which to commune or contemplate.

In the evening I mounted a bus, fully believing that I was off to the domestic airport to make a phone call. I wasn't and I didn't. Instead I spent an hour and a half circumnavigating Rio. With all its bright lights, it is a very pretty town at night but I did not even sight the airport. However, I did learn how to get to the botanical gardens if I should want to go there. The next day I found the right bus and the airport and was very pleased with myself. Then I walked across the fly-over to the downtown area and again nagged the airline about an earlier ticket. Still no luck.

The way that many people rode buses for free amazed me. All you had to do was enter via the front, thus avoiding the turnstile. Over sixty-fives, if they were game, could freeload, also small children, those in school uniforms or just carrying books, and women with babes in arms. No credentials were checked. Brazilians seemed very tolerant of each other. I suppose they had to be when there were so many poor people. I saw conductors look the other way when young lads got on the bus, limboed under the turnstile and didn't pay. And drivers would allow vendors onto the bus to try to sell some small item to passengers. The vendors would recite their spiel up and down the aisle, offering you one lolly or a packet of gum, and then alight without paying. One day a well-built young bloke got on selling batteries. He'd had one leg amputated at the knee and he hopped along without a crutch. I had previously decided that buses were only for the fit and strong and not for the infirm or feeble but this lad made his way along the jolting bus with his box of batteries, sold some, and then hopped of.

I went to the beach at Ipanema, which is further on from Copacabana, and walked along the foreshore for a long way. This was not exactly a deliberate venture; although the breeze was pleasant by the sea, this day was quite hot. I was looking for a map shop that I still have yet to uncover. Maybe next time.

In a cafe near the beach I saw an example of the Ugly Tourist that I hadn't seen for a long time. I had hoped that they all might have died out. This one was a late-middle-aged, American female old enough to know better. She and her poor doddering husband were making a frightful scene about the kilo menu. She demanded loudly to know what was in each dish – and there were at least twenty dishes – what it cost and how the system worked. It was hard to believe anyone could be so thick. You load your plate and pay ten real per kilo. Simple. Not for her. Later when I went to pay the cashier, she was there making another scene about how much it cost it and how she should pay. Then she said to the cashier, 'That's all right. Now tell me what that is in my money.' I imagined the cashier trying that trick in her country. Would she give him the price in reals?

It was late afternoon when I got on a bus to return to my hotel. I had not previously taken one at peak hour, and now I realised why people said that most robberies occurred on buses. Standing squeezed in a solid mass of humanity in a lurching swaying vehicle, I thought, Now is the hour. Drivers of northern buses had been horrendous, but at least they had not been doing their stuff in heavy traffic. Imagine a four-lane highway with four buses across it, all flat-out performing like cars racing in a Grand Prix, passing each other, swerving all over the road, in the centre of town. I decided that drivers get their jollies from upsetting their passengers and if they can't scream around corners and roar down narrow streets – I was in one that actually mounted the kerb and drove with half its wheels on the footpath – or if they get stuck in traffic where they have to slow down, they display their frustration by jerking the brakes so that the passengers fall about the bus anyway. But then, they were very good to me whenever I was lost.

That night as I was passing through the hotel foyer, I was arrested by a gruesome sight on the television – a Rio city bus lying on its side while white-coated attendants rushed about taking passengers from it on stretchers. In the background were piles of black plastic bags that looked suspiciously like they contained bodies, while to one side the fire brigade blasted blood off the road with a massive hose. Until then I hadn't imagined that a local bus could have a fatal crash. After watching this, I thought about it all the time as I rode about town.

A couple of days later Murphy took the day off. When I

rang the airline for my daily nag, a perfectly agreeable woman not only understood everything I said but also offered me a seat in two days time. That left me forty-eight hours to cram in everything that I wanted to do. I set off immediately and in downtown Carioca found Rio's library, the Biblioteca Nacional. An imposing nineteenth-century, four-storey building, it has a superb foyer containing a wonderful marble staircase flanked by graceful columns. I had thought that I might be able to use the internet there but a sweet receptionist with good English told me that it was only for students – and no stretch of the imagination could inveigle me into that category, except perhaps as an extremely slow learner. The receptionist gave me the address of an internet cafe in the Rio Branco, the main street. She said it was most easy to find. And I did!

Next on my list was the magnificent municipal theatre and opera house – the Teatro Municipal – an exact one-quarter scale copy of the one in Paris. Another impressive late-nineteenth-century creation, its exterior had everything possible in the way of domes and cupolas, as well as great bronze eagles on its roof. I went inside and mingled with its many statues as I listened to singers on stage practise for a coming opera. The voices followed me as I wandered through the fabulous and extensive restaurant, a fantasy reminiscent of a Cecil B. de Mille biblical extravaganza. Built on two levels, with seating downstairs and a bar and grand piano up top, the whole caboose was tiled in bluish turquoise. The walls were interspersed with wonderful French glass lights made by Henri Lalique that were supported by carved, wooden animal heads and separated by marble columns.

The tram that runs across an aqueduct built in 1723 and ascends to the lovely residential area of Santa Teresa was another must. I had read that the station was somewhere near the cathedral and had seen the aqueduct, a big white procession of arches that stuck up high above the surroundings, on previous forays around the town. I found the aqueduct and followed it to its source. From a distance the aqueduct appeared far too skinny and fragile to carry such a boisterous object as a tram. It looked as though it was made of plaster, but now that I was about to trust myself to it, I sincerely hoped it was concrete.

The tram cost seventy cents and was very comfortable. However, it had not occurred to me that it would not be fully enclosed. It sides were actually open and from your feet up there was nothing to stop you pitching out into the abyss. The tram driver arrived, put one foot on the running board, stopped and blessed himself, moving his lips in silent prayer. I thought, Well, that's him taken care of, but what about us?

The tram was metal with lots of shiny brass fittings and lovely old polished wooden seats, but I was wearing slippery silk trousers and I shot back and forth on my seat like a jack-in-the-box each time the tram lurched. Trams seemed to do a good trade – every one I saw was full. The paying customers sat on the seats, but as soon as the tram started off, the non-payers jumped on the outside and, hanging onto the side rails, swung precariously in the breeze. Much as I like a free ride, there was no way I'd have done that, for when the tram took off it circled a garden then clanged out onto the narrow aqueduct where it pitched from side to side alarmingly. The city beneath me seemed kilometres away. Good grief, I'd had apprehensions about the cable car and yet here I was, terrified, on a wobbly tram a long way from the ground, rocking about on a high, skinny edifice. As I slid back and forth on the seat I clutched the back of the seat in front of me for all I was worth.

Our driver, Pedro, was a happy soul with a bright smiley face and he knew absolutely everybody on the route. As the tram wound around and up the very steep hill, all along the way he called greetings to people, or stopped the tram so that they could get on, giving extra help to women with babies or heavy middle-aged ladies, who I'm sure wouldn't have made it onto a bus. He always made certain that his passengers were safely on board before he started gently off again.

Suddenly, half-way up the hill, there was a loud explosion and a great flash of flame, followed by sparks and smoke, shot from the controls. Pedro, unperturbed, stopped the tram and, reaching up into a wooden box above his head, fiddled with some knobs. We waited for the smoke to clear and after a while off we went again. By now our pace was down to a crawl, which gave Pedro time to chat to everyone we passed. He knew all the school kids, who rode free, by name. One curly-headed blond girl was obviously a favourite. He stopped the tram and waited until she had finished talking to him before taking off again. At one stage I pulled my camera from my bag and he stopped so that I could take a picture. The tram had a big brass bell which, to my delight, Pedro dinged loudly every now and then. This ride was so relaxed and sociable after the nightmare bus journeys that, once I survived the aqueduct, I thoroughly enjoyed it.

I decided that it would be mainly the rich who lived on this hill. Some of the houses, which were built rather precariously either on the slope above or below the tram line, were extremely grand. Some were Mediterranean in style, others had turrets like castles and many looked ancient. It took forty minutes to reach Santa Teresa and return again and it was the nicest thing I did in Rio.

Back safely on terra firma, I celebrated with a divine lunch in the kilo restaurant at the tram station. Fortified, I set off once more in tourist mode, this time to seek a ride across the harbour on a ferry and visit the market. Where the market was alleged to have been, I found a car park. Perhaps it had moved or become defunct or perhaps, perish the thought, the accursed book had got it wrong again. It couldn't have been me.

I boarded the ferry easily enough. Built like a landing barge, it romped up to the wharf and disgorged a mob of people from its maw like Jonah being spat up by the whale. I rode the ferry across the fantastic Rio harbour, the Guanabara Bay, and back again, passing a stupendous bridge that crosses to an island a long way out. Rio has one of the finest natural harbours in the world and this, as well as Brazil's other great ports, has greatly contributed to the wealth of the nation. A Portuguese navigator, Gaspar de Lemos, discovered Guanabara Bay in 1502 and, thinking it was a river, named it Rio de Janeiro. The French established a settlement here in 1555, but this was taken over by the Portuguese in 1560. In 1760 Rio replaced Salvador as Brazil's capital and remained so until 1960, when Brasilia secured the title.

I started my last day in Rio by waiting on the wrong bus stop for half an hour before I twigged and tootled down to Central and, finding the right bus, asked the driver to put me off at Sugar Loaf. I had finally mustered the courage to ride the cable car, but I suffered severe misgivings when I saw that my ticket was dated the thirteenth and my jitters didn't improve when it came to the moment of truth and I had to step aboard. I really didn't want to get into that wobbly thing. On a scale of nought to ten, the bus through the Andes took the ten for terror, but this horror was at least eight. Once in the cable car the ground was a dreadfully long way down and you were supported merely by an itty-bitty rope, which from the blessed dirt looked about as thick as a piece of cotton. The box-like car swayed alarmingly as I stepped on – and you don't get a seat. I wanted to lie down and hide my head, but had to stand and look either out, or under my feet. Either way there was nothing. I had a vivid sensation of being suspended out in space with only a great emptiness around me.

As you got out of this wavering capsule, you had to jump over a gap and, looking down, you saw the earth thousands of metres away. One slip and I'll fall down there, was all I could think. I wasn't the only coward either. Another woman was even worse than I was. Her friends dragged her protesting into the cable car, but she wasn't going to look. She kept her eyes shut tight whimpering, 'Is it over yet?' I tried to console her, which took the edge off my terror, but, as if one ride wasn't enough, when I got off the first time I discovered that, wait, there's more. From the first peak you go on to another even higher. The view was spectacular, a vivid panorama of Rio and her natural beauties, but I wondered why in the name of heaven anyone, except a sadist, would have conceived the idea of building this device.

Not satisfied with this mental torture, I then took the cog railway up to the summit of Corcovado – the Hunchback – mountain on which mountain stands the enormous statue of Cristo Redentor, Christ the Redeemer. This necessitated going back into Central and again asking a bus driver to put me off at the right place. This time he said, 'No, no, no.' Then he said more. I actually don't know what he said. I just let drivers rattle on and waited for developments, hoping that they would push me off at the appropriate time. I would never have found my way anywhere without someone to help me. But this time it turned out that the driver was chasing another bus for me. When he caught up to it, he said, 'Quick, get on this one.' Then I was braving a third extremely high and ter- rifying ride in the space of twenty-four hours.

To be honest, looking down from this one was the least frightening of them all. I don't know how a cog railway works, but I sat in a double train carriage that was pulled up a moun- tain on a wire. We ascended steeply. At first there were a few houses and then we were going through a national park that was very beautiful. On both sides of the railway line the park's lush green vegetation crowded closely, one side going up the mountain and the other down. You either looked down into many glorious greens or up to the green-covered hillside. Plants and ferns – ones that at home are pampered, petted darlings cosseted in the house – scrambled wildly over walls and clambered madly up trees. There were all manner of many coloured flowers – big red blooms like hibiscus and strelitzia; salmon pink, pale pink or mauve busy lizzies that romped over the ground in pretty profusion; lilac and purple flag iris; and bushes that had blue and white flowers like plumbago. The top half of the train's windows had no glass and through them I could breathe in the smell of the forest, that luscious, damp, green scent of fresh foliage, a wonderful earthy smell that I adore.

The train made several stops on its long climb to the top of the mountain and now and then picture-postcard vistas down into the blue bay appeared through gaps in the foliage. I had read that you could reach the summit by road, but it was not recommended – in fact, it was said to guarantee that you would get robbed. I could imagine that bandits hung about in the forest. It was very dense and would have been scary to venture into alone. The railway disgorged me at the end of the line, from where I had to walk up about a million steps to reach the top. At intervals on the way I encountered a snack bar or someone selling souvenirs. Then, there it was, Corcovado, the enormous statue of Christ with arms outstretched. Built in 1931, it stands forty metres high and weighs seven hundred tonnes – thirty tonnes in the head and eight for a hand. Once again I wondered why this had been built. Why not go down into Rio and spend that money housing the homeless or erect some ruddy public toilets so that the stench of urine is not the strongest memory tourists take away from the city?

My day of departure arrived. The airport bus proved difficult to find so I engaged a friendly taxi driver. He told me I should not be standing in the street with my bags in this area as it was too dangerous. When I asked why, he said that there were not enough police and too many robbers. Then we flashed at the speed of light to the Aeroporto International. At the plane check-in a sympathetic girl said she couldn't put me in the exit seat I requested (they have more leg room) but, even though the plane was full, she managed to leave the seat next to me empty. I had told her that I had a bad leg. This is true. I have two bad legs if you go by looks.

The plane was ninety minutes late. Finally, at eight-thirty I was allowed on board, only to sit and sit until an announcement was made: 'We will be twenty minutes delayed.' Half an hour later we taxied to the runway where we again sat until another announcement: 'We will be one hour delayed due to a technical problem.' That could mean anything.

I debated getting off. I wonder if anyone ever has. A technical problem could mean that there was an engine on fire or all the wheels had fallen off. By the time they decided to move the plane I was almost ready to quit. I was very nervous. They did not say the problem was fixed and no one asked me if I still wanted to go on their faulty air-machine. I didn't, I wanted out. Here I was, flying with a South American airline I didn't trust anyway, and now they had confessed to a defective plane. Once you are up there, there is no way out.

Dinner distracted me for a while, but it was soon interrupted by the seat-belt light coming on, followed by turbulence, rain and lightning. Oh boy, now this. I imbibed quantities of the red wine on offer as a general anaesthetic.

To my great surprise we landed safely in Buenos Aires. It was cold in the airport where an announcement informed me that there was an hour's delay. What's new? I really didn't want to spend twelve hours flying over the Andes and the Pacific Ocean with this mob in this suss plane but I got back on it anyway. The flight was rough at first but I was served another dinner and more red wine.

The female flight attendants wore a cross between a football jersey and a waitress's pinny with butcher's stripes, but despite this lack of sartorial elegance, the service was superior. With two seats to lie across and the therapeutic effect of the wine, I managed some sleep, but it was still an interminable night as I woke often and thought of all that ocean underneath me. At intervals I would get up for a drink and a sandwich; breakfast, consisting of lots of sweet rolls and cake, was served before we arrived in Auckland. From the air New Zealand looked green and pleasant, but as long as it was solid earth I didn't care if it was desert. Back on the plane I had another breakfast, with less cake now that we were onto Australian tucker.

In Sydney I breezed through customs only to be bailed up by a sniffer dog, a dear little spaniel, who thought my bag was suspicious. I managed to convince the authorities that he could smell the bananas that I'd previously had in it, and then I was free to go home.